Heinrich Zschokke, Frederica Rowan

Meditations on Death and Eternity

Heinrich Zschokke, Frederica Rowan

Meditations on Death and Eternity

ISBN/EAN: 9783744660860

Printed in Europe, USA, Canada, Australia, Japan

Cover: Foto ©ninafisch / pixelio.de

More available books at **www.hansebooks.com**

COMPANION VOLUME

TO

MEDITATIONS

ON

DEATH AND ETERNITY.

MESSRS. TRÜBNER AND Co. have much pleasure in announcing a second series of Meditations selected by Her Majesty from the same work as the "Meditations on Death and Eternity," which have been received with such distinguished marks of public sympathy. This second series (which, like the former, is translated by MISS FREDERICA ROWAN, and will be published with the Queen's most gracious permission) consists of Meditations on Life and its Religious Duties.

Messrs. T. & Co. having observed an announcement of a "companion volume" to the "Meditations" issuing from another quarter, beg to inform the public, they are instructed by MISS ROWAN to state that the selections translated by her and published by them, are the only ones that have the royal sanction.

60, PATERNOSTER ROW,
15th Dec., 1862.

MEDITATIONS

ON

DEATH AND ETERNITY.

MEDITATIONS

ON

DEATH AND ETERNITY

TRANSLATED FROM THE GERMAN

BY

FREDERICA ROWAN.

Published by Her Majesty's Gracious Permission.

London: 1863.
TRÜBNER AND CO.,
PATERNOSTER ROW.

THE MEDITATIONS contained in this volume form part of the well-known German devotional work *Stunden der Andacht*, published in the beginning of the present century, and generally ascribed to Zschokke.

They have been selected for translation by one to whom, in deep and overwhelming sorrow, they have proved a source of comfort and edification.

June, 1862.

HER MAJESTY having graciously granted her permission to publish these selections (originally printed for private circulation only) the Translator now presents them to the general public.

TABLE OF CONTENTS.

	Page
IS SLOW DECLINE OR SUDDEN DEATH MOST DESIRABLE?	1
FEAR OF DEATH. PART I.	12
FEAR OF DEATH. PART II.	24
GOD IS LOVE	36
THE CONSOLATION OF THE PATIENT SUFFERER	48
THE SICK	61
A FORETASTE OF HEAVEN. PART I.	72
A FORETASTE OF HEAVEN. PART II.	82
THE WORLD A MIRROR OF ETERNITY	92
THE EXISTENCE OF ANGELS	104
DEATH IS MY GAIN	117
ETERNAL DESTINY. PART I.	129
ETERNAL DESTINY. PART II.	139
THE DESTINATION OF MAN	150
IMMORTALITY	164
WHY MUST THE FUTURE LIFE BE HIDDEN FROM US?	175
A JOY IN THE HOUR OF DEATH	187
THOUGHTS AT THE GRAVES OF THOSE WE LOVE	198
THE THOUGHT OF ETERNITY	210
INTERPRETATIONS OF ETERNITY:—	
GOING IN TO THE FATHER	222

INTERPRETATIONS OF ETERNITY:—	Page
THE FUTURE LIFE	236
INTERPRETATIONS OF ETERNITY:—	
RETRIBUTION	250
INTERPRETATIONS OF ETERNITY:—	
REUNION	265
INTERPRETATIONS OF ETERNITY:—	
REUNION	280
INTERPRETATIONS OF ETERNITY:—	
REUNION	292
MEMORIAL FESTIVAL OF OUR TRIUMPH OVER DEATH	305
THE TRIUMPH OF HOLINESS	315
THE CONNEXION BETWEEN LIFE AND ETERNITY	328
GLORIFICATION AFTER DEATH	342

MEDITATIONS.

IS SLOW DECLINE OR SUDDEN DEATH MOST DESIRABLE?

Saviour! by Thy death wound's power,
Strengthen me, when that blest hour,
Which weigheth crowns of victory,
To my death-bed draweth nigh.

Then, Peace, with soft and silent wing,
Round my couch thy shadow fling!
Ghost of my sins! avoid the bed
Where I, dying, rest my head,
While the fading life-light pales
As my quivering eyesight fails.

Come, my angel, from God's throne,
Bring me my celestial crown;
Then waft me, with thy waving palm,
To heavenly joys, and angel calm.
(Matthew vii. 20, 21.)

WHAT a painful shock do we not all experience at the intelligence of the sudden death of a friend, or even of a mere acquaintance, whom we may have seen and spoken to but a few hours or a few days before, and whom we believed to be in good health! We are

B

struck with terror; we find it difficult to realize the fact; it seems to us incomprehensible, impossible; it is as though we had expected that God, the Ruler of life and death, would, in regard to us and all that concerns us in this world, have made a merciful exception to the general course of things.

But what is it that terrifies us? It seems to us dreadful that a human being should, unexpectedly and without any preparation, be torn from amid all his plans and projects, and be ushered into another world. We at once picture to ourselves in imagination our own soul in the place of that of the departed person, and feel the silent awe with which it must be seized at the mighty change that has been wrought in the course of a few seconds, when it finds itself, without any forewarning, drifting away from its common occupations into the unknown world beyond the grave. We shudder at such parting without leave-taking, without the last pressure of the hand of affection.

Different are the impressions produced by the spectacle of the slow extinction of one whose illness can only end in death. It is true, that in such case we are better prepared for the loss we are to sustain; but, nevertheless, the slightest sign of improvement revives our hope that the malady will not prove fatal, and the dearer to us the person who seems about to depart, the more willingly, and more fervently, do we give ourselves up to hope. And when death does ensue, our grief is not the less poignant because we might have been prepared for all that was to come. It is true that the sufferings of the sick are seldom as intense as our heated and self-torturing imaginations depict them to us; but who can watch the formerly so blooming, and now so emaciated form, the pale cheek and sunken eye, without being moved with deep pity? Who can listen to his groans and sighs, to the quick, feeble, or heavy breathing, without wishing that a merciful God would soon put an end to this state, and give the sufferer rest in that sleep of death, which is, after all, inevitable?

Thus we are terrified by sudden death, while we are pained by the spectacle of slow decline.

But which of these would be the most desirable, if wishing could be of any avail, when the goal of every hope and every desire has been irrevocably fixed? Is sudden or slow death to be preferred?

This is a question which at first sight, indeed, seems idle, as our opinions can have no effect upon that which must and will take place. But, nevertheless, the subject has great attractions for every mind, and to meditate upon it cannot fail to be instructive and consolatory, if it tend to destroy the many prejudices which are entertained in regard to it.

For instance, are there not many mortals who look upon sudden death as the greatest of evils, because they believe that whosoever is thus stricken down, is carried away in the midst of sins which he has not had time to repent of, to eternal damnation? Are there not many who for this reason in particular pray to God to deliver them from sudden death?

But such belief can hardly be other than the fruit of superstition and of an unworthy conception of the greatness and justice of God. For, if sudden death were in reality the greatest of evils, how could God—whose children we *all* are, to whose grace and mercy we *all* lay claim—favour some human beings in this most important matter (if it be really so,) and not others? When an earthquake or a flood suddenly destroys with one swoop hundreds of lives, are there not likely to be among the number as many virtuous and upright men as there are deep-dyed sinners? If sudden death were the direst of misfortunes, would not an all-merciful God in distributing it exercise some discrimination? What have the millions who breathe out their lives slowly on a bed of sickness done to deserve their being thus favoured?

We may indeed say to ourselves,—On the bed of sickness the evil-doer has time to repent of his sins, and to turn anew to God. But are we not all sinners? And if repentance, brought about by the fear of death, can set everything right again, would it not be opposed to the Divine love of God, which embraces all alike with fatherly tenderness, if He were to deny this happiness to many thousands while He granted it to others? Would even an earthly father, a human mother, exercise such injustice towards their children? No; your conceptions of the highest of all Beings are faulty, because you entertain erroneous views of the value of death-bed repentance. When a criminal in his prison cell, full of fear of the coming punishment, repents of his misdeeds, would you at once place him in moral worth on a level with the most pious and virtuous of men? If a child, who has long caused you sorrow by its disobedience and manifold naughtinesses, perceiving that you are at last determined to put a stop to the evil, and to carry out the threatened punishment, burst into tears and repent because of its fear of chastisement, would you reward it in the same way, bestow upon it the same pleasures, as upon the docile, industrious child, who, looking up to you with tender love, has always obeyed your will? Your sense of justice would recoil from this. Then how can you suppose the All-Just One to be less just than you would be? How can repentance born of the terror of the moment, be of the same value as a life virtuous throughout? Christ Himself has, with deep earnestness, warned us against this error. Neither tears, nor words, nor prayers, will avail, but *deeds, works of penitence!* "Wherefore by their fruits ye shall know them!" Saith the Lord, "Not every one that saith unto me: Lord! Lord! shall enter into the kingdom of Heaven, *but those who do the will of my Father which is in Heaven!*" (Matt. vii. 20, 21.)

Sudden death is not, therefore, to be feared as the greatest of misfortunes, because it deprives us of the opportunity and of the time necessary to express our repentance and to utter a few prayers. The Divine Son did not teach—Repent at the hour of death; but He said, "Whoever takes up my cross during his lifetime, and follows me, he is my disciple!" "Be perfect, as your Father in Heaven is perfect." But such perfection cannot be attained when sickness has worn down our strength, but only by persevering struggles against our sensual desires, by self-consecration according to the Words and Spirit of Jesus.

If, then, it be blameworthy to *fear* sudden death for the reasons assigned, it is no doubt equally blameworthy to *wish* for it from sheer cowardice. For, in reality, what can it be but cowardice, or fear of the sufferings of a deadly malady, and the approach of death itself, that makes so many wish to be carried off as quickly as possible, when their time shall come? To *live* to endure adversity requires greater courage than at once to seek death. Of all the circumstances that dishonour the suicide, there is none that adds so much to the baseness of his dastardly deed as his dread of life. For this reason it was that Divine wisdom implanted so deeply in the breast of man the love of life and the fear of death—that the weak and timid race, overwhelmed by its earthly trials, might not fly too soon to seek refuge in the grave. Those trials and sufferings were necessary to turn away the mind from sensual objects, and to lift it up and make it grasp higher ones—but the love of life was not the less necessary. Without these fetters large countries would often have been converted into deserts, and the ends of God and the destiny of man would have remained unfulfilled.

The wise man will see the same reasons for deeming a slow as a rapid death desirable; but he will never see cause to fear either. For he knows the Lord that created him; he knows the voice of the Lord, who speaks to us even in the hour of death, saying, "Fear not: for I have redeemed thee, I have called thee by thy name; thou art mine." (Isaiah xliii. 1.)

Fear not death, whether it come early or late; whether it come slowly, through the exhaustion of illness, or the decay of age; or suddenly, in the strength and enjoyment of life, or on the field of battle, or by some extraordinary and unforeseen occurrence. For thou mayst indeed look forward to death, as at night we look forward to sleep; but thou wilt not know when it comes, as little as thou art conscious of the exact moment when thou sinkest into sleep. They who shall see thee die will be conscious of it, and shudder. They shudder because the love of life, with which God has inspired all creatures, recoils from that which is parting from life. But thou wilt as little see thyself die as thou hast ever seen thyself fall asleep. Thou seest not the film gathering over thine eyes, thou art not alarmed at the increasing pallor of thy face, at the coldness of thy limbs, which fill the imagination of those who surround thee with dismal images.

Fear not thy dissolution, for thou knowest who has redeemed thee: it is Christ Jesus who has shown thee the way to heaven, and who has revealed to thee the will of the Father; by doing which faithfully thy spirit will be ennobled and rendered worthy of entering into a realm of glory. Thou knowest, when thine hour cometh, who it is that has called thee by thy name, and has said, "Thou art mine!" It is the almighty, the all-loving Father, who has created thee, who has singled thee out, not for eternal suffering and destruction, but for eternal bliss.

Fear not then, even shouldst thine end be rapid. Constant and exaggerated terror of death is not only unworthy of a Christian, but even of a heathen; for this useless self-torture is in itself more painful than death can ever be. It wears out the spirit, deprives us of all capacity for joy—which is in reality the true supporter of health and life—weakens the body, and hastens the approach of death, while we are endeavouring to flee from it. It is well known that fear is one of the most dangerous poisoners of life. Fear is in itself deadly, life-consuming. He who is ever dreading death, dies a thousand times, and suffers each day of his life, while when death is really at hand he will not be conscious of its coming.

Therefore, cheer up, divert thy mind, occupy thy fancy with other images; for it is only thy diseased imagination that conjures up before thee these dismal shadows, not thy rational conviction. Try to turn aside thy thoughts, which are so prone to cling to this painful subject, because thou hast too often led them in this direction. Every cheerful hour that thou enjoyest is a healing draught, and adds to the length of thy days.

Fear not death, should it even be thy lot to die suddenly. Who knows what his end may be? Who can in any way foretell whether he may not be cut off by a fire, by the falling of a tile from a roof, by a cannon ball, by an attack of apoplexy, or by some other untoward accident? Therefore, prepare thy house—keep thy domestic affairs, thy worldly concerns, in order, so that, if thou be called away suddenly from the midst of thy friends, everything shall be found after thy dissolution arranged with such perfect care, that there shall be no neglected parts, no confusion. The praise of the living will follow thee; the blessings of thy loved ones will reach thee in the eternal abodes; thou wilt have fulfilled one of the most sacred duties towards those who are bound to thee by the ties of blood. We may always take it for granted, that he who kept his domestic affairs in order, was found prepared in those more important matters also that lay between him and God. Live and act each day so that after thy death, were it even to take place the next minute, thy family shall not be left in want, and no blame shall attach to thy name. For the good name of the departed must ever be the most blessed inheritance to those he leaves behind. Arrange thy affairs so that they may at any moment be laid before the eyes of strangers, as is always more or less the case after our demise.

Prepare thy house! If thou leadest at all times a life of piety, innocence, benevolence, full of active well-doing, and free from hatred or anger, such as Jesus thy Saviour taught thee, then sudden death can only be to thee a sudden benefit. Why shouldst thou dread to appear before God? Art thou not ever in His presence? Hast thou not been, even from thy birth, one of His children, whom He holds in His arms, whom He watches over and protects? True, thou tremblest before His judgment. He knows thy shortcomings; but He knows also thy earnest efforts to correct them. He sees also the honest fight which, in order to be worthy of Him, thou fightest against the temptations to sin; he sees how often thou hast resisted and overcome thy tendencies to avarice or sensual enjoyment; He witnesses thy endeavours to make amends for every fault by noble actions. Ought a child to fear to appear before its loving parent, even though it have not yet conquered all its faults? Has not Jesus revealed to us the infinite mercy of the Father in all its beauty? Has He not given us assurances of His grace and His forgiveness?

He who ever walks before the Omnipresent in the loving spirit of Jesus, he need not tremble before the Omnipresent; and to him sudden death is but an unexpected benefaction. Such rapid passing away deprives death of its sharpest pangs; the sight of the weeping loved ones that surround us, the thought of the sorrow of those who are absent, which render so difficult our inevitable departure from this world. For to a loving heart, what bitterer grief can death bring than this? Who could behold without deep pain the affliction of those he is about to leave? Who could remain unmoved, when they draw nigh to stretch forth for the last time the hand of faithful love? Who could remain untouched, when they surround the death-bed with mournful lamentations?

Even the many solemn preparations for the possible occurrence of our demise, the anxious listening and watching of our dear ones, and the many other distressing circumstances which generally surround the dying, add to the agony of these last moments. Therefore, God often sends to His children sudden death. He relieves them from the afflicting necessity of witnessing the fruitless, and sometimes immoderate grief of those who remain behind.

Death itself, the falling asleep, has no bitterness. It is not a suffering, it cannot be so, for *it is the end of all suffering*, in which pain must already have ceased. It is the sickness alone which is distressing; but sickness is not death, it only slowly introduces the latter. He whom God calls suddenly from this world is even spared the trials of a bed of illness. He dies without having tasted of death. Between his earthly and his heavenly life scarce a moment intervenes. Without care, without fear, without pain, he passes from this life into a better and higher existence, like one who passes from dreaming to waking. He knows nothing of the struggle between death and the instinctive love of life; in him there is no longing to remain with his loved ones, no repining for what he is about to leave, no anxious looking forward to what awaits him.

No, I do not look upon sudden death as a punishment of God, but as one of His sweetest boons. Thus He called unto Himself an Elias and an Enoch.

How could that be an evil, O Thou, the Allgood! that cometh from Thy hand? Lord of the seraph and of the worm, Ruler of life and death, I am in Thy hand; do unto me as Thou deemest fit, for what Thou dost is well done. When Thou didst call me from nothing into life, Thou didst will my happiness; when Thou callest me away from life, will my happiness be less Thy care? No, no, Thou art Love, and whosoever dwells in love, dwells in Thee, O Lord, and Thou in him. Thou, Lord, art my light and my salvation! Why should I tremble? Thou art the Lord of my life; what should I dread?

FEAR OF DEATH.

PART I.

It is fulfilled! once—to the Cross fast bound,
   His bitterest hour past—the Saviour cried,
His flesh transpierced with wounds, His head thorn-crowned,
   Cried He to Him in whom He could confide;
Nor vainly cried He, for the hour drew nigh
That ended all His mortal agony.

It is fulfilled! Though yet a short delay,
   I also once must cry, and that ere long;
Then shall I go where tears are wiped away,
   Where sickness cometh never more, nor wrong—
The heart that's filled with love and trusting faith
Knows what it still may hope for, e'en in death.
                  (2 *Cor.* v. 1—5.)

IF we mortals could foresee from our cradle all the events and sufferings that await us, many would tremble more at life than at the closing act of it which we call death.

Life has often been metaphorically represented as a journey begun without our willing it, and ended without our willing it. On we speed with restless haste. We set out in the dim dawn of morning, emerging from the unknown depths of night, and hurrying towards another night. From beginning to end it is the work of God.

Minutes vanish, hours fly past us: fain would we linger among the first flowers that smile to us in the rosy morn of youth! But a hidden power urges us on, the flowers fall withered from our hand, the hot mid-day sun of life is already glowing above our heads. We discover shady spots, whose refreshing shelter invites us to repose; and gladly would we rest. But, no! we must speed on. We endeavour in vain to hold fast the joys we find by the wayside. They escape. Already the sunset reddens the sky, and behind the lurid glare night is stealthily approaching. Willingly would we pause to enjoy, in longer draughts, the coolness of the lovely evening. But onwards! onwards! cries an unknown voice. We cling in vain to the objects we meet, to stay the speed of our progress. It is but a futile effort, they are carried along with us down the rapid stream. The colours of the sunset fade; darkness envelopes all things; light is extinguished; earth vanishes; our senses rest; the journey is accomplished. We are surrounded by night; men have forgotten us.

Such is our lot. We all know it. You do not shudder at the night from which you have emerged into this life—why should you shudder at the night into which you are to pass? Are these wonderful transformations of existence your own work? No; they are the unalterable consequences of the wise laws of a Higher Power.

What, then, is that which we call to die? To go out like a light, and in a sweet trance to forget ourselves and all the passing phenomena of the day, as we forget the phantoms of a fleeting dream; to form, as in a dream, new connexions with God's world; to enter into a more exalted sphere, and to make a new step up man's graduated ascent of creation.

We know naught of the world beyond this; nor can it be revealed or expressed to mortal man, because it exceeds all his previous experiences, and he lacks the senses wherewith to comprehend it. How could you explain to one born blind, the feeling of delight awakened in you by the contemplation of a beautiful form, or by the spectacle of early morn in spring among flowers? If the soul of an animal should ever be clad in human form, and with this should receive the light of reason, would this new human soul, do you think, long to return to its first animal state, when in dull monotony it could only brood over the present as it passed by, and know of naught but what was immediately before it?

Why, then, do we fear death, which is but the certain transition to a better state? Why do we, when we think of dissolution, treasure more highly our existence as it is; although there are but few among us, who, if they had the choice, would care to live their life over again with its many hours of suffering, its follies and its self-torturings, unless they might be allowed to introduce some changes?

There are two sources from whence spring the fear of death, which more especially deserve our attention.

1. The Deity Himself has intimately interwoven with our whole being an instinctive love of life. Hence the general revolt of our nature against dissolution in all its forms.

Were it not for this strong and almost unconquerable love of life; were it not for this natural shrinking from death, the earth would already now be a depopulated desert. Man has to encounter in this world numberless dangers, which would long ago have destroyed him, had not the love of life given him courage to resist them, and had not this courage, in its turn, given him the power to conquer them. To many a man his self-inflicted sufferings, or even his blind fear of misfortune, soon render life intolerable, and he would sink down before he had attained the goal of his journey, did not his dread of the dark mystery of the grave make him gird himself up, and reconcile him to the labours of the day. Already, dark despair with dim-eyed frenzy approaches the brink of the abyss, and resolves upon passing over into the quiet land of death; but life puts on new smiles, and hope, which ever accompanies it, plucks the dagger from the upraised hand. It is the DIVINE WILL that we should live to ripen for a higher destiny; therefore have we been bound to life by the tenderest yet strongest ties.

Without this passionate love of life, the continuation of our existence after death would be indifferent to us, and we should never earnestly set about preparing ourselves for higher perfection. But the passion for life is implanted in us, and with it follows the desire for continued existence even after the change in death. And to the hope of eternity is joined the feeling of the necessity of rendering ourselves worthy of a higher life hereafter.

Thus this inborn love, this instinctive clinging to life, becomes to us a Divine revelation of the continuance of our existence after death. And not only has the Christian received this spirit-stirring revelation through Christ Jesus, but to all nations of the earth it has been vouchsafed.

The wildest savage who roams the woods in still

undiscovered lands, looks with the same joyous hope towards eternity as did the sage of antiquity.

But man errs grossly when he allows this instinctive love to degenerate into an unnatural and tormenting passion for life, which leads him to entertain an unreasonable fear of death, and to place an exaggerated value upon existence here on earth.

In many cases it is only a morbid state of the body which causes us to surround death in imagination with shadowy terrors—a tendency to melancholy, which, when permitted to gain ground, harasses us with a constant and blind dread of dissolution. Not the real change which takes place in death, but the false images of it which float before the imagination, are calculated to awaken terror; and these man has himself created for his own torment.

This distressing tendency of mind is frequently nothing more than the result of a too sedentary life, and the consequent thickening of the humours of the body, and the obstruction by these of the delicate play of the nerves. It may sometimes be more readily overcome by exercise, work, and amusement than by the best-founded consolatory arguments. The condition of a person who is in constant dread of illness or of death, is very sad, and it would be advisable to consign him to the care of a skilful physician.

We ought never, either to ourselves or to others, to depict death and the grave in more sombre colours than in reality belong to either. Gloomy images of this kind only serve to disturb the imagination, and they exercise a baneful influence over weak minds.

The dying are as little conscious of the transition from life to death as the weary are aware of the transition from the waking to the sleeping state. We have known many persons who on the last bed of sickness, have awaited with full consciousness the moment of dissolution, and have even predicted it. Their imaginations had not been previously excited, they fell asleep smiling and without a fear, as should every Christian who believes in God, and who treasures up in a pious heart a full trust in His infinite goodness. That change which the spectator who stands by the bedside sees in the face of the dying, they see not themselves. Illness may be painful; its cessation cannot be so.

When we shudder at the sight of the lifeless corpse, which lies before us cold and stiff, pale and breathless, having no sympathy with our feelings, no pity for our tears, as though it had never belonged to us, and never known us—this shudder is caused by self-deception only. If we look narrowly into ourselves at such times, we shall find that we pity the dead for all he has lost. But *he* knows of no loss. We picture to ourselves how tenderly he loved us, how he would fain have remained with us, how he has been separated from us by an unknown hand, and how vainly we sought to keep him back. But the dead knows naught of this, and even in his last days and hours these sad thoughts and feelings were far less vividly present to him than they are generally to persons in health. He has vanished from the realm of this life, and has left to us his ashes, his earthly raiment, this icy statue, which we loved when it was animated by the soul, but which never belonged to him, and which will now return to the elements out of which it was gradually built up.

Not to death itself belongs terror, but to the fancies we connect with it. Carry your mind away from these to the simple fact, and it will lose most of its gloom in your eyes.

Another unnatural deviation from the instinctive love of life that God has implanted in us, is the passionate clinging to life which many persons evince, and the undue value which they attach to it. Life has no value except in as far as we use it for perfecting our souls, for enriching our minds with nobler qualities, and for spreading happiness around us. When we can no longer do this; when, as in extreme old age, all hope of again being able to exert ourselves in this way ceases, then this life has lost its highest value, and a new existence becomes desirable.

Exalted souls, ye know of nobler possessions than life! Ye who have gone to meet the hero's death for the freedom and welfare of your fatherland and thousands of oppressed fellow-citizens; ye who, to uphold the truth of Jesus Christ's religion, have courageously chosen the path of the grave; ye who have preferred death to a life without dignity and without virtue—ye knew the true value of existence. Ye died courageously in the service of virtue, in the performance of heavenly deeds. Your death is more enviable than the life of thousands! Ye blessed ones, ye teach those that remain behind what their lives ought to be. (Matt. xvi. 25.)

Life has no worth except through our virtues, through the happiness that we prepare for others. He, therefore, who, like the animal, only lives to satisfy his hunger and his thirst, without any effort to prepare his mind for a future nobler existence; he who lives merely to tickle his palate with daintier viands and more exquisite wines than other men; he who lives but to clothe his body in finer raiment than other men, to satisfy his vanity and to display his miserable pride—futilities that must vanish on the brink of the grave—his existence has no worth, his death deserves no tear.

Frequently, again, the passionate clinging to life is but a consequence of too great a love and anxiety for those we may leave behind us. We tremble at death because it will tear us from the arms of a beloved husband or wife. We shrink back from the grave because, when we shall descend into it, dear children will stand around it,—poor orphans without education, without protection, without support.

For this reason we often see that young persons, who have no innocent dear ones depending on them, die more composedly than parents, whose eyes are fixed lovingly upon their children. But even in such cases the mind of a Christian ought not to be overwhelmed by the fear of death. It is not thou, O father, nor thou, O mother, who hast hitherto protected thy child; it is God! God is the Father of the orphan; the same God who watches over the life and the well-being of the humblest worm. If He wills the welfare of thy children, verily no human power shall prevail against them. If God should call thee from them, hasten joyfully to the Heavenly Father; the time will come when He will call thy children also.

2. The second chief source whence springs the fear of death, is the turning away of men's hearts from the eternal truths of religion.

You are, it is true, baptized in Christ; you confess Him in the Holy Supper; you perform the customary rites of religion; but do you also walk in the spirit of Christ and of His commandments? Are you conscious of your God, and at one with Him in the depths of a pious heart? Do you at all times walk in the ways of the Lord? Do you at all times aim at being just? Do you do all the good that is in your power? Have you made peace with your enemies? Is your conscience troubled by the remembrance of secret sins?

The religious man stands highest in the human scale on earth. With his eyes fixed on eternity, with his hand stretched forth to do good, he walks in and with God; calm amid storms and tempests, blessed with the peace that God alone can bestow. But never does the sublimity of religion appear in a more beneficent light than in the hour of death, or even when connected with the mere thought of the tomb. It is then that its most blessed power is revealed.

A sensual, uncultivated man, when he thinks of death, feels the fearful isolation of his spirit, and anticipates the annihilation of all that he possesses. What is his spirit when deprived of that which has hitherto constituted its delights? He has never contemplated a higher destiny; what is to become of him then when he loses the earthly things, which alone he knows and values? He is descending into the grave, and behind him he leaves merry feasts, gilded honours, costly garments, the flatteries of parasites, the obsequiousness of dependents, the heaped-up treasures which covetous heirs rush to divide. Poorer than the beggar that used to hang about his door he stands before the portals of eternity—he has lost his *all;* he knew but *one* world—his earthly home. What is now to become of him?

O religion, O sweet peace of conscience, and thou O union of my soul with the Most High, do not abandon me! Alas for him who only stretches forth his arms towards you, when all earthly things are melting away! Alas for him, who does not fix his eyes on a higher existence until he feels this sublunary world giving way under his feet!

O Jesus, in Thy holy revelation I will live, and in it I will die. Blessed is the power of Thy word; to it the power of death must yield. I live to Thee, and I shall not die. There is no death, there is no grave; it is but change and glorification. God is no God of death; He is our life. He created life, and my spirit is His work. My spirit is life, while it animates my body, and remains life, when the dust which for a time clothed it as a garment, and which was to it as an instrument, returns again to dust.

Heavenly and eternal Father, Source of all being, Thou from whom I spring, unto whom I shall return —Thine I shall ever be! Sweet is life, in truth, but death has, nevertheless, no terrors; no fear of it shall overwhelm me, shall turn me away from Thee and from the path of virtue. I hold as naught the days that I do not adorn with good deeds; I hold as naught a life which I cannot glorify by virtue.

And me also, me also, O God, Thou wilt call unto thyself when my hour comes, when my earthly goal is reached. Blessed shall I then be if I can say unto myself, *I have fought a good fight;* as far as my powers allowed, I have completed a life of well-doing; *the crown of eternal life awaits me also!*

And when in the last hour I have to taste the bitterness of death, to drain the final cup of trial; when my stiffened hand can no longer bestow a blessing on my loved ones, from whose sorrowful eyes the tears of parting are falling on my pillow, my closed lips can no longer utter words of love, of love true unto death; when the stir of the world and all the sweet sounds of life cease to fall upon my ear,—then, then, O Lord! I commend my soul to Thee. Joyfully I turn away my dimmed eyes from those who are dear to my heart, for I know they are in Thy keeping. Thou abidest with them as Thou abidest with me, for evermore in the regions of eternal life.

No, I fear not death, *O Father of life!* For death is not eternal sleep; it is the transition to a new life, a moment of great and glorious transformation, an ascension towards Thee.

Yet we cannot deem unpardonable the tear that is wept over the bier of a beloved object. O Source of all Love, Thine eye penetrates our inmost being. Thou seest the bleeding heart of the mother standing by the coffin of her child, which carries with it into the grave her brightest hopes. Thou knowest the heartrending grief of the father who has, by the death of a beloved son or daughter, been bereft of every happiness in this life. May Thy Spirit, the blessed Comforter, penetrate our souls, and inspire with its strength our poor human hearts! Alas, we are but mortals! We are overwhelmed by the power of the moment—Angels would in such moments praise Thee!

Finally, the death of our loved ones sweetens our

own death, which leads us towards eternal reunion. The affectionate words of Christ are an earnest to us of a more joyful futurity. We also shall one day be with our loved ones in paradise. Amen, O God and Father! So be it. Amen.

FEAR OF DEATH.

PART II.

Away, pale fear of death, away!
   Rejoice thyself in death my heart,
The cold corpse will rejoin its clay,
   And grief shall end, and pain's sharp smart,
And the well of tears shall dry
When the dust in dust shall lie.

Thou healest every wound, O death!
   Thy touch at once each sorrow charms—
As departs my failing breath,
   Flee I unto angels' arms.
Though enclosed within the grave,
Light and freedom shall I have.

Father, for each earthly pleasure
   Heartfelt thanks from me receive.
Thanks, should grief o'erflow the measure,
   Father, still my soul shall give—
Shouldst Thou take them both from me,
Yet more gladly praise I Thee!

                  (2 *Cor.* v. 1.)

A COLD shudder seizes me at the thought of death, and every fibre of my body seems to struggle against the feeling of dissolution and separation. And yet however much my whole being may revolt against it, like others, I must die. I see pass by me to the grave the corpse of the child faded in the bud, and of the old man worn out with years. The ashes of the maiden, called away in her early bloom, mingle with those of the man, whom some dire event, some unforeseen accident, has cut off in the prime of his manhood and activity. And my corpse, too, will one day be laid among the rest.

Why am I alive? Why should not death be as familiar to me as life, as both come to me without my will and without my knowledge?

Sobbing with grief, the faithful husband stands by the coffin of his dear partner, his second self, her whom he called the better half of his heart; with similar grief a devoted child remembers an affectionate father, or a gentle, loving mother, who has been taken from him, alas! too soon; painfully fall the tears of the sorrowing bride on the cold clay of her beloved, whose death is to her the death of every hope in life; deep is the sadness with which father or mother contemplate the little grave which covers the remains of the darling child, whose innocence and grace so often delighted their hearts, and filled their views of the future with soul-elevating images.

Wherefore do I weep? And wherefore do you weep, who have lost beloved ones? Is it for the dead, because they have to leave all that is dear to them—to leave a life which has bestowed so many pleasures, and promises so many more? Oh, uncalled for compassion! Do we pity each night our dear ones when they fall asleep, or do we pity ourselves when we go to rest? Yet what difference is there between sleep and death? True, he who falls asleep feels a profound assurance that with the rising sun he will awake again with renewed strength; while the dying has not so near a hope. But when he awakes he will find instead of you the long lost dear ones that have gone before him; he will find his God, who will be more to him than you could ever be, poor orphans! he finds a blessed state that will endure for ever; nay, he will in a short time even find you again. For what is the duration of even the longest life on earth? Ask the old man of threescore and ten, and he will tell you,— "So little have I retained of my life, that it seems to me but a summer night's dream of threescore minutes and ten." Then, wherefore do we weep? Even sleep causes separation; and the separation in death, is it for a much longer term?

Nay, we ought to be able to say good night to our dying friends with the same calm composure with which we take leave of each other in the evening, when, looking confidently beyond the night, we enjoy in advance the pleasures of the coming morn; or we ought to whisper our friendly farewell as though they were about to set out on a safe journey to a pleasant land, to the house of our Father, the home of our loved ones, whence an invitation has gone forth to them, and whither we shall follow ere long.

In truth, when divested of all the gloomy subordinate circumstances with which my imagination invests death, it is not so terrible. No one would think of it as dreadful had he never seen a dead corpse—the pallor, coldness, and stony impassiveness of which causes a shudder; did he know naught of death but that it is a transformation of our souls, a passing away to a happier and more blessed home.

It is to our imaginations we owe the gloomy thoughts that most distress us; in the fulness of our health and strength, and our love of life, we fancy ourselves in the place of the dying, and thus we experience grief that he knows not, and endure pains that he does not suffer. We fancy ourselves in the dark tomb, and behold the members of the body being converted into dust, and the grave seems to us the end of all life.

But if we set aside these terrific images, the offspring of our own brains, which have no existence in reality, we shall find little difference between sleep and death. Numbers of persons, who in their lifetime have entertained a most unreasonable fear of death, have ultimately passed away with a cheerfulness and serene composure which they never expected.

It is still more unreasonable to picture to ourselves the moment of the soul's parting from the body as especially painful. Whether this disruption causes suffering to the body no one is able to tell. The spasmodic twitching of the muscles (which in many cases indeed does not take place) is distressing to behold, but is painless as a sensation. With the exception of falling asleep, nothing is so similar to the passing away in death as the sinking of a person into a swoon; yet he who faints experiences little or no suffering before unconsciousness ensues. Perhaps, if artificial stimulants were not applied to restore to his nervous system the power of serving the soul, he would pass from the swoon into death without any further sensation. Such also is the condition of all those who, reduced to unconsciousness by excessive cold, are eventually restored to life. Their limbs are benumbed, their blood flows slower and slower, and finally the body stiffens as in death. The only sensation they experience is unconquerable drowsiness, and desire to lie down and rest; and though they may be perfectly conscious that sleep is likely to end in death, they nevertheless brave it that they may enjoy the delight of sleep.

It is thus established that the moment of dissolution has in itself nothing that is terrible, that very few persons are clearly conscious of it, and that it is the imagination of the survivors that invests it with horrors. And yet even in this case it is not the act of dying itself that seems so terrible, but the thought, What shall I be when I have ceased to belong to humanity, when I have been stripped of my human form? It is this uncertainty as to all that is in store for us, that fills us with awe. The darkness that envelopes the future makes us rejoice doubly in the broad daylight that surrounds us; we learn to appreciate that which we possess; and we tremble at the thought of exchanging all that is familiar to us for a state of which we can hardly form a conception.

Had the wisdom of the Creator vouchsafed to us in this life a knowledge of what is to come in the next, verily the grave would cease to be a barrier, and a small number only would await patiently the natural hour of death.

But the very uncertainty in which we are left constitutes the strongest tie that binds to life the impatient and the frivolous, who are apt to be thrown into despair by the slightest adversity, and prevents them from cutting short the term of trial appointed for them. It is this that surrounds death with such awe, that all who are not bereft of reason shrink back from it.

But even this uncertainty is only terrifying as long as the future world seems far off; in the hour of death it changes character. Then it is the life that lies behind us that appears dark and vague; while the future, with its new existence, is irradiated by the light of certainty. The dying man makes up his account with the world, once more bestows his blessing upon his dear ones, and turns away from all that he loves best, in order to shut himself up within himself, and to pass over into the happier existence. The past has no charms for him; he is attracted solely by the new world, on the threshold of which he stands.

However, it is not to all that death loses its terrors. It is with reason that the sinner trembles when he beholds it in the distance, and still more so when he finds himself inevitably face to face with it.

But who is the sinner? Every one to whom this earthly life is all in all, and to whom the Divine element in it is nothing; every one who lives for this world as were it never to end; every one who thinks more of the gratification of his senses than of the improvement of his immortal spirit; every one who wastes year after year in endeavouring to increase his earthly possessions and dignities, who lives but to adorn his person, to enjoy frivolous pleasures, to triumph over his rivals and opponents; in a word, to secure to himself such earthly goods as seem to him most desirable, while he feels it irksome to devote a moment to the perfecting of his undying soul.

When such a one dies, his soul is in death even poorer than in the first hour of his birth, when at least it possessed the jewel, innocence. He dies, and his spirit sinks into nothingness; for earthly goods were *everything* to him, and he himself was but an instrument of rude passions. What becomes of the soul, if made the slave of the body, when the body, its master and idol, has been converted into dust? What becomes in death of the accomplishments of the body, the artistic language of gesture, the sportive wit of the moment, the capacity for over-reaching and seducing others, the power of flattery, the thousand little arts of vanity and conceit? They perish with the flesh. But the poor neglected spirit, and the forgotten eternity—they endure! Fearful as it may be, they endure; and the consequences of sin, and the account to be rendered, and the judgment, and the righteous before God—they endure.

Lost one! my soul is moved with sorrow at thy lot. Angels may well weep over it; but thou hadst warning. God, nature, reason, the events of the world, joy, misfortune, men, books—all preached it to thee, all recalled to thee thy higher destiny; all warned thee, now louder, now more gently, now in threatening tones, now in imploring accents, to remember the *one thing* needful. Lost one! thou didst smile proudly, and thy pride was thy god. Thou wert ashamed of being good—called it visionary enthusiasm, romance, folly to ask of thee to be truly, humanly noble, by rising above thy dearest passions! Lost one! thou hast prepared thine own destiny, and no angel will alter the eternal laws of nature or of the world of spirits. God is just, and no prayers, no sweat of agony on thy pale forehead, can save thee; thy life lies wasted behind thee, thy spirit passes, without a hope of a better lot, into the new existence. Thou hast enjoyed thy goods, and thou hast thy reward.

Yea, most assuredly, a dreadful certainty awaits

him who in this life has lived but for the present, as though it were not to be followed by a hereafter! But equally certain is that which awaits the righteous man who has quietly pursued the path of duty and virtue, and who has preferred the well-being, the peace, the happiness of those around him to his own.

He enjoys certainty. His heart tells him, thou shalt not die entirely; eternal love watches over thee. Nature tells him so, when through her wonders he beholds, as through a veil, God in His majesty, His infinitude, and His mercy. His religion, as revealed by Jesus, teaches it. He knows that our earthly mansion, our frail body will be destroyed, but that we have a building, built by God, a house not made with hands, eternal in the heavens. (2 Cor. v. 1.)

What are the terrors of death to a noble mind? A play of the imagination, at which, not the soul, but only what is earthly in us, trembles. Has not Jesus Christ conquered for us the terrors of death? Did He not open for us joyful admission to the Father, when He taught us to be perfect as our Father in Heaven is perfect?

Though the body may shudder when about to be reduced to ashes again, and it ceases to be an instrument of the soul that until then had animated it, the spirit of the righteous is at the same time seized with holy transports: for it sees throughout the entire universe LIFE only, nowhere death; it sees the mutual relations of all things, sees no link wanting in the great chain of beings, which the almighty hand of God has woven.

Millions before me have fought the battle and won the victory, and millions will do so after me. Shall

I alone, then, shrink back with vain and cowardly fear from a death which is not death? Nay, let us depart courageously and cheerfully by faith, if not yet by sight. (2 Cor. v. 7.) These friends, these children, these loved ones to whom my heart clings so tenderly, when I part from them will it be for ever? Nay, it is but separation for the length of a summer night. Their congenial souls will remain true to mine. The kind though mysterious hand of Providence, which made us find each other in the gloom of this life, will re-unite us again in the bright daylight of eternal being. God, whom the eternal Son, whom Jesus calls Love, Love the purest and the highest, will not destroy and tear asunder that love which He himself created. No, the all Holy One, in whose likeness we may grow through love and virtue, will not allow love and virtue to fade with the dust, from which they do not spring.

If, then, it be my Father's will that I should depart hence earlier than ye, whom He confided to my care— ye beloved ones, whom He bestowed upon me, to gladden my life,—my last look will dwell upon you with tender blessings, while eternity is beckoning me away. The tears of sadness ye weep at my death-bed shall be to me the last test of your faithful love, which so often shed happiness around me and which can never die! Ye will cease to weep for me, but not to love me; and even in its heavenly abode, even amid the pure transports it may there enjoy, my soul will continue to love you—that sentiment which God implanted in it, I will lay again before His throne. "Weep not," I will whisper to you in my last hour; "that is not death where innocence, virtue, and holiness live. Sin only is the death of the soul. Flee sin, hold fast to God, act divinely in as far as your powers will allow, and we shall belong to each other and remain united there as here."

Yes, henceforward I will walk more steadily in the path of righteousness, and the terrors of death will vanish before the consciousness of my growth in goodness, as mist disappears before the rays of the morning sun. How cheerfully have not numbers of noble mortals voluntarily encountered certain death for truth and right, for their country and for the good of humanity! They died in the good cause as martyrs to their own nobility of soul. Ye, exalted minds, ye prized sacred objects higher than a life without merit —prized the duties of the spirit higher than a few brief hours or years spent in the sensuous enjoyments of earth. Ye esteemed death in the cause of God a gain; it was to you but as a change of garment, and in reality was but this: you cast off the perishable raiment, to clothe yourselves in the imperishable.

Ah, enviable fate, to breathe out the spirit in the arms of God, while sacrificing an empty, worthless life in the fulfilment of duty! Jesus! such was Thy death, the death that redeemed the world! Ah! could such be the death of all Thy followers, could mine be such! May it be my lot to give up my spirit in the midst of well-doing, and while surrounded by the blessings of a world rendered happier through my exertions!

Finally, what attractions has this earth that should make parting from it so difficult? The desire of the righteous is to be for ever growing in righteousness. Can the opportunity be accorded here below for this continued growth? No, this holy craving can only be satisfied after they awake in the higher existence.

And the joys of this life—though I am far from holding them lightly, for they are the gifts of God—how fleeting are they not! How quickly do we not tire even of the greatest pleasures of earth! What have we gained, when we have obtained all that we have lusted for? What, but the constant repetition of a drop of honey mixed with a drop of gall? None of this world's pleasures is quite unalloyed.

Thou fearest death, O feeble mortal? What then wouldst thou gain by an unusually prolonged life? Thou wouldst see the friends of thy youth, thy children, all thy loved ones, descend before thee into the grave; thou wouldst find thyself at last alone in the world, a forlorn stranger, no longer having aught in common with it. Thou wouldst stretch out thine arms longingly towards those that had gone before thee, and thou wouldst weary of the empty hours of thy earthly existence. Thy protracted life would become to thee but a painful burden, which thou wouldst willingly consign to the arms of death, that thou mightest hasten free and joyful towards the beloved spirits that await thee yonder where no sorrow, no parting, no tear is known!

Yes, O my Saviour, I will become what Thou demandest of me—a true child of God, useful, loving, delighting in well-doing, without hatred, or vanity, or covetousness, pure as thou wert, divine Friend of man! Then for me the grave will have no terrors; then death will be to me only the easy passing from dreaming to waking.

And when I shall awaken into the eternal, more

blissful existence! O Jesus! Revealer of eternity! O God, bountiful Dispenser of the never-ending bliss of our spirits! what holy transports fill my being at the mere thought of what I shall then enjoy! The grave is my cradle, death is my awaking, the sunset of this life is the sunrise of existence in the regions of eternity!

Ah, ye dear ones, who have gone before me! ye tenderly beloved ones, whose sacred memory I still honour here on earth with my tears: how my heart yearns for you!—And I shall once more be with you. Though more perfect than I, ye still love me as I love you. It is love that binds together the spirits of distant worlds, that forms the link between heaven and earth; therefore its flame can never die out in my heart! And this love shall sanctify me, this hope of reunion shall be my safeguard against all temptations to sin. Towards you are directed all my wishes—fain would I again blend my being with yours. Therefore will I devote my whole soul to God and virtue, that through God I may find you. I fear death no longer! It is but the messenger of God, sent to liberate me, to lead me to you.

    Soon! oh soon! shall all be done—
      Peaceful rest I, Lord, in Thee;
    Thousands have the victory won—
      I, too, shall win the victory.
    Louder in death than nature's voice,
    My heart outcries, Have faith!—Rejoice!

GOD IS LOVE.

Could we silence every tongue,
  Love! thy praise would still be sung.
Sun and moon, and stars above,
  All bear witness, God is Love.
Silent heights, depths, earth and heaven,
  Soul! by thee is witness given.

Labour's impulse—peaceful hour—
  Joy in living—come from Thee.
I—what am I? whence my power?
  Gave a foe this strength to me?
Say—are speech, ear, sight and feeling
Tokens of love, or hate's revealing?

Oh, I feel Thee—and before Thee,
  Father of Love, in praise I fall;
For that I *am* I will adore Thee—
  Join the chorus, creatures all.
Love gave me life—and from above
Bestows all good—because 'tis Love.

                (1 *St. John* iv. 3.)

"GOD is Love!" How constantly is not this thought—the most comforting of all to an anxious human heart—reproduced in the prayers and writings of Christians, and yet how few quite comprehend it! and, more deplorable still, how few have full and unswerving faith in this blessed truth!

Heaven and earth proclaim it, for every law of nature bears witness to it; reason, also, bids us put faith in it—the revelations of Jesus Christ preach it—

and yet how vague and uncertain is the belief in it in the most human hearts!

All the nations of antiquity have said it: God is the wisest and purest Love. The most enlightened as well as the least civilized peoples of the present day profess it. Yet all have witnessed many fearful events seemingly in contradiction with this faith. They have seen dreadful wars that have struck down the hopes of nations—wars which have been permitted by God: and they have been terrified at the thought that these evils were sent by the God of Love. They have seen floods and inundations devastate whole countries; they have seen earthquakes shake the earth to its very foundations, cities and villages engulfed in the fiery abyss, and millions of human beings destroyed in a moment. They have seen mountains give way and bury under their ruins populous regions; they have seen a single tempest sweep every ship from the seas, and famine and pestilence convert smiling landscapes into deserts—and with doubting hearts they have asked: can all this havoc be the work of a loving God?

No! cried a voice in their bosoms; and yet the dreadful events would force themselves upon their memory. Hereupon they endeavoured, by the light of their immature reason, to solve the apparent contradictions in the government of the world, and thus they came to believe, not only in the loving Father of all, but also in an EVIL BEING, who is ever contending against His goodness. Their childish imaginations created two deities of almost equal might, and placed both, as antagonistic powers, on the throne of the universe. They loved the Good Deity, and brought

Him thank-offerings; and they feared the evil deity, or the Devil, and endeavoured to allay his enmity by prayers.

In this manner the ignorant heathens interpreted the origin of evil in the world, which their weak understandings, and their imperfect conceptions of the greatness of God, could not reconcile with His goodness. In consequence, the idea of a mighty evil spirit, opposed to God, was introduced among the Jews also, when they dwelt among the heathen during the Babylonian captivity; and this notion of a Devil, as the author of all evil in the world, was again transmitted from the Jews to the Christians, Jesus and his apostles having, when addressing Jews, made use of figures of speech which would be likely to be understood by the people.

This ungenerous notion, so incompatible with the omnipotence and omniscience of God, is perhaps hardly worthy of a refutation. There is no God but God! He, and He only of all beings, is the Lord of the living and the dead. He alone rules the destinies of the worlds, as those of the humblest worm in the dust.

Thus thinks the Christian. But unfortunately the conceptions which a great number of Christians form of the all-loving God, are not therefore more exalted, but frequently (hard as it is to believe) even less pure than those of the heathen. When the heathen found it impossible to reconcile the goodness of God with the evils of life, he invented, as a means of explaining the contradiction, a second deity, an evil being, but he did not accuse the God of goodness of being the author of evil, and did not attribute to Him low human, or rather animal passions. Many Christians, on the contrary, who as such believe of course in one God only, seeing the many ills that afflict humanity, explain these by conceiving of God as a God of vengeance, as an angry God, a jealous and inexorable God, who punishes the faults of a moment (for is man's life on earth more than a brief moment?) with the sufferings of eternity, and who takes revenge for the sins of the fathers on their innocent offspring—actions which, if committed by a human being, would rightly be considered as execrable and unjustifiable.

These ideas of the Most High originated at a period when the human race was still in its infancy, and when men hardly formed a higher conception of God than that of a very powerful human being, and when they even depicted the Deity in human form. These are remnants from the time when Moses exhorted the Israelites, and when he was obliged to use expressions that could make an impression on their hard hearts. For what were the children of Israel, at the time they were led out of Egypt? Were they not rude and ignorant, without instruction, without education, accustomed only to bondage under their Egyptian masters, obeying only when they felt the lash over them? Did they not make unto themselves idols of gold and stone, and worship these as they had seen the Egyptians worship their idols? Did they not even do this after Moses had preached to them that there was but one Almighty God, and no other God?

To be able to guide such a people and to accustom them to strict obedience to the heavenly precepts, Moses was obliged to address them in accordance with their usual modes of thought. Children must be spoken to in terms different from those which would be used to grown-up persons, and ignorant, uncivilized nations cannot be addressed in the same language as thinking, highly cultivated peoples.

However, even after the Israelites accepted the laws of Moses, and faithfully conformed to them, these ruder conceptions of God, meant only for their fathers, when they came out of the Egyptian bondage more than a thousand years previously, continued to prevail among them. And as the first Christians had been for the most part Jews, it followed as a matter of course, that they took their conceptions of God over into Christianity with them. And thus they have descended from generation to generation, even unto our day, and have been maintained, partly by the circumstances of the times and society, partly by the circumscribed knowledge of many teachers, partly by erroneous interpretations, and applications of certain passages in Holy Writ.

We, however, will hold fast by that alone which Jesus Christ taught and revealed. And He, the eternal Son, described the Father as the purest Love, in whom there is no particle of evil—as the all-perfect Being, in whom consequently no human passion or weakness can dwell, who is alike incapable of jealousy, of anger, of vengeance, and of repentance. He blames the outbreak of such passions in man—how then could he find them praiseworthy in the highest Being, in Him who is most emphatically Love and Goodness?

But how, if God knows neither anger nor vengeance, but only love, how has evil come into the world? Who, then, is the author of all the misery and suffering we behold on earth? Thus asks the doubting Christian, suffering man, who knows not how to account for the existence of so much woe. If God is the Author of all things, is He not also the Author of evil? And how am I to reconcile this with His Wisdom and Goodness, nay, even with His Justice?

What can I answer to this, poor doubter, other than *in the entire universe there is no evil but sin?* And sin is the work of man, springing from that freedom with which God has endowed him, to will and to do right or wrong.

Now, as in the Divine creation everything is just and good, all that is wrong and unjust, so to say, isolates itself; and when man wills evil, he feels the suffering that attends this *dissociation*. This suffering, however, tends to reform and enlighten him, so that he may no longer act against God's order of creation. And to God's ordinances belong, not only the laws of nature around us, but also the laws within us.

We are, therefore, ourselves the principal authors of our sufferings, by rushing, in our blind passions, headlong against the eternal and unyielding rules of creation. Thus a child is the author of its own pain, when, from ignorance, it wounds itself with dangerous weapons; but the pain is the beneficent teacher of prudence. Again, a child is the author of its own suffering, when from wilfulness, disobedience, obstinacy, or thoughtlessness, it partakes of things that are injurious to its health; but this suffering is the beneficent inculcator of forethought and virtue.

The Divine laws that rule on earth, are, that we should grow daily in wisdom, in knowledge, in virtue, and in godliness. Pain and suffering are man's guides to perfection. And even had wisdom and virtue never been preached to men, nature's silent language would have taught it to them.

It is true there are many evils in life which cannot be said to be the consequences of our acts. When hailstorms destroy the growing corn, when war lays waste our homes, when the plague devastates the country, when floods or earthquakes swallow up flourishing cities and their inhabitants—what can poor helpless men do to stay the powers of nature? how can they struggle against the might of God? And yet these are terrible evils—and yet God is Love.

Yea, even amid the most fearful and destructive phenomena of nature, let it be proclaimed, God is Love.

For, after all, what is it that those terrible revolutions destroy? The earthly form of man—not his real self, not his immortal spirit. And can we call the end of all earthly evils an evil? And is not death the conclusion of the earthly and the commencement of the higher existence? Now, when thousands and thousands of human beings, fathers with their children, husbands with their wives, die at the same moment, struck down by some natural catastrophe, in accordance with the plans of Providence—is there in the event itself, any very great difference from death caused by sickness or such like? Would not those that perished, at all events in a few years have gone home to the eternal Father? If death is not an evil, then neither is earthquake, or flood, or pestilence, or any natural event which is destructive of human life, an evil to those who are thereby removed from this earth. It is only to the survivors that the grand spectacle of the destruction is terrific. But why? Because they see therein a proof of the weakness of mortal man, and they tremble at the thought of the power of the Most High. But does this give us reason to despair of God's love? If that were so, then every case of death would afford similar reason. But who would be guilty of the folly of doubting God's love, because men draw nigh to the goal of their destination?

The sufferings endured by the victims of the catastrophes alluded to are often more painful than the death which puts an end to them. But these bodily pains, which are founded in the order of nature, afford no reason for attributing to the Deity cruelty or a love of vengeance. Such sufferings are only temporary, and when bodily pain grows beyond endurance it generally terminates in a swoon, and the patient becomes insensible. God's beneficent hand has thus ordained it; and more than this, He has ordained that by the side of every mortal affliction there shall grow compensatory joy, which the sufferer may cull if he chooses. Life on earth is but a many-coloured series of changes.

But the physical pains which we endure during our earthly career, are, like all other suffering, beneficent teachers. They warn us not to forget how fleeting, how mutable, how unreliable is everything that belongs to earth, and is born of earth. They warn us not to attach too great value to these things, and rather to occupy our spirits with that which is unchangeable, eternal and divine. He who does this, can never be quite stricken down either by poverty, or sickness, or abandonment, or the death of his loved ones, or any other misfortune. He is exalted above the fluctuations of earthly happiness, and looks towards eternity.

There are other Christians who think that, having conceived of God as an infinitely perfect Being, they must not attribute to Him any human qualities, not even the most sublime and loveable virtues which grace humanity. For, they say, that which is the most exalted in man, and which presents itself to the human mind as such, may, in the Deity, be no more than imperfection. Thus they maintain that, although that which we call love may be the highest jewel, the paradise of human life, we can nevertheless not conceive of such love as moves us, as an attribute of the Deity; for we stand much too low in the scale of beings to be able to comprehend the perfection of God.

To many persons this mode of viewing the matter may seem most likely to be the true one; but if I ask them, does it give them peace and happiness? they must answer, No: for if we divest God of the attribute of love, we stand indeed alone in the world, with no one to turn to for consolation, and life becomes a dark and insoluble riddle. Those who think thus do not deny God, it is true; but they deny the possibility of our forming a just and adequate conception of Him.

Miserable men! you confess that your views fail to render you happy: but why is this? Because you are at variance with yourselves or with your own reason. Bring your reason again into harmony with yourselves and with the universe, and you will reconquer your peace of mind.

It is true that we cannot approach even to a faint conception of the full measure of God's being. But it is as true that GOD IS, as that you are. And this once admitted, your reason cannot but add, that He is the most perfect of all perfect beings. For all imperfection is the reverse of divine.

It is undeniable that human reason, when forming to itself a conception of the Highest Being, must divest this Being of all feelings and passions which have their origin in earthly nature—such as anger, hatred, rancour, cruelty, or vengeance. For how can we form to ourselves an idea of Him as the most perfect of all beings, if we do not attribute to Him the highest perfection within our power of conception? Why, therefore, this self-contradiction? Why this hesitation to ascribe to the highest Being the highest perfection? How do we gain any knowledge of God, except through the great works of His creation? Is not our reason the gift of God? Is it not through this reason that He has revealed Himself to all nations? Do we not behold before us His works, in which He has given us a standard, though an infinitely small one, by which to measure His greatness?

If you refuse to conceive God as a perfect Spirit you cannot conceive Him at all. Then God has made your reason a lie, and has surrounded you with meaningless phantasms. If you conceive Him as a Being lifeless, yet wonderfully animating and setting in motion the whole universe—as a powerful machine devoid of self-consciousness, but which causes the worlds to roll in their measureless orbits, and makes the sap to rise in the veins of the most insignificant lichen, according to eternal laws—then you make self-conscious man more perfect and more divine than God; and reason, truth, and revelation you reduce to empty sounds.

If, on the contrary, you conceive God, *your* God, the God of the *Universe*, not as a lifeless Being, who performs His wonderful works unconsciously (it seems madness even to suppose this); oh, then, honour in Him the sublimest idea which He affords you of Himself. You fear that, sublime as it may be, it is unworthy of His Majesty. Nay, those ideas which He has Himself enabled us to form cannot be unworthy of Him. See, the high Heavens, star-spangled with innumerable worlds, paint an image of themselves on the retina of your eye; and yet how small is your eye and how immeasurable are those distances, how illimitable that space, which the most highly cultivated reason suffices not to calculate or to fathom! Nevertheless it is through this miniature picture on the glossy surface of your eye that you are alone able to discern them, and admire them, and thus also the infinite God! He mirrors His perfection and His greatness, which no mind can compass or fathom, on the eye of the mind.

Love for what is great, good, beautiful, holy, perfect, prevails throughout the spiritual world; a loving Wisdom reveals itself in all the wonders of heaven and earth; and what God speaks to you through the evidences of His power, would you deny it? You dare to pronounce man sublime in his holy love, and you hesitate to declare God to be the purest Love? When man willingly sacrifices life and all its joys for love of God and virtue, how exalted does he not appear to us!—And yet you can doubt that God is Love! Does, then, man bear within himself something more divine than God?

Away with these fallacies, bred of human sophistry and one-sided science. Thou, O God, art Love! Not in vain hast Thou endowed us with this sentiment and this feeling which links soul to soul, the living to the dead, and is but a ray of Thy infinite perfection, which mirrors itself faithfully in the spirit of man. Thou art love, and naught but love! Does not the whole creation proclaim it? Do not the events of my own life bear witness to it? Does not Jesus Christ, the Divine Enlightener of man, declare it?

Thou art Eternal Love! Thou wilt never disunite what Thou hast united in Spirit; Thou wilt never, O Father, separate us, Thy children, from Thyself. Thou didst not in vain send Jesus to us, to guide us to Thee. Thou wilt never, O Father, dissever the loving spirits which Thou hast led together here on earth. As they belong to each other here, so will they belong to each other hereafter. They will be reunited in Thee, Thou Centre of all that is spiritual and of all that is blissful!

Oh, exquisite thought! oh, inspiring hope! God is Love, and whosoever dwells in love, can never feel forsaken, and can never cease to exist!

THE CONSOLATION OF THE PATIENT SUFFERER.

> Be strong, my soul, although to-morrow,
>   Each earthly joy were from thee torn—
> Have courage, though the bitterest sorrow
>   Should leave thee comfortless to mourn.
> Upraise thee, groveller, from the dust,
> In soul to grasp thy God, and trust;
>   Be worthy of the glorious lot
> Which He who died for thee, the Son,
> Has for thee from the Father won.
>   This life's a dream that lingereth not.
>
> Striv'st thou with zeal to bless thy kind—
>   Still on thy country's good intent—
> Were the whole world against thee joined,
>   Ne'er of thy righteous zeal repent.
> Let neither wile nor mock of sin
> Stifle the still small voice within,
> Nor hinder thee from deeds of love.
> Thy heaven is in the realms above.
>   (2 *Tim.* iv. 7, 8.)

THE most virtuous Christian ought already here on earth to be the happiest, yet this is not always the case. It is true, Religion sheds her soothing balm, her heavenly peace through the hearts of her worshippers, so that even in the deepest depths of their miseries they cannot be utterly wretched; she affords them an anchor in the wildest tempest, a star to guide them through the darkest night. But there are hours, there are days, when even this anchor seems to give way, when even the light of this star seems to grow dim. There are hours and days when even the consciousness of our uprightness, the sense of our own worth, the remembrance of our virtues, far from soothing our distress, only increase it, nay, overwhelm us with an excess of anguish. In such an hour it was that Jesus, bowed down in the dust, shed drops of bloody sweat, and cried: "O my Father, if it be possible, let this cup pass from me!" In such an hour it was that He stammered with dying accents on the cross: "My God, my God, why hast Thou forsaken me?"

Sufferings of an unusual nature may indeed at times even shake our faith. When we find that we—though full of resignation to the ways of Providence, of unwavering trust in the eternal love of God, of affectionate sympathy for the weal and woe of our fellow-beings, and though devoting ourselves industriously to the duties of our office—are visited by misfortune and affliction, while bad men bask in the smiles of fortune, revel in well-being, rise in the world, though totally devoid of merit, and know no sorrow and no suffering—ah, how pardonable is at such times the groan of the deeply depressed Christian: "Of what use is my virtue, of what avail are my prayers so full of heartfelt devotion, of what avail my endeavours for the good of others, or the many sacrifices I have so frequently made to principle? See, vice is exultant; and virtue is scorned. The railer against God triumphs; fear of God, innocence of mind, are scoffed at as folly; and the worshipper of God weeps lonely in the dust. No one approaches lovingly the poor deserted sufferer; even God's mercy seems to have turned away from him. Is then the order of the world, such as God created it, antagonistic to all that is called religion and piety? Are noble hearts predestined to suffer? Does the Ruler of the universe crown only unscrupulousness, base crime, and cunning shamelessness?—Where am I? Why was I taught by Jesus to treasure a pure heart as above all price, when this heart is, more than any other, exposed to every grief?"

What has the pious Christian done, that the thunder-cloud of war should burst destructively over his cottage? Perhaps his sons, the hopes of his life, have been murdered, his daughters dishonoured, his goods destroyed, his means of subsistence taken from him. As a helpless beggar he must struggle with want all the rest of his days, and totter to the grave without a friend to comfort and sustain him; while worse men than he have enriched themselves by fraudulent means, and pass through life honoured, loved, and flattered. What has the child been guilty of, who is tortured by sickness which it has not brought upon itself, and has to drag on through a blighted life with an unhealthy body? He grows into youth and manhood—but of what avail are his ardent prayers for health to the Hearer of all prayer? They are not answered. Of what avail is his pious heart, his keen desire to be useful to others? He lives and dies in helpless misery, while others in the enjoyment of blooming health seem only to have received the fulness of strength from Heaven, to enable them to inflict the more evils on the world.

Yes, who can venture to deny it? There are sufferings in the world, the spectacle of which tempts us to doubt the rule of an all-just Providence, and the value of piety and virtue; when our faith and trust give way, and unconquerable melancholy takes possession of the soul.

But even during such moments of despair a friendly voice from Heaven cries to our heart in the words of Jesus: " Come unto me, all ye that labour and are heavy laden, and I will give you rest." The only fountain of consolation therefore, when reason fails to supply such, is the religion of Jesus. Whither, indeed, should we flee when the world deserts us, but to the arms of God, in whose Might we dwell?

And however furiously the storms of life may rage around us; though every door of escape may seem closed against us; though the light on our path through life be extinguished; though the last friend depart from us; though our grief and distress may have reached their climax; life and death be struggling for mastery within us—God is still our God! Whatever happens is still His work, and the work of the most exalted Love. That which He withholds from our earthly part, will form the strength of our immortal soul; that which we have lost and may still lose, was and is only transitory, and to lose it we must all be prepared; but our spirits are enriched by the bereavement, are brought closer to God thereby.

Therefore, courage, unswerving principle, and faith, even in the hour of bitterest trial! HE will not abandon thee, HE will not forsake thee, though all earthly blessings fail thee, if thou do not forsake HIM! Who has ever promised thee, that the things of this world should be other than fleeting? Who has ever promised that thy sweet dreams should prove eternal? And even if, like Job, thou hast been deprived of thy best, thy all; what is it that thou hast lost?—Mere dust and ashes! "The Lord giveth, and the Lord taketh away!"

If thou keepest up thy courage and thy faith, thou hast lost nothing; for God is All in all, and all else is naught. And God will be near to thee, for thou art His creature; thou art an object of His care, of His love! God remains near thee, even when the world to thy dimmed eye is shrouded in darkness, and the wings of death are waving above thee—for the goal of thy spirit is eternity.

Blessed wilt thou be, if, at the end of thy life's journey, thou canst say, with proud consciousness of how thou hast passed through every trial: "I have fought a good fight, I have finished my course, I have kept the faith."

It is an error to believe that virtue can be *rewarded* with earthly goods, with riches, honours, health, and all kinds of human enjoyments. No, the spirit cannot be rewarded with what belongs to the flesh; its rewards must be spiritual. The spirit's nature is immortal; its joys must be immortal like itself. Only in as far as we are human, that is to say, sensuous beings, do we seek for sensuous pleasures. These, however, fall to our lot, or are withdrawn from us, quite independently of our virtue and piety. They are the results, partly of our prudence and judgment, partly of our honest industry, partly of the confidence with which we have known how to inspire others. They are partly, or indeed entirely, the consequences of the wise ordinances of the Ruler of the world, according as He finds one or another auxiliary means better adapted to the qualities of our souls.

It is, therefore, erroneous to conclude, that because a man is visited by corporeal privations, and suffers from the loss of earthly goods, that this is a punishment of God. It is likewise a mistake to look upon wealth, honours, and other gifts of fortune as rewards bestowed by God. The noblest, most faithful Christian is often subject to the greatest privations. The most audacious rogue, who mocks at religion, often accumulates the largest fortune. A more glorious recompense awaits the righteous; a more terrible punishment than mere bodily privations awaits the sinner.

It is true that parents encourage their children in obedience by bestowing earthly rewards on them; it is true that princes requite the merits of their subjects with riches and honours—not that virtue can be paid for in so much money; but because princes, not being divinities, cannot requite services, cannot testify their esteem, except through the bestowal of earthly tokens.

On the other hand, the sufferings to which as mortals we are subject, are either self-imposed—in which case, they are the painful consequences of the abuse which we have made of the gifts and capabilities with which God has endowed us, of transgressions against His rules, and thus they are indeed punishments inflicted by sin upon itself—or they fall upon us without any fault of our own; and in this case, it is God's will that they should be to us what the gifts of fortune may be to others: means for ennobling and perfecting our souls. And thus all suffering at length conduces to the triumph of the victorious spirit, and opens to it a more glorious career in Eternity. God is just! Throughout the creation there is nothing wrong or unjust. Everything leads upwards to a glorious end. God the Rewarder lives! And what, after all, are the sufferings of this earth when compared to the glory to which they consecrate us, by endowing our souls with higher strength, power and dignity?

Besides, the wisdom of the Most High has so ordained it, that no pains connected with earth can endure for ever. Only he who suffers damage in his soul, who fails to improve his spirit,—only he loses eternally; because he neglects that which is eternal. Habit deprives even the most appalling evils of their terrors, and makes the heaviest burdens lighter. No suffering endures for very long. For every wound, however painfully it bleeds, time has a soothing balm. Night is ever followed by morning, storm by calm. We are dwelling in the realm of the transitory; and as no joy endures for ever, so also sorrow, want, and anxiety are but fleeting clouds in our sky.

Sustain thy courage, persevere in well-doing, keep thy faith and trust in God, and thou wilt come triumphant out of the struggle, thy brows encircled by the crown of glory, which God, the Rewarder, bestoweth.

Thou art pining in helpless poverty, and can see no end to thy tribulations. Thou hast laboured honestly and industriously, and yet hast laid by no store, and each succeeding day makes thee tremble more and more for the future. Though faithful in the fulfilment of the duties of thy vocation, though trustful in thy prayers to the Giver of all good gifts, thou nevertheless sinkest deeper and deeper into poverty and misery. Instead of diminishing, thy difficulties increase every day with fearful rapidity; thou seest no means of rescue. Before thy family lies a future full of pain and privation—before thyself a life robbed of honour and happiness. Yet man thyself, O unhappy mortal! and though all forsake thee, forsake not thou the path of virtue. Though every hope break faithlessly away from thee, do not loose thy hold on God! Save the innocence of thy soul, and thou wilt have saved everything. Many have been more deeply involved even than thou, and yet have been wonderfully rescued by Providence. Fight a good fight, and keep thy faith. Even when all have forsaken thee: God is still thy God.

And thou, who never sparedst labour or pains when thou couldst promote the well-being of thy fellow-citizens; who didst sacrifice the best years of thy life, fortune, time, and rest to the welfare of others—why dost thou chafe at the heartless ingratitude of men? They requite thy love with shameless calumny, thy noble-mindedness with baseness, thy sacrifices with scorn, thy fidelity with contempt and desertion. Malice triumphs, prejudice prevails, thou succumbest. Yet be of good heart, fight trustfully the good fight to the end. There is ONE who does not misjudge thee; there is ONE who will deal justly by thee. He is the Omniscient, the Rewarder! Did Jesus do less than thee? Did the world reward Him better?

Thou who art stricken down in the prime of thy strength by painful illness, that deprives thee of all enjoyment and all hope in life—despair not! As regards thy earthly prosperity, those hours are indeed lost which thou sighest away on thy bed of pain; but to thy soul they are not lost. In these bitter moments of agony thou art securing higher gain. Thou who once stood there so proudly in the fulness of thy health and strength, who wert so rich in plans for the future—thou acknowledgest now with fear and trembling the hand of a Mighty One above thee, which rules the fate of worlds, and of the meanest creature. It is His will that has fixed thy destiny. It is true thy wealth will suffer, now that thy arm fails that kept it up; it is true thy children, almost uncared for, move like orphans round thy bed, casting sad and anxious glances at thee; it is true deep sorrow gnaws at the heart of thy loving spouse, though she endeavours to hide it from thee—yet do not despair! A strong arm upholds thee,—the arm of Divine Providence. And should even thy illness become still more painful, thy fortune still more impaired, thy prospects still more hopeless, God is still thy God! Fight the good fight in thy hours of suffering, and keep thy faith. Not as thou seest it, but as God ordaineth it, will be the fate of thy children. And shouldst thou be doomed to part from thy loved ones, should the tears in the eyes of thy dear relatives be the first tears of the last parting,—then blessed art thou! The Father of all is calling thee a few moments earlier into the better world. We shall follow thee in a few brief hours, after another short dream. Why sorrowest thou with faithless anxiety for those who will linger on earth but a short time after thee? Who cared for thee, when no mortal watched over thee? Is thy God not also the God of thy dear ones?

And thou, who with loving heart hast attached thyself, as thou thoughtest, to a congenial mind, and sought the happiness of life in this friendship only—why art thou so downcast? Because that heart deceived thee? Because those lips only feigned the love, which thou gavest with all thy soul? Because those eyes falsely smiled on thee? Because thy faith was responded to with base perjury, and thy tenderness requited with shameless treachery? Unhappy mourner, thou hast indeed lost much; thy experience has perhaps for ever embittered thy gentle heart, and robbed thee of thy faith in mankind. The treachery thou hast met with has perhaps filled thy heat for ever with disbelief in human virtue. Thou hast no longer a friend in whom thou canst trust, to whom thou canst devote thyself. Thou standest alone in the world; and without friendship life has no attractions for thy delicately moulded soul. Nevertheless, bear up manfully. Thou, also, prepare to fight the good fight of the Christian; be generous-minded to the last! God is faithful, though none else be so! If the whole world deceive thee, there is ONE who never deceiveth. He is thy God, the God of truth and love, the God who endowed thy soul with its tender yearnings. Even shouldst thou be doomed to pass through life without an earthly friend, ONE Friend remaineth to thee—the Eternal Father, thy Creator! If those who are dearest to thee abandon thee: let this play of shadows, this constant shifting of the sublunary scene, strengthen thy spirit in self-dependence, and lead thee closer to what is eternally true and lasting— to God.

Wherefore weepest thou, sorrowing widow, by the coffin of thy husband? And thou, faithful child, on the grave of thy father, thy friend? And thou, disconsolate mother, by the bier of thy infant? What is it that they bear to the grave? Is it not merely the mortal coil? Or can spirits die and moulder away in the ground? Why fixest thou thine eyes, sore with weeping, on the earth? Ah! that which hath fled from thee, that which thy eye seeketh, is not there! Lift thine eyes to Heaven, let them penetrate the boundless universe! Thy friend is there. The mysterious power which animated the dust, and which we call soul, the same that so often smiled lovingly on thee through tender eyes, that spoke to thee from friendly lips, now with solemn earnestness, now with joyful mirth—it has gone to God, is with God, has entered into more glorious connexions, into higher spheres of action, is more elevated, freer, happier, more perfect than thou! Why, then, turn thine eyes upon the grave? the ashes that lie buried there were only a borrowed raiment, did not belong to the immortal being—were but an instrument useful for a short time here below, now no longer needed. The soul has finished its course in this world, has fought the fight, and kept its faith. Henceforth it wears the crown of immortality!—Man thyself, O mourner, and thou, also, prepare to fight the good fight. The loved one whom thou hast lost will one day advance to meet thee at the gate of eternity, to greet thee as a glorified companion, and will cry unto thee: Here also God is thy God!

Oh, God! oh, Father! Thou art also my God, my Father; why, then, should I be bowed down with grief? Why weakly yield myself up before my course is finished, before I have fought the good fight to the end? Oh, give me strength, give me power! whatever suffering Thou mayst impose, I will bear it, for it will bring me nearer to Thee!

Father, for each earthly pleasure
   Heartfelt thanks from me receive—
Thanks, should grief o'erflow the measure,
   Father, still to Thee I give.
Shouldst Thou take them both from me,
Yet more gladly praise I Thee.

In the sweet and smiling spring,
   When true friends around me stand,
Though each hour new joys may bring,
   Hopes fulfilled as soon as planned—
Yet I sadly seem to see
All earth's joys are vanity.

What to Earth and Time, though bright,
   Is the joy that can enchain?
No, my spirit strives with might
   Immortality to gain.
Only *one pure* joy I see—
Holy, and in God to be.

Soon, oh, soon! shall all be done,
   Peaceful rest I, Lord, in Thee;
Thousands have the victory won,
   I, too, shall win the victory.
More loudly yet than thunder's voice,
My heart outcries, believe—rejoice.

Yes, I believe, till life shall close,
   The God I trust will ne'er forsake.
On Him, in hope, will I repose,
   Altho' the last fond tie should break.
Can I but hold Him for my own,
Then shall I never stand alone.

Look, Lord, with pity on my tears,
   Behold my cares—my fallen state;
Comforter, come, relieve my fears.
   Oh, I am left so desolate!
Sustain me, Helper; ease my smart;
Send joy and peace into my heart.

THE CONSOLATION OF THE PATIENT SUFFERER.

  And yet, oh Father, not my will,
   But Thine alone be done on me.
  Tho' like the patient Jesus, still
   I wander through Gethsemane,
  At last, my God, when all is done,
  The glorious guerdon shall be won.

THE SICK.

> In silence will I bear the pain
>   Which God has sent me by His will—
> Ne'er will I murmur nor complain;
>   Although He wound, He loves me still—
> In sickness not the less God's child
> Than if the world around me smiled.
> True to Himself, God changes never—
> Wise, mighty, merciful, for ever.
>
>   (*St. Matt.* xxv. 36.)

AMONG the manifold misfortunes that may befall humanity, the loss of health is one of the severest. All the joys that life can give, cannot outweigh the sufferings of the sick. Give the sick man everything, and leave him his sufferings, and he will feel that half the world is lost to him. Lay him on a soft silken couch, he will nevertheless groan sleepless under the pressure of his sufferings; while the miserable beggar, blessed with health, sleeps sweetly on the hard ground. Spread his tables with dainty meats and choice drinks, and he will thrust back the hand that proffers them, and envy the poor man who thoroughly enjoys his dry crust. Surround him with the pomp of kings; let his chair be a throne, and his crutch a world-swaying sceptre; he will look with contemptuous eye on marble, on gold, and on purple, and would deem himself happy could he enjoy, even were it under a thatched roof, the health of the meanest of his servants.

Hence the sight of a sick person is painful to all. Who can behold without pity and emotion the wan cheek, the dimmed eye, and the emaciated form? Even the rude warrior checks his ruthless passion at this sight, and spares the sufferer.

A sick person is a sacred object to every Christian, and ought to be so. Even levity grows earnest at the side of the sick-bed.

Perhaps thou wert once thyself such a pitiable object; if so, remember the days of thy suffering. Thou didst then gain great and weighty experiences. Come with me in spirit now to the bed-side of a languishing fellow-being, and renew there the thoughts and resolves of those days.

But if thou hast not yet learnt what it is to lose health, the day may come when thou shalt make that sad experience. Prepare thyself like a sage against that time of trial. Learn to love the sick and to nurse them with tender care, that thou, like they, mayst one day be thus honoured and tended.

Disease is not necessarily connected with life. Originally man was made perfect in all his parts. Thousands go through life without ever having experienced any derangement of their physical organization. To them even approaching death brings no illness. They die because the last drop of life's oil in their lamp has been consumed; they sleep away in sweet weariness, like the reaper in autumn when his daily task is completed.

If we have not inherited the germs of disease from our parents, it is generally to our own imprudence or thoughtlessness that may be attributed the loss of life's best gift—the health of our bodies—the partial destruction of the instrument through which our souls are to work and do useful service.

In every case, observe the nature of thy body, and regulate thy life accordingly. Observe its laws in thy nourishment, thy drink, thy pleasures, and thy mode of working in thy vocation. Never forget that one single hour of intemperance may be the parent of long years of suffering. Never forget that one moment of guilty self-forgetfulness in the midst of joy, suffices to poison thy cup of bliss.

Man's body is not his inalienable possession; it is a loan from the hand of God, which we shall one day have to give up—an instrument of the spirit, without which the latter cannot fulfil its appointed work on earth. If man deserve punishment for sin, then assuredly he deserves it when he sins against his own body; for he thereby robs himself of the joy of life, and of the capacity, for a long time, and perhaps for ever, of doing as much good as he might otherwise do.

Not only do we, by carelessness of our health, render ourselves incapable of fulfilling adequately our duties to God, our country, and our fellow-citizens, to strangers, and to friends; but we may even, though subsequently apparently restored to health, in reality have hastened the approach of the hour of death. The man wanting in moderation—whether it be, that with careless presumption he exposes himself unnecessarily to danger, or that by exaggerated care he render himself over-delicate—may be said to be a self-murderer, though against his will and desire.

Again, the germs of disease are often transmitted from parents to children: the maladies of one generation thus become the ailments and sufferings of a distant posterity. Therefore guard reverently the health of your bodies, that your children may not one day upbraid you with their diseases; that the follies of one brief moment of your existence may not become a source of misery to your children's children! It is this that the Scriptures allude to, when they say: the sins of parents are punished unto the third and fourth generation.

Often place yourself, in spirit, by the bed-side of the sick. It may be to you a school of wisdom. When the sunken eye and deathly pallor of the poor sufferer make you tremble, the resolve will be strengthened in you, to avoid everything that may injure your own health.

But watch not only over thyself; watch also over the health of thy companions. Tempt not others to immoderate pleasures; lead them not into dissipation that may breed disease. What satisfaction will it be to thee, when thou hast robbed them of the sweet bloom of health, when thou hast become, as it were, the destroyer of their best joy in life?

Nevertheless, this is a point in regard to which even good people, without malice and without premeditation, but in the tumult of pleasure, so frequently err. Their example and their encouragement excite weaker persons to indulge in undue gratifications. In the very endeavour to give their friend a proof of affection, they frequently become his poisoner, his destroyer. Neither the malice nor the cruelty of man is so dangerous as his thoughtless levity.

Honour, O Christian, in thyself as in others, the

sanctity of health! Perform towards the sick the holy duty of benevolence!

Be a friend to the sick, as was Jesus, that sublime example of what we ought and what we ought not to be. Did He not go, with helping hand, to the bedside of the sick? Was it not He who lovingly called unto Him the lame and the blind, the leper and the man sick of the palsy? Was He not the refuge of all sufferers? Did they not let themselves be carried unto Him, when they learnt that the Divine friend of suffering humanity was nigh? Thou, who callest thyself Christian, be a Christian in truth —follower of Jesus, be what Jesus was!

It is true, thy hand can perform no miracle; but it can perform acts of kindness! Thy arm cannot raise up the hopelessly sick, and place him again in the blooming realm of health, nor can it stay death; but it can lovingly support the weak. At thy bidding, it is true, all pains will not vanish; but thy words may comfort, may give counsel and cheerfulness to one whom every earthly joy fails because he lacks health.

"I have been sick, and ye have not visited me!" will be the words of Jesus to those who have uncharitably left the sick without tender care.

Help, more especially, the poor sick stranger! Those that are at home will be tended by their sorrowing relatives. The rich will not lack nursing, for every one will be willing to minister to them, and they have the means of procuring for themselves all that they require, and everything that may tend to soothe their sufferings. But who is there to minister to the poor? Perhaps not even an unfeeling hireling. Who is there to take care of the suffering stranger?

F

Ah, perhaps, no one, while his brothers and sisters are grieving over him at a distance.

You often long to be able to do some good. You think, perhaps, that when you have charitably given alms to the beggar in the street, you have done enough. But how little is this! God has given you more, far more than this; and yet how helpless and poor did you not come into the world? Go, and give more than alms. Remember the words of Jesus, and let them resound in your hearts: "What ye have done to the least of these, ye have done to me."

Go forth and visit the abode of poverty and misery, and behold there the hungering father and the starving mother on the comfortless bed of sickness, with no one to nurse them, no one to advise, without a doctor and without medicine, surrounded by terrified and weeping children: there is the post of honour for thee; there is the field in which thou art called to sow blessed seeds for eternity; there is the path that will lead thee to glory. If God have bestowed upon thee in rich measure, or even in moderation, the goods of this earth, then seek out the poor families in thy neighbourhood; inquire how they live; find out if there be any sick among them, and if so, be thou their ministering angel!

In many cases the alms which you fling to a professional beggar in the street, are no more than an encouragement to his laziness, a premium to his want of thrift and order. But could you behold with your eyes the interior of many a poor home, those eyes would weep tears of blood. It would startle you to discover such nameless misery in a hovel at the side of the pomp and luxury of the neighbouring palace. You would shudder at the thought that, in a Christian city, there could be so much unalleviated suffering—so much unknown sorrow among so many thousands of joyful beings. Though the sick Lazarus, covered with sores, may not in our day always be found outside the rich man's door, endeavouring to stay his hunger with the crumbs that fall from the rich man's table, he may be found in a dwelling close by, where his groans are heard by the Omnipresent God alone.

If it be in thy power, remember the sick stranger with charitable institutions for his benefit. It was one of the most praiseworthy customs of our forefathers that, when blessed with riches, they applied part of these to founding pious and charitable institutions. God bestowed upon them bountiful superfluity, and by their last testaments they gratefully returned a share of it to God. Their pious hearts, which called God the Father of all, were open to love of their poorer fellow-men; and when the time came, the needy were found numbered among their heirs.

In many places, this excellent, truly Christian custom is only occasionally followed; in others it has ceased to exist. Our fathers died, but to this day thousands of sick persons, who are nursed in the institutions founded by their benevolence, send up grateful prayers for their unknown and long deceased benefactors. Will future generations pray thus for us? Oh, ye wealthy of the earth, your children's children will glance with indifference at the marble mausoleums you have erected for yourselves. They will smile contemptuously at the futile vanity which made you surround yourselves with pomp even in the grave. A grateful tear shed by a poor sufferer who had been relieved in an institution which perpetuated your kindness, even after your death, would have been of more worth than the cold drop which the artist's chisel fashions on the marble statue above your graves. This tear will crumble away with the stone in which it is cut; the poor man's tear will be registered in heaven.

Let us return to the good old custom of our fathers; let us remember on our bed of sickness those helpless sufferers who have no one to take care of them as we have; and let us contribute to allay their pains, even after God has put an end to ours.

Honour, wherever thou meetest them, the sufferings of thy sick fellow-creature. Wert thou not his friend before, become so when he suffers. Wert thou even once his enemy, go to him, and be reconciled. If he have offended thee, go to him and pardon him his trespass, that he may part from thee and from life with a more cheerful spirit. If he have reason to be angered with thee, go to him and seek his forgiveness. Let no one depart from thee in anger, that in eternity there may be no being willing to stand forth and accuse thee.

Sooner or later thou mayst thyself be thrown upon a bed of sickness. No balm, no draught will then be so potent to soothe as the thought, that no fellow-being bears anger against thee; that though many a kind heart will send a sigh of regret after thee into eternity, not one will curse thee!

Glorify thy Christian faith in thy hour of suffering, by patience and pious resignation to the will of thy Creator, who has ever guided thee, and who will be thy guide henceforward as heretofore. And glorify thy faith in God's Providence by quiescent trust, and calm abiding, and cheerful resignation. Wish not for dissolution, neither fear the quiet sleep of death. Millions have died before thee, millions will die after thee; it is the Divine law that rules the universe; it is for the good of the world. Thou hast indeed died many a time already. As often in thy life as thou hast fallen asleep, thou hast tasted death, for it is but the last sleep. It is not thyself that sleepest away, but only thy body. Thy soul sleepeth not; it keeps vigil with God, it lives near Him, it draws nigh to more blissful spheres, and smiles at its own past fears.

And suppose thy illness should not prove deadly, but that thou art destined to recover. Is this, then, so great a happiness? Thou wilt step back from the open grave only to approach it again in a few years. Thy earthly dream will be prolonged for a few moments, and thy entrance into the glory of the better world which awaits thee, according to Jesus' promise, will be delayed for a few days.

Even on thy bed of sickness, cease not thy works of charity. Even on thy bed of sickness do good without ceasing. Shouldst thou in the days of health have neglected to do it, do it now while there is yet time. Let not a day of thy life pass by without an act of Christian love. The remembrance of thy well-doing will be thy happiness in death.

But in sickness as in health, at all times alike, the true Christian is ready to exchange the transitory for the eternal. Not that it would be right to dwell constantly upon the subject of death. Nay, it would be folly to mar by sad thoughts the many blessings which we receive here below from the bountiful hand of God. But live as if thou wert to be called away from this world suddenly and unexpectedly. Prepare thy soul, that it may be ready to depart at any moment. Put thy house in order, that when sickness and death overtake thee, thou shalt be found to have fulfilled thy every duty towards those that depend on thee. Put thy house in order. Attend at all times to thy avocations with such care and fidelity, that thy relatives, when they lose thee, may not have to sustain a double loss—a twofold trial. When in health, thou providest for those that belong to thee with tender solicitude; but reflect, would they be provided for, if, this very day, some untoward accident should suddenly tear thee from them, and to-morrow they should stand alone with tearful eyes, without thee to lean upon? Flatter not thyself with the hope that thou wilt have time during long and lingering illness to put thy house in order. Dost thou not each week see men called away in the prime of their manhood? Dost thou not see others whom protracted illness has deprived of all power and desire to attend to serious business?

The true Christian proves himself such by being ever ready, ever prepared in all his relations, whether as a citizen of this world or of eternity. He passes cheerfully and composedly through life, for his accounts, both as regards this world and the next, are at all times made up.

Thus let it be with me, my God and Father! The best Christian is the greatest man on earth. He looks with equal calm to the past and to the future; he stands in equally happy relations to both. He is a true hero, for while gratefully enjoying the pleasures of life which thou, O Father, vouchsafest to him, his spirit dwelleth in anticipation in the realms of eternity. He is above every accident, for none can take him by surprise; he is greater than any fate that may befall him, for, trusting in thee, O my God, his spirit soars above all sublunary things.

Such let me be, let me become! Let my death be such that it may teach others how to live; and let my life be such that it may teach others how to die joyfully! Thus lived, thus died, my Saviour. He who won heavenly bliss for me, Jesus, my Divine teacher. He was the faithful friend of the sick; their adviser, their comforter. I will be the same, as far as my feeble powers will allow.

> Yea, Father! be Thou my relief
> My comforter in pain and grief—
>   Make sickness' self a gain to me;
> Draw my heart—all sad hearts that bleed,
> Through all their pangs, in every need,
>   Unto Thy love—and unto Thee.
>
> Jesus! to Thee my heart appeals—
> Oh help! for Thou art He who heals.
>   The sorest pain canst Thou make light,
> Our sickness e'en Thou send'st to bless—
> Thou art our refuge in distress,
>   Our tears are ever in Thy sight.
>
> To Thee my trust, my faith, shall hold.
> Oh never let my love wax cold,
>   Health, sickness, whatsoe'er befall.
> Then can no pangs my spirit shake,
> I joy to bear them for Thy sake.
>   My grateful heart gives thanks for all.

A FORETASTE OF HEAVEN.

PART I.

Let everything that liveth praise the Lord!—
Deep in our spirit the responsive chord
Awakes devotion, and a holy joy
Which knoweth no alloy.

Try Him, and prove Him, and see how bountiful He is.
Truth and compassion,—tender love, are His.
Reigning for ever, o'er us and around,
Still is His mercy found.

Let everything that loveth, love the Lord!
High on His throne, by all the saints adored,
Seraph and cherub—all the heavenly host—
Happiest, who love Him most.

Thirst then, *our* souls, like the blest souls above,
Holy and happy—evermore to love
Him who created us, who keeps us still
By His most gracious will.

All hail! We love Him evermore. The dust
Loves its Consoler—puts in Him its trust.
All eager longings He will satisfy—
Tears He Himself will dry.

(St. Matt. v. 8.)

I WILL lift myself out of the slough of this world, I will rise above the storms of this life, and lay hold on those higher things that afford lasting peace of mind, indestructible happiness. What is to me the noisy tumult of the world, amid which I never feel perfectly satisfied; where every light has its shadow, and where every joy has its attendant woe? Can I there live entirely to myself, entirely possess myself? No, I am there the victim of every evil; of care and trouble, and vain wishes, of wrecked hopes, of sad events, and of wearisome pleasures. I am never less lonely than when, alone, engaged in silent meditation, I lift up my soul to Thee, Lord of all destinies. I pity those who have never enjoyed such an hour, and happily their number is small; for even to the most frivolous worldling there comes at length a moment—perhaps, indeed, it comes sooner to him than to others—when pleasure palls upon him, when he feels society a burden, or at least when he derives but little gratification from it; when he yearns for something different, when, meditating on the worthlessness of the life of trifling he leads, he begins to have a presentiment of a better state and ardently to desire it.

And yet he fails to lay hold on it. For it seems to him incredible that it should be in the bosom of the highest wisdom, in the sanctity of religion, that he is to seek for it. Religion, as he feels it, inspires him with too little respect. It is to him no more than a confused medley of vague and disjointed sentences and precepts, which have remained in his memory since childhood, but which he has never reflected upon or endeavoured to systematize. He wonders that people should affect to find therein matters of such importance, and perhaps he smiles compassionately at their folly; and he returns, though with failing heart, to his former mode of life, to his accustomed amusements, soon again to weary of them, and soon again to feel that he has no joy in such existence.

So far, indeed, he is right: the disconnected fragments of biblical phrases learnt by rote in childhood, which he calls his religion, and which he discards from his thoughts the moment the church service (which he attends merely because it is customary so to do) is over, that is in truth a poor religion. But this has no affinity with the religion which Jesus the Messiah revealed to us. His religion is not a matter of memory, nor a matter of routine, but a living power of God in the human soul.

However, thousands drag on through life in this way, following their craft, their art, their trade, their studies; allowing themselves, in times of war as in times of peace, to be consumed by fleeting pleasures and long-enduring pains. They commit their happiness, their contentment, to the rule of chance; believe that they can after all do nothing towards securing it themselves; and are totally ignorant that it is in man's power to be lastingly happy—to enjoy, here on earth already, a foretaste of heaven. At length, possibly, they learn to despise all pleasures, and sometimes become discontented grumblers whom nothing can satisfy—haters of their kind, and despisers of their own life, because they have not learnt to know true pleasure.

There are again others, wiser than these, who, strengthened by religion, or animated and exalted by nobler sentiments, do not deny the value of this worldly life. But they deplore the fleeting character of all pleasure. "I also was at one time thoroughly happy, and enjoyed a foretaste of Heaven," say many. "I seemed to be steeped in happiness. But—how soon did not my dream vanish! Yes, it was but a dream, and now it lies far behind me in the realm of the past, like a fading shadow. Soon the very memory of it will be almost lost to me. I shall then continue my way through the monotonous dulness of every-day life, as through a desert."

Let every man take a retrospect of the days that lie behind him, reflect upon them, and then ask himself, "Which period of my life was the happiest? Which was the sweetest moment I ever enjoyed?"

Many of us will at once recall to mind the innocent days and delights of childhood, those days when life was coloured with the rosy light of morn. Then the merest trifle seemed a treasure, a flower was a jewel in our estimation, and a walk our greatest happiness. Everything was invested in our eyes with a higher significance; our own joyous souls seemed to infuse themselves even into the lifeless things that surrounded us, and we talked to and loved objects that could not return our affection. With happy carelessness we skipped over the thorns in our path, and whatever wounded us was forgotten as soon as the tear was dry that the pain had called forth. Oh, what brilliant prospects all thoughts of the future then conjured up! What great expectations did not others entertain in regard to us, and did we not ourselves entertain as to what we should perform in later years! "Yes; that was the happiest period of my life!" many will exclaim.

I believe it; yet, when I look nearer into the matter, it seems to me that each age has its own pleasure which God has ordained for our enjoyment. It cannot be our destiny to remain children for ever—who indeed would wish it to be so? Who would desire to return to that dream of the past, out of which we see every child longing to emerge, that it may take part in the pleasures of an older age? It would be sad were there no higher felicity in life than that of the child, for that we can never recall. It seems to me that that only can be the highest happiness which each human being may, with a resolute will, renew at any time.

But let us examine more closely what constituted our happiness when we were children. Was it the outward things that surrounded us? Was it riches, pomp, and honours? Ah, no! Seated on a heap of sand we thought ourselves richer than kings; with a few boards we built ourselves palaces; a little picture would fill us with delight. Why was this? Surely the source of these joys lay *within* us, not in the outward world. We were *content* with what we possessed, and like the bee, we sucked honey even from the lowliest flower. We took no care for the morrow; for we believed that each day had its own joys, and we thought only of the present. If we had raiment and food sufficient, we asked not for more. We had light hearts; and although we knew then, in reference to the smaller things of life, as well as we do now, in reference to the greater, that much that was disagreeable had to be encountered, that many tears would necessarily be shed, that many fears would be excited, yet we never dwelt long on what occasioned us dissatisfaction, but on the contrary only felt the happier for having escaped from some cause of fear, only rejoiced the more when we had been relieved from some state of pain. For this reason we seldom repined. We were joyous because we anticipated not evil, *because our hearts were pure and our consciences unburdened.* Let us recall to mind the bitterest moments of our childhood! Were they not those in which we had for the first time done wrong, and in which we feared discovery, and looked forward with trembling to the punishment that awaited us? But this very fear served as a correction. We resisted the sin the next time it lured us. When the punishment had been submitted to, the guilt expiated, we again skipped merrily through life.

Alas! wherefore have we forgotten the wisdom of our youth? wherefore have we become more full of folly in old age than we were in childhood? Wherefore do we with unpardonable self-deception, instead of seeking our happiness and welfare *within ourselves*, expect it from circumstances that lie beyond us, and which after all only assume, in regard to us, the character with which we ourselves invest them? Why do our thoughts attach themselves with senseless obstinacy to all that is disagreeable, rather than to that which is innocently pleasurable? Why are our hearts no longer so contented as at that time, when we extracted pleasure from trifles? Why is our position not sufficiently exalted, our income not sufficiently large, our apparel, our furniture not costly enough, although all are far better than the humble cottage that once satisfied us? Why is it that we are for ever troubled by a secret and never-ceasing anxiety, a restless consciousness of wrong? Why is it that we never enjoy a pleasure without being aware of some admixture of bitterness in it?

Because we have deserted the wisdom that belongs to the age of childhood! Neither the world, nor the people that surround us, have changed since then; the change is in ourselves. We have been untrue to ourselves, and have attached ourselves to outward things as though they could give us back the lost happiness; and we pursue them with blind ardour, yet never feel the bliss of former days. It is not an Angel, but our own vanity, ambition, covetousness, and luxuriousness, our own pride, cunning, envy, and hatred, that have driven us forth from the paradise of youth—" Except ye become as little children," said Jesus Christ, the Wisest of the wise, " ye cannot enter the kingdom of Heaven !"

If, therefore, thou believest the period of thy early youth to have been the happiest of thy life, forget not why it was so. It depends upon thyself whether the heaven of thy childhood shall spread over thy later days also. Become again what thou wert then: simple, pious, forgiving, loving, content with little, and the foretaste of Heaven which thou then enjoyed thou wilt again experience. Thou wilt then understand Jesus, the Wisest of the wise, whose words thou hast perhaps often perused, but without entirely comprehending their deep wisdom.

There are, however, many persons whose happiness in childhood has been disturbed by sickness, by the cruelty of a step-father or a step-mother, or by other misfortunes, and who cannot, therefore, reckon those years among their happiest. But if thou belongest to these, which was the most delightful period of the other portion of thy life? Perhaps that in which thy heart first opened to love, when the privileged day had come, and as youth, or as maiden, thou madest thy first independent step in the world. Thou still rememberest those hours of sweet reverie, thy hopes, thy longings. Heaven and earth seemed to grow brighter under the influence of the inexpressible feelings which then moved thy heart. Thy every thought was devoted to the beloved object. Everything connected with it assumed higher value in thine eyes. A look was enough to make thee happy; the simplest gift was prized by thee above a crown; the first flower received from the hand of thy beloved thou wouldst not have exchanged for the costliest jewel. Thou didst enter a second time the heaven of thy childhood, but with new feelings, with a new spirit. What a Divine halo seemed spread around everything, and how full of noble virtues the beloved object! How often in thy humility thou didst deem thyself unworthy of the love granted thee! How earnestly thou strovest to improve thyself, and to please by higher qualities! How much bliss was there not often in thy sorrow, and how much comfort even in thy pains! What elevated resolves passed at that period through thy soul! How thou didst blush at every vice, at every impure thought and action!

"I, also, was once in paradise!" cry many in whom the memory of those bygone days is revived. "I was full of happiness! And yet it was no more than a delirium of the imagination, a foolish self-delusion. Too soon, alas! I awoke from my dream, and, when more calm, I perceived that the many perfections I had beheld in the beloved object either did not exist at all, or only in very small measure."

Yes, such was thy experience; but, nevertheless, those days count among the happiest of thy earthly existence. Where, then, was the source of the bliss that filled thy heart? It was not in the *outer* world —for thou hast just confessed that thou hadst deceived thyself; nay, the heavenly being that thou lovedst was *within* thee, and thou didst paint its image on the outer world. Thou didst love the Perfect, noble duty, the grace of goodness, the sublimity of truth—not perfidy, not vain-glory, not riches, not rank. Thou lovedst, and thy love lent beauty even to the defects of its object.

The awakening of first love is but a revival of the innocence of youth, and of the reverence for the Divine element in the nature of man! And that Divine element which thou reverest was in thyself, and thou now callest it delusion, because thou failedst to find out of thyself that ideal of every perfection that thou believedst to have discovered within thyself.

Why hast thou never since then enjoyed an equal measure of happiness? Why hast thou cast away with the delusion, the bliss-inspiring love of the Divine and the Perfect? Why hast thou not sought the ideal within thyself, since thou couldst not find it elsewhere? Why dost thou not exert thy powers to gain for thyself that rare perfection, that grace of goodness, that sublimity of truth, the conception of which caused thee so much delight? Why dost thou cease to adorn thyself, as before, with nobler qualities in order to please thy beloved? Why dost thou not now, as then, shun everything impure, every vicious passion, every vice? If thou didst, thou wouldst still be full of bliss, for the world would honour thee, and the approval of God would raise thee above all the pains of earth. Ah, degenerate man! hadst thou remained true to thy youthful ideal of perfection, thou wouldst even to this day enjoy a foretaste of Heaven!

But thou hast been untrue to thyself, to the nobler

nature within thee. Thou didst not find in others all the perfections which thou worshipped; and in consequence thou forgottest thyself, thou becamest base and bad as others, perhaps even worse than they. To this dost thou owe that thy Heaven has fled from thee.

O Lord, my God, Creator of the heavenly bliss enjoyed on earth, I also was once full of bliss, and I enjoyed the foretaste of higher things. Ah! in like manner as Thou gavest it to the first human being, made in Thine image, Thou bestowest to this day with inexhaustible bounty a paradise on each earth-born soul. How long he shall retain it depends upon himself. It is his as long as he remains virtuous, as long as he does Thy will, as long as he continues to be pure in heart, as long as he does not desecrate the Divine element within himself. But the impure desire for outward happiness drives him out of his Eden, and he sees Thee no longer. His eyes are fixed greedily on the goods of this lower world, as are those of the unreasoning brute, instead of being uplifted to the Heavenly gift, as beseems those who are made in Thine image.

A second time the way to the lost paradise has been opened to us by Thee, O blessed One who took pity on the world, Saviour, Divine Teacher, by Thee and by Thy word! Why do we close our ears against Thy voice? The greatest desire of all men is to be perfectly happy; in the days of childhood, and of sweet adolescence, the magic power of virtue affords us a foretaste of the highest bliss—why do we not, O Jesus, truly understand the wisdom in Thy words: " Blessed are the pure in heart, for they shall see God?"

A FORETASTE OF HEAVEN.

PART II.

If I trust in God alone,
If I feel He is mine own,
If my heart until I die
Ne'er forget His constancy—
Nought of sorrow can I know,
Feel nought but love, devotion, joy o'erflow.

If in Him my soul is blest,
Willingly I leave the rest;
Tread in faith my pilgrim road,
Trusting only in my God.
Earthly troubles, faint and dim,
Fade into nothing while I rest on Him

Where in God's own sight I stand,
There only is my fatherland;
Every gift He sends me thence
Is proof of my inheritance.
Kindred and friends long mourned in vain,
With youth renewed, there shall I meet again.

(*Rom.* v. 3.)

YEA, I know it, I believe it, and I feel it; I see it in every event of my life, in the various destinies of my fellow-creatures, in all the splendid works of nature —that sublime and eternal temple of God—that the all-loving Father has created us children of the earth for perfect happiness, that we may already here below enjoy a foretaste of Heavenly bliss; but that the source of our delights, as the source of our pains, is in our own bosoms—springs from our virtues or our vices.

How unutterably happy must not the man feel whose heart has not one thing to upbraid him with in respect to any of his relations in life; who does not permit his mind to be unduly disturbed by cares of any kind; who does not allow either unbridled anger, or unrestrained affection, to lead him into any excess! In him dwells a sublime calm, of which ordinary men can hardly form a conception—that calm which is the true peace of God.

Have you ever passed a fine spring morning alone amid the new-born beauties of nature? When, at such a time, you have been roving in the shade of peaceful groves, through the green canopy of which the rosy waves of sunlight broke; when the soft breath of morn was wafted across the verdant landscape, and the numberless flowerets shivered, and the dew on the leaflets glittered in the tears of joy which Heaven had shed at the Holiness and Goodness of the Creator; and the cascade leaping from the rock, and the river in its bed, and the forest on the hill, sent forth solemn murmurs; while high up above, and deep down below, the air resounded with the wonderful song of birds, and the buzzing of insects— oh, what were your feelings? Did not a sense of inexpressible delight flash through your bosom? You drew a deep breath; your body seemed etherealized, you felt as if you must join your voice to the voices of the air, as if you must mix your tears with the tears of heaven; you longed for the wings of rosy morn to soar up high into the empyrean, or to sink into the green depths of the forests, or to lose yourself in the blue haze that veiled the unknown distance. You longed to pour your love through the entire world.

Did you ever lie down on the top of a mountain, whence you beheld a wide landscape with its fields and cottages spread in silent repose before your eyes? In your bosom also perfect quiet reigned! You forgot all your domestic cares; no sorrow weighed on your spirits, no unpleasant remembrance disturbed the beneficent calm, no passion dared to intrude to break the holy peace of your soul, and a voice within whispered, " Blessed were I, could I for ever remain thus !" What you then felt was a fleeting foretaste of Heaven, which sometimes even passionate, unquiet spirits are allowed to enjoy, in order that they may look into themselves, and earnestly reflect how they might perpetuate this tranquil and blessed state. What you then felt was the peace of God, which the virtuous and wise, which the true followers of Christ, experience even in the midst of the greatest tribulation, and which raises them above it. You were happy in the moments alluded to, because you learnt then to forget yourselves, because you were free from the mundane desires, which regained possession of you as soon as you re-entered your homes. But woe to him who, in order thoroughly to enjoy life, must learn to forget himself! This is a proof, either that his heart is burdened with the consciousness of many sins, or that it is oppressed with cares and unsatisfied wants, springing from his vanity, his frivolity, his covetousness, or other impure tendencies; or that when he acts he does not act wisely, and that what he possesses he does not possess with wisdom; but that he allows himself to be consumed by a thousand vain and petty cares, and creates for himself sorrows which he will eventually discover to have been unnecessary.

The true disciple of Jesus never needs to forget himself in order to be cheerful in his very innermost soul. On the contrary, it is when he examines his inward being, and his relations to the Father of all life, that he feels most happy. The present day may have its storms, but the future only smiles the more brightly to him. He is with God, and God is with him. Whether he be of high or humble station, rich or poor, praised or blamed, to him it is all the same; for the source of his happiness is not in the outward world, but within himself. And he is with God, and God is with him. And "blessed are the pure in heart: for they shall see God," here already, in their foretaste of the higher bliss of Heaven.

Almost every stage of human life has its heavenly moments, in which mortal man feels himself, as it were, involuntarily raised above himself. Not what we possess or what we earn, not what we eat and drink, not our apparel, not what men think of us, but a pure heart is the true source of happiness.

Have you witnessed, or have you read of how persecuted innocence has been rescued? how some meritorious benevolent man was long misjudged, and overwhelmed with accusations by his enemies, until at length the world learnt to see its own injustice, and every one sought to make some amends? Do you recollect how that recognition of long oppressed innocence made your heart swell with emotion; how a quiet joy took possession of you, as though it were your own innocence that had been vindicated; how the happiness of that virtue which had at length received its reward, called tears of silent satisfaction into your eyes? On that occasion you shared in spirit, with the person whose innocence was made manifest, a foretaste of Heaven. It was from your own virtuous feelings that sprang the joy you experienced. It was the germs of true happiness within you that were moved; it was the source of your eternal welfare that began to flow. Ah! why did you choke up this spring with the rubbish of lower desires and petty cares? Why did you not put forth your full strength to rise in future above all low tendencies, and make a resolve to remain for ever the elevated being you were during those brief moments of emotion?

Childhood has its Eden. Adolescence has its hours of paradise. But at a later age also we behold from time to time a ray, as if from a better world, flashing across our path, and lighting up the commonplace things around us. These are foretastes of Heaven, which Providence sends to poor mortals, to stimulate them to strive after that which can alone render lasting such blissful moments.

Hast thou known the feelings of a mother kindled by the smile of her child standing before her in the fresh bloom of its loveliness and grace? when in silent but holy love she bends over this angel of her life, and seems with her kisses to draw its pure soul over into her own? Hast thou known the delight of a father, when he beholds for the first time the new-born babe that owes its existence to him; when the infant smiles upon him for the first time? when the joyous child lisps its first word? when he sees it growing in health, industry, and virtue? Ah! the delights of those heavenly moments he would not exchange for all the treasures of the world! and the mother too feels this most deeply, and says, "Take all else from me, and I am nevertheless blessed!" Queens may be inexpressibly miserable, and beggar-women unutterably happy!

Such feelings are vibrations of the purest chords of the heart. Alas! why do we so often leave them untouched? What is it that draws us all so irresistibly towards the sweet world of childhood? What is the hidden power which, at the sight of an infant, moves even the barbarian, and which wins at once the stranger's heart? It is the guileless trust, the sweet innocence, the winning grace of childhood, that charms us. It is the spotless purity of the angelic nature; it is the vague anticipation of a brilliant future for the child, and of how deservedly—should these young beings preserve their purity and their virtues in a later age—they will become objects of the world's devotion. We honour in the child the undesecrated sanctuary of the heart, which as yet has no presentiment of evil. It is not the outward form, it is not flesh and blood, that excites our love and admiration; but the purity, the something Divine that speaks to us from the frank and open eye, the ingenuous countenance of the child. It is our own inborn sense of virtue, which, unconscious to ourselves, animates us at such moments. In intercourse with the innocent little ones, we ourselves become more innocent, more noble and more wise; we are ashamed to appear before them in all our imperfections; and he who has not the courage to conquer his faults at least tries to conceal them. Verily, we may frequently learn more, improve more in wisdom and goodness, in the society of children, than in intercourse with the wisest of our acquaintance. "Suffer little children to come unto me," said Jesus; "for of such is the kingdom of Heaven."

The experience of every age thus proves and makes manifest that the highest happiness of which man is capable, does not depend upon whether he has much or little, but upon *whether he has a pure heart*. In the moments of his highest bliss his sense of virtue is always most strongly excited. In such moments he is good; he rises above selfishness, malice, false pretences, and impure desires. In such moments he willingly shares with others what he possesses, he would fain make the whole world happy; he forgives his mortal enemy, and embraces all mankind in his love.

It is the power of virtue that is strong within him and that bears witness to the truth of Jesus' promise: *Blessed are the pure in heart: for they shall see God!*

Be pure of heart, and all the sources of heavenly bliss within you will be opened up, and you will enjoy constantly that foretaste of Heaven, which hitherto has only been vouchsafed to you in your highest moments. For they were your highest moments, simply because while they lasted you had risen to be better men. Why did you not remain ever what you were then? Why did you become untrue to yourselves?

You were untrue to yourselves in giving yourselves up again to the outward world, and expecting from it pleasures which it does not afford. You deliberately became unfaithful to yourselves, because you cared not to be masters of yourselves; but preferred surrendering the mastery to things which could in no way contribute to your peace of mind. You abandon yourselves to excessive care connected with your outward circumstances, forgetting that it is your inward condition that is the chief object of life, and that when this is not what it ought to be, all outward honours, all comforts and luxuries, all pomp and grandeur, will be powerless to make you happy. Like madmen, you sacrifice life for death, peace of mind for constant anxiety, cheerfulness for sadness, the consciousness of innocence for pangs of conscience, the pride of independence for the shame of dependence, the sense of security for never-ceasing fears. Perhaps you have often sent up the prayer: "Give me, O God, a pure heart; and let Thy Holy Spirit inspire me." But no sooner was the prayer uttered than you again gave way to anger against your brother, than you again hypocritically deceived some unsuspecting person, than you again allowed a sufferer to leave you without being comforted, than you again began to amass money by unrighteous means, and allowed jealousy to fill your heart with hatred and malice. And what have you hitherto obtained in return for your many anxieties? Perhaps physical infirmities, which prevent you from enjoying what other advantages may be yours; perhaps a few more possessions than previously, but perhaps, also, fewer joys than when you had less worldly goods; perhaps a post of honour which exposes you to malicious attacks of envy, and heaps upon you responsibilities and cares. Is that a foretaste of Heaven? Can these gains bear comparison with the happiness you enjoyed in those higher moments, when you possessed none of these, but when you were pure in heart, and your mind was free and fearless?

He who is thoroughly happy within himself covets not other joys, asks for nothing more than to remain for ever as he is. If outward circumstances make man happy, why then is he, even after he has attained the desired end, ever craving for something better, something different? Why, then, is he always pursuing happiness as the child pursues the glowing colours of the rainbow, without ever reaching them?

Pause, wonder, reflect upon the heavenly hours thou hast enjoyed in life, and ask thyself how they came to thee. Not to rank, nor riches, nor fine clothes, nor meat, nor drink, didst thou owe them, but to thy pure heart. Thou wert a better man in those hours, and therefore all that surrounded thee was better. Abandon the mistaken road towards happiness, and strive again to possess that which alone can lead thee back to thy paradise.

Live with God in childlike purity. Never allow thyself to be too much absorbed in care for outward circumstances. Do thy duty, keep thy conscience clear; for all else trust in HIM, who knows best what is good for us. Root out thy faults and evil tendencies: when a child thou hadst them not, and therefore thou wert happier then than now. First of all cast from thee the desires that cause thee most uneasiness; correct, by steadfast perseverance, those defects in thy disposition and thy conduct, which are the chief sources of disquietude to thee. Man has great, nay, incredible power over himself, if he will but exert it. Think not of gratifying thyself; but consider each day what good thou canst do to others. Demand what thou hast a right to; but on the other side, never in the smallest way do injustice to others. And in order that thou mayst continue to improve, study earnestly the spirit and precepts of Jesus. In these thou wilt discover the highest wisdom, and from them learn the way back into thy lost paradise. There thou wilt find thy God again, and even in the severest trials of life, an inward peace, cheerfulness, bliss, of which no mortal can ever deprive thee. "Blessed are the pure in heart: for they shall see God!"

Merciful and eternal God, Love inexhaustible, Father of the universe, my Father! if I have but Thee, all that life may bring is but a shadowy phantasm. If I have but Thee, I shall pass without fear through light and through darkness, and shall find my way, and shall not falter, though want and death may threaten. If I have but Thee, I am sufficiently rich, though all fail me that others call riches; I am sufficiently exalted, though all the world look down upon me; I am strong enough, though thousands conspire against me; I am safe, though disasters may befall me, and all my earthly possessions be lost. If I have but Thee, death itself cannot rob me of my joy, should it even tear from my bleeding heart all the beloved souls to whom I am attached. Ah! death is *Thy* angel messenger, he brings them to Thee, and in the bosom of Thy love I shall find them again. If I have but Thee, I possess all things! Amen.

THE WORLD A MIRROR OF ETERNITY.

The Lord is King! He reigns for ever—
The Lord is God! He ceaseth never—
He was—He e'er shall be—He is—
Who shall dare change what He commands?
The universe rests in His hands—
　Fails He to hold, it perishes—
Yet still unconscious of decay
The globe revolves from day to day;
In the eternal seas of air
Floats yet this earthly ball, so seeming fair.

How long, ye nations, will ye try
His patience, "and His wrath defy?"
　Triflers on earth—His love forgot—
How long ere yet His anger burn—
Omnipotent, although ye spurn
　His power, and comprehend Him not—
A Father and a Judge alike,
Though merciful He yet can strike—
The earth rests only on His will!
And ye, too, scorners!—yet delays He still.
　　　　　　　(1 *Cor.* xiii. 12, 13.)

How gloriously does not the God who beams upon us from the Heavenly revelations of Jesus, harmonize with the wonderful God who majestically reveals Himself to me and to all nations, at all periods of time, in the varying beauty and grandeur of nature! Mysterious and grand He appears in His action on the world of spirits. Mysterious and grand in the order of the myriads of flaming worlds, which move in their eternally prescribed orbits, without ever diverging from their paths or coming into collision. Mercifully He reigns in the realm of immortal spirits, where His call to happiness penetrates all beings, and His justice rules; mercifully in the sublunary world, where His love is extended even to the lowliest creature.

The longer I consider and weigh the revelations of the Eternal Son, the longer I dwell upon the spectacle of the infinite creation, the more conscious I become of the proximity of God, the more vividly I feel: this is not mere mechanical activity. In all the forms of this sublunary world, through all the play of the hidden spiritual forces, there is revealed a Will full of Almighty Power, an Almighty Power full of Wisdom, a Wisdom full of Holiness, full of Love—and this is God! But the nature of God I cannot fathom. A God whose nature I could fathom would not be God, for even the nature of my own soul is a dark riddle to me. Seek not to know wherein consists the essence of the Highest Being; for the essence of even the meanest creature that He has made is an insoluble mystery to thee. Audacious mortal, the longer thou gazest at the dazzling brightness of the sun, the more it blinds thee!

Our knowledge here on earth is but partial, said St. Paul, the wise Disciple of Jesus; "now we see through a glass, darkly, but then we see face to face; now I know in part, but then I shall know even as I also am known. And now abideth faith, hope, charity, these three; but the greatest of these is charity." (1 Cor. xiii. 12, 13.)

Yea, this world, which is for a short time assigned to us as a habitation, is to me as a darkened mirror of eternity. I see here in part that which I shall one day behold with delight in its wonderful totality. What I hope here, will there be fulfilled; and that which is here but an obscure foreshadowing, will there surround me as a bright reality. And the God of Life, whose glory I behold here only in reflection, will be revealed to me in full effulgence, when my immortal spirit shall be immersed in Him and in His bliss.

The world is to me a darkened mirror of eternity. That which I experience in detached fragments in this life, betrays to me what I shall one day experience in a more perfect life. For in the Divine creation all is unbroken unity; all things are connected; there is no interruption of continuity. In the chain of the infinite universe there are no missing links.

The here and the hereafter, life and eternity, are but ONE, form but ONE WHOLE, without interruption. Were my eyesight sufficiently strong, I should discover in the minute seed which a single blade of grass suffices to conceal, the gigantic tree which at the end of a hundred years will overshadow a whole valley. In everything there is progress, development.

God has diffused throughout the wide universe a vital force, a secret power of animation. This all animating power manifests itself on every side, yet how rarely do we notice it! All things are imbued with it, and it is constantly renovating the form of whatever is undergoing dissolution. It acts with wonderful energy in the innermost germ of every seed, draws nourishment from all the elements, attracts towards itself the crumbling dust of ages, spreads fresh life through it, and produces a new plant, whose beauty charms us in spring, whose radiant colours dazzle our eyes, whose fragrance delights us, or whose fruits afford us delicious nourishment.

This vital force resides in every part of animal nature, so that the part is hardly separated from the whole, before, in the midst of decay, new life begins to develop itself.

Thus our earthly body likewise is imbued with this vital force. In every minute part of our bodies, also, the wonderful power diffused throughout the universe is at work. It is placed at the service of our spirit as long as the latter dwells in the body. For the benefit of the spirit it animates the delicate nerve tissues, and causes the blood to flow through the labyrinthine passages of the arteries and veins; for the benefit of the spirit it draws nourishment from the elements, brightens the eye, sucks in the fragrant breath of the flowers, and carries the tones of the outer world into the innermost recesses of the soul.

When, however, that which is immortal within us outstrips the earthly coil; when the thinking, freely willing, spontaneous power within us, which is subject to special laws of its own, and which we call our spirit, our real self, takes leave of the body, then the vital power ceases to perform its functions, and the body perishes.

But, in the same manner as these forces and life-impulses always find new materials which they work into new forms, so also the noblest of all forces, the immortal spirit, called to freedom, to bliss, and to eternal endurance, doth clothe itself in a new vesture. It neither sleeps nor dies when its first body passes away; and it will not fail to find a new veil in which to shroud itself, when called, perhaps, to act more gloriously, more perfectly, in the sphere of eternal existence. It must be so,—for *naught perishes*. What is death? Nothing more than transformation. The dead flower is transformed into dust, which in time becomes parts of other flowers. And in like manner as the blind life-force, acting according to the eternal laws of God, continues without ceasing, so also the free spirit of man, when relieved from its earthly coil. Thus this world is to us as a darkened mirror of eternity.

What eye can measure the boundless universe of God? The strongest telescope of the astronomer fails to discover its limits. Beyond all the stars or worlds which we discern through his instrument, we behold the faint gleams of the pale light of still more distant and unknown realms of space, which may be the reflection of still remoter stars, located in parts of the infinite universe which will ever remain hidden to man.

The wonderful rapidity with which light travels has been calculated; the relative distances have been measured between the sun and the planets that revolve round him, and which borrow their light from him; but to express the relative distances of the greater number of stellar systems, words and numbers fail us. Stars which we see glimmering in the heavens because their light is still travelling towards us through immeasurable space, may have been long extinguished. New suns may have come into existence at inexpressible distances from us, which we do not see because the light from them has not reached our eye. So immense is the universe!—Nay, not the universe, but merely the small part of it which we can discover from our earth; and this small part, according to the suppositions of the most distinguished astronomers, is far from the glorious centre round which the worlds revolve. The earth, the sun, the myriad stars, float in the great ocean of space, and revolve round a greater sun which, however, remains hidden from our mortal ken. Each hour the globe we inhabit moves fifteen thousand miles, and each day three hundred and fifty-five thousand miles, onward in space. Hourly and daily the sun, with the eleven planets (worlds like our own) and eighteen moons (all of which cannot be seen by the naked eye) belonging to his system, in like manner move along with inconceivable rapidity, without our being able to perceive it. So immeasurable are the distances that separate these worlds belonging to one and the same system, that even after a century's observation, we are hardly able to discern their motion round another—to us unknown—sun.

And these numberless spheres, almost all of which are of infinitely greater magnitude than the globe we inhabit, are intimately connected with each other, in spite of the enormous distances that separate them. Similar to each other in form, they mutually dispense to each other the light which they irradiate, and which is perhaps the same as that which flashes from the thunder-cloud, and which beams so brightly in the Aurora Borealis.

Ah! what is the finest masterpiece from the hand of the first human artist compared with the great, the wonderful, the boundless universe whereon God is enthroned! And all these worlds form a unity—are the intimately connected, closely related parts of a continuous whole! From immeasurable distances the one acts upon the other. The moon moves our seas to ebb and flood, and influences the weather on our globe; and in like manner our earth is influenced by the sun, which holds in dependence upon itself all the spheres floating in space at distances of hundreds of millions of miles from it. In virtue of the as yet undiscovered, and probably ever to us undiscoverable, matter that connects the countless worlds, they are constantly influencing each other. Thus all form but one whole; all are connected by the Almighty Hand of Divine Majesty! And thus this world, little as I know of it, is to me as a darkened mirror of eternity. In this boundless ocean of the universe, wherein nothing is ever annihilated, I also dwell. Like all that belongs to it, I can never cease to exist in it. I also am an inhabitant of the Divine edifice, and the All-Holy One, on whose breath hang myriads of suns, I may call Father! My Father! Here, as there, I am within the bounds of eternity! There is no difference, for all is one! The hours, the years which pass over my head on this earth, are parts of eternity, drops in its ocean, in no way separate from it!

When I learn from the observations of distinguished astronomers and natural philosophers, that the size of the sun is more than one million and a half greater than that of our globe; when I learn that the sun probably consists of earths and rocks similar to those of our sphere, that mountains and valleys really appear upon its surface, that it is not, as it seems, a glowing ball of fire, but that it is surrounded by an indescribable luminous vapour in the same manner as our earth is surrounded by clouds;—or when I learn, that even tolerably strong telescopes show upon the surface of the moon entire ranges of strangely formed mountains and valleys, interspersed with dark spots, supposed to be oceans and plains;—or when I hear that in the sphere which we call our morning and evening star, mountains have been discovered, which far surpass in altitude those of our earth, I am seized with reverential awe, and my mind is lost in amazement at the incomprehensible vastness, at the wonderful construction of the universe, in which I perceive so many globes like our own, and probably—nay, certainly—inhabited like our own by living beings. Beings, the noblest of whom acknowledge and praise God —ah! perhaps more truly and worthily than I do.

Then I see the world as in a darkened mirror; then arise in me feelings never before experienced; then I become conscious that I belong, not alone to this earth, to this fleeting, insignificant life, but also to other kindred worlds; that I have brothers, more perfect and more happy, dwelling in immeasurably distant regions of the grand universe. Language fails me. My thoughts are confounded. I seem to have a presentiment of the infinite. I stand in the midst of eternity. I am immersed in its awful depths!

What manifold forms of life and existence may there not be in those great worlds, that roll so majestically through space! What an ascending scale of ever greater perfection and happiness, of which I, poor mortal, cannot form even a distant conception! Even here on earth I behold and admire the manifold differences which prevail in great and small things. Even here I behold strange inequalities. What variety of mental capacity and of power of enjoyment, even among animals! What an inferior creature is not the mussel clinging to the rock on the sea-shore, when compared to the May-fly rising on golden wings through the balmy air of spring! What an exalted position does not the sagacious elephant, the intelligent courser, the dog, the faithful friend of man, maintain at the side of other individual species of the animal race! And what is the instinct of animals compared to the reason of man! And can we suppose that after calling man into being the creative power of the Creator was exhausted? Can we suppose that man is the most perfect of created beings in the universe, because he is the highest and most glorious being on this globe? What is this earth of ours? Why, one of the smallest stars in the firmament. And even our sun, though one and a half million times larger than the earth, is but one of the smallest when compared to the suns which, placed at distances from us that no mortal can calculate, yet appear as stars of the first magnitude. If I may be allowed to draw conclusions from the comparative magnitudes of the heavenly bodies, oh, then, man must be one of the meanest and most insignificant of Divinely created beings; then there exist in the infinite creation, in the abodes of eternity, beings of far higher nature than ours, before whom we should appear but as the dust at our feet; and whose wisdom, holiness, perfection, happiness exceeds ours as much as our wisdom, holiness, happiness exceeds that of the lowly worm which we unconsciously trample under foot.

Yea, there are creatures, of higher nature than myself, far more holy and perfect, who, like myself, pray to the Highest of all Beings. Revelation mentions them as angels, as the exalted spirits of Heaven, as Cherubim and Seraphim. There are worlds above ours. There are inhabitants of the boundless universe, in comparison with whom I am a mere nothing. And had no revelation taught me so, I should have learnt it from what I observe even on this earth. Yea, verily, the world is to me a mirror of eternity; and though but a darkened mirror, the images I behold in it are mighty enough to stir up my innermost soul.

Only a darkened mirror, and yet how much do I not behold in it! My knowledge here below is but partial, yet how elevating even in its limited form! When my mind loses itself in the infinitude of Divine creations, I feel my insignificance, my nothingness, and yet at the same time a sweet pride and consolation come to me in the thought, that I, also, am worthy of God the Creator of the universe; that something Divine lives and thinks within me!

Alas for me, when from this sublime height, where I seem to have a presentiment of God, I look down upon my past life! Alas for me, what have I been? What have I done? The sorrows I have known, have they been nearer those of the angel or of the brute? Have I striven more to secure the sublime and intense gratification which the seraph enjoys in the consciousness of his perfection and holiness, or the sensual gratifications of my earthly body, which are common to the lower animals as well?

Blushing, I cast down my eyes before the incorruptible judge within me; before the Omniscience of the All Holy One. Fain would I hide myself—hide the whole course of my life, that no eye might behold it! For I have looked into the darkened mirror of eternity, but failed to be impressed by what I saw. I had an intuitive perception that a higher destiny awaited me, and that I must consecrate myself to it during my earthly life; but I did not raise myself up into the sphere of the angels, but sank down into the slough of animal life. I laboured for my body only; took heed for naught but meat and drink; stretched out my hands with child-like folly after pomp and earthly glory, evanescent as dust; I neglected myself, lived not for my soul, my real self, but for my perishable body, which is mine only for a time. I looked into the darkened image of eternity; but, like the animal whose drooping head allows it only to gaze on the earth, I never lifted my face towards Heaven. The applause of men, so contemptible and so little enduring, I prized more highly than the consciousness that I was making myself worthy of God and my eternal destiny. Ah! how unutterably foolish I have been! how despicable I seem to myself! "Be perfect, as your Father in Heaven is perfect!" So saidst Thou, my holy, my Divine Teacher, Jesus Christ, who filled the spiritual world with Thy light, which was not of this world. Woe is me! I heard Thy voice, O faithful Shepherd of men, but I did not follow its call!

Alas! like my knowledge, so was also my willing but partial and imperfect. But is it ever to remain so? Shall I become still more imperfect than I am? Shall I be precipitated from the place which I now hold in the scale of God-created beings? Eternity! Eternity! In thee dwells Eternal Love; but woe to me, sinner that I am, in thee dwells also the Eternal

Judge whose Justice deals with us according to our deserts!

Console me, ye lovely daughters of Heaven—Faith, Hope, and Charity! Accompany me along the paths which I may still have to traverse. Strengthen me, O Faith in God! and raise my mind above earthly cares and earthly wishes up to its true destination. Save me when my soul vacillates between time and eternity, when it is tempted to prefer the animal to the Divine. Save me when passion is nigh mastering me, and when sensuality threatens to carry the victory over principle and duty. And thou, O Hope, Divine gift of God, promise held out by the lips of Jesus Himself, abandon me not in the most anxious hours of life! And when I sacrifice everything for the sake of righteousness and the purity of my soul, should I be poor and forsaken because of my virtue, and become a laughing-stock to men—oh, then, Hope in Eternity and Mercy, do not thou forsake me!

And thou, loveliest of all virtues, parent and source of every spiritual perfection, Charity, love to God, and love to man, penetrate me so that in thee I may live, and breathe, and have my being. Only he who dwells in love, dwells in God; only to him who dwells in love, who is thoroughly imbued with love, is eternity opened here on earth; only he enjoys here below already a foretaste of its bliss. For He who dwelleth and ruleth in eternity is the all-animating Love, is God!

THE EXISTENCE OF ANGELS.

Alone by reason's glimmering light
   We dimly search out nature's plan—
But all to *Thee* was clear and bright,
   Long ere creation's dawn began—
Together linked, some scattered beams
   Of truth our weary toil may claim,
But to *Thine* eyes, these fitful gleams
   Glow like a golden sea of flame.

The countless hosts that throng each sphere,
   Each blooming flower—each hidden gem
Revealed before thy glance appear,
   And by their names Thou callest them.
Thou piercest to the germ within,
   Doubts, dangers—ne'er can 'scape Thine eye;
Thou knowest all that is, has been,
   And *can* be in futurity.

Such glorious knowledge is in Thee,
   I tremble at the wondrous height :
The wondrous depth o'erpowers me,
   As I stand praying in Thy sight.
I faint—I falter—God! Thy ways
   Are measureless; unless *Thou* teach,
Not even the Archangels' gaze
   Can sound their depth, their height can reach.

                        (*Matt.* xviii. 10.)

AT a very early period already the human race showed a tendency to believe in the existence of higher beings, who, though created by God, were infinitely superior to man. This belief was very natural. Because the better acquainted men became with the various parts of creation, the more convinced they were that in nature there are no gaps; that everything embraced in it forms one great continuous chain, in which the lowest link, *i.e.* the most imperfect being, is connected with the highest, though only through innumerable other links, gradually rising in the scale of perfection; that between the broken fragment of lifeless rock and man, lies the long progressive series of plants and animals; that the lifeless stone first touches in its crystalline form the lowest family of plants; that certain plants, on the other hand approach very near to animal life, such as it is seen in the water polypus and the coral; that in the endless scale of living beings the less perfect is always followed by the more perfect, until at length the most perfect animal touches the least perfect, most animal-like race of human beings, who are only raised above the sagacity of the dog, the elephant, or the ape, in as far as a faint spark of reason glimmers within them.

On observing this remarkable and regular gradation of beings, the question would naturally arise in man: Though I may be able to discern all that lies below me, does it follow that there is naught above me but what I know? The most sagacious among animals are indeed aware of my existence, but can they form to themselves even a distant conception of what it is to be a man, or of what man can acquire and perform through means of his mental capacities? And can I venture to presume that the most perfect man touches immediately in the scale of beings, the Deity who rules the universe.

Impossible! The deeper I look into God's creation,

the more His glory and His boundless power are made manifest to me, the more vividly do I feel how infinitely inferior I am to the All High, how far I am removed from Him. And can I suppose that the immense interval that separates man from the Power that rules the universe, is left unoccupied; that the continuity of nature which I observe wherever my mind can penetrate, has here been suddenly interrupted; that between God and man there is naught but an infinite desert? This is inconceivable!

In like manner as in the planetary system smaller moons revolve round the earth; in like manner as our planet and other planets revolve round the sun with other moons; in like manner as the sun, accompanied by all the planets and their moons, and probably together with many other suns which we call fixed stars, moves in space around an infinitely greater sun which our eyes have never beheld; in like manner as this again, with all the surrounding suns, planets, and moons, sweeps around a still more glorious centre, in periods of time for which human language has no numbers: so also there must be placed between human nature and the Deity myriads of higher beings, supermundane natures, nearer akin to God than poor mortal man! In ordinary language we comprise all these beings under the name of angels, but we know not wherein consists their higher nature, nor do we know the number of grades which there may be between the least perfect angel, who is nearest akin to the most perfect man, and the most glorious of created beings, who enjoy unutterable bliss, feeling themselves in close proximity to God.

The Holy Scriptures also speak of the existence of

these lovely natures, without affording any idea of what they are and wherein their advantages consist. The Scriptures only mention their superior happiness, and say that they are the servants of the Most High, the doers of His bidding. Jesus Christ, also, who withdrew the curtain from as much of the sanctuary of the super-terrestrial world as He thought the eyes of mortals could bear to behold—Jesus, also, speaks of the higher spirits which intervene between us and the Most High. But He only speaks of them as beings standing nearer the throne of the Eternal Father than we, and taking a loving interest in the welfare of human spirits, in like manner as kind-hearted mortals often constitute themselves friends and protectors of beings inferior to themselves. (Matt. xviii. 10.)

Now, although it would be vain labour to endeavour to form a conception of the nature and happiness of the higher spirits, it is nevertheless an interesting occupation for our thoughts to dwell upon what we know of the spiritual in this earthly existence, and to draw thence conclusions as to the spirits that rank above us. For in the world that we know we find as great variety in the spiritual forces or invisible powers as in the material things. Among such spiritual forces or essences, the existence of which we know only through their effects, we must indeed count not only human spirits and animal souls, but also those powers which we usually denominate blind forces of nature, and which dwell in all things, not only in the animal and in the plant, but in stone, in water, in fire, and in all elementary substances.

Is not heat a special power which expands and

changes everything that is brought within its influence? Is not light a special power, which, while stimulating our eyes, speeds on in all directions in straight lines and with inconceivable rapidity?—Who has not beheld with wonder the mysterious power of the loadstone, which it communicates to iron? It works according to eternal laws peculiar to itself. The magnet attracts towards itself light iron materials from a certain distance; and the iron needle rubbed with loadstone, ever points one of its extremities, and always the same one, towards the northern quarter of the globe. In consequence hereof it becomes the trusty and unerring guide of the seafarer during the storms that drive him out of his track on the ocean, and also of the miner, who labours deep down in the bowels of the earth, far from the light of day.

Is not that strange something which manifests itself as lightning in the clouds of the air, and as a spark emitted by the coat of various animals when stroked—which betrays its existence in certain fishes of the sea by a violent shock, and which men of science call forth by friction from various substances in the form of a flash of lightning, or of a tremendous shock—is not this a peculiar power?

All these and many other forces of nature are, in a manner, spiritual—that is to say, they are present in the various bodies, though imperceptible to our senses, until called forth by certain circumstances. Then they reveal themselves by some change produced in the bodies, and our senses take cognizance of their presence. In like manner the spiritual power of man remains hidden, until revealed in word and action.

These blind forces of nature are diffused through all matter. They work for, against, and with each other. They fill the air and every field of space. Through them only we obtain cognizance of the existence of the stars. They are in consequence spread through the boundless ocean of all creation; lifeless, that is, imperceptible in themselves, and only active and vivid when brought into connexion with certain bodies, just as the spirit of man only manifests its existence when united with a body.

We call the effects produced by these hidden forces natural phenomena. We, as well as every animal, every stone, every plant, are imbued with this spiritual something, without knowing what it is in itself, and how it works. It remains ever hidden beneath the plan of its phenomena, in like manner as the spirit of man is unknown to itself, but only learns from its effects on the body, or its action through the body, that it is present.

Finally, all that we know about these blind forces of nature is, that their influence contributes greatly to maintain the life of plants, and also the mere vegetable life of animals and men. It is they who give heat and colour to our blood, and who suffuse the flowers with varied tints. It is they who in the dark caverns of the earth form various metals and minerals, and transform the latter into regular crystals.

Nevertheless all these forces together are incapable of producing a single blade of grass, with its fibres, its cells, its air-valves and spiral tubes. The blade of grass only comes into existence through means of a seed of its species. In this seed alone lies the possibility of the future plant with all its forms, as for instance in the acorn is the germ of the future majestic oak.

But what is it that develops itself so beautifully and wonderfully in and with this germ? What is it that forms out of the volatile substances borrowed from earth, water, and air, marvellously regular tubes, valves, veins, fruits, down, leaves, roots, all organized with perfect wisdom? What is it that produces in human and animal bodies, bone, blood, sinews, and nerves; that regulates the internal parts, makes the blood flow according to laws of its own, and establishes the relative position of each part to the whole? The human spirit dwells in the body without knowing what is passing within it, or how it is that everything moves within it according to rational laws.

Here there is evidently something more than the mere blind natural forces, such as magnetism, light, and heat. Here is a higher power, which, though still not self-conscious and still following blindly the laws of the Creator, yet already builds up instruments for definite purposes.—I call this more exalted and powerful something, the vital force.

This vital force—which develops the bodies of men, animals, and plants, which builds and sustains according to eternal laws laid down by the Creator—is totally different from the simple blind powers of nature. A flint-rock will never become a rose-bush, the seed-pods of a fruit tree will never grow into gold. Each remains after its kind what it is, and the vital power develops itself according to the laws of creation. In like manner as it draws towards itself, and transmutes earthly materials for the construction of the bodies of plants, animals, and men; so also it uses, as it were, for the completion of its purpose, all the æthereal or spiritual substances, *i.e.*, the simple powers of nature alluded to above. It uses these, however, only as means, and thus proves that it is a higher power than they.

The connexion between the vital power and the natural forces is, however, so intimate, that the former, failing the aid of the latter, remains inactive. If heat and light be not admitted, the vital force in the vegetable germ cannot develop its activity, cannot make use of its instruments above and beneath the earth, to gather up new materials.

Thus we recognize in the realm of creation known to us, two kinds of spiritual essences: the blind powers of nature, and the true life-power in plants and animals. But the power which calls forth life, or rather, which in itself constitutes that which in plants and animals we call *life*, is as little self-conscious as is the force called heat. What does the growing hair on our heads, what does our body with all its limbs, know about itself, except through the activity of the indwelling soul?

The plant has life, so has the animal; but the latter has also a soul, that is to say, possesses an innate power of perception, and of judgment to a certain extent, and likewise a power of feeling hatred and affection, anger and joy, desire and repugnance. Animals have also the power of willing; but plants, which do, indeed, in rare instances manifest a faint indication of sensation, do not show the most distant appearance of a will.

Therefore the animal kingdom ranks as far above the world of plants, as the self-determining soul ranks above the mechanical vital power, or as life ranks above the blind powers of nature.

Yet the animal soul is intimately connected with the vital principle in plants, and the activity of both often manifests itself in a similar manner. Just as the plant, following laws of which it is not conscious, draws from earth, air, and water, the nourishment it requires, so does the animal soul act in obedience to mysterious instincts, which it has not the power to resist. These instincts, however, originate in the peculiar construction of the animal body. Thus horned cattle pass by those herbs which are not congenial to the nature of their bodies, and seek for those which will afford them healthy nourishment. Thus hunger makes the wolf ferocious, while the instinct that incites them to pair, makes even the fiercest beasts gregarious. All the sensations and desires of animals arise out of their bodily structure, their acts are influenced by this alone; that which is agreeable or painful to their bodies, they like or dislike.

How different from the mere animal soul does the exalted spirit of man appear! This is not only conscious of its own existence, but clearly so. It not only takes cognizance of the things that surrround it (the animal soul does as much), but it recognizes the more subtle relations between them, with their causes and consequences. It investigates the wonders of the lower creation, it masters the elements through its powers of invention, and presses them into its service; its transplants the produce of the vegetable kingdom into foreign soils; it conquers the strength of the most powerful animals; it calculates the movements of the heavenly spheres through space, and bears within itself a revelation of the Deity.

Of all this the animal knows nothing. The soul of the most sagacious brute is incapable of rising to the height attained by the thoughts even of a young child. The animal soul has indeed a will, but it only wills what its body desires, and acts only in accordance with the bodily instincts. The spirit of man on the contrary, when its innate nobility is uncorrupted, acknowledges a higher law than that of bodily instincts; it obeys, not the flesh in which it dwells, but itself alone, that is to say, the laws of its reason, whereby it distinguishes between good and evil, right and wrong. He who obeys only self-imposed laws is free. Therefore the human spirit is capable of freedom, and the animal soul, being the slave of sensual instincts, is in consequence essentially different from it. The human spirit is akin to the Divine, the animal soul is akin to the flesh.

But the spirit of man is nevertheless, through the earthly bonds in which it is held, closely connected with the animal soul. Frequently the spirit is hardly master of itself; the animal soul connected with its body overwhelms its more exalted power, and thus arises a twofold law in the human breast. Man does not always do that which the spirit wills, but on the contrary, often does that which it abhors. Therefore St. Paul, the inspired apostle, said:—

"But I see another law in my members, warring against the law of my mind, and bringing me into captivity to the law of sin which is in my members." (Rom. vii. 23.)

Further, the human spirit, in spite of its consciousness of immortality, is also herein similar to the animal soul, that although it takes cognizance of the things that surround it, it has no knowledge of its own nature. It is familiar with all things, but is a stranger to itself, and cannot say how or wherefore it exists. All earthly matters it surveys and organizes with wonderful acuteness, but the spiritual world it cannot fathom, though it is itself spirit.

Does the chain of the higher forces and essences end with the spirit of man? Oh, if so, how short were it not! Who can believe, when everything in the universe bears the stamp of infinitude, that the circle of the higher powers should consist only of the blind forces of nature, the vital power, the animal soul, and the spirit of man?

Nay, feeling the inconceivably great distance that separates my spirit from the Deity, I am willing to believe in the existence of manifold powers and forces of a higher nature—spirits more full of knowledge, goodness, and power than ours, or Angels as we term them in ordinary language.

These higher powers are, perhaps, or even probably, as closely akin to the human spirit, as this is to the animal soul, or as the latter is to the vital force in matter, or as this again is to the dead forces in nature; at all events there can be no doubt that these spirits, kindred to our own, are as far above us in power and capacity, as man is above the animals, as animals are above plants, and plants above minerals.

It seems almost as if I could picture to myself the clearer insight of those higher spiritual existences, which rank next to ourselves in the scale of beings. They must be able to look deeper into the mysteries of God. While we mortals are endowed with the capacity of understanding and representing earthly matters, but are left in ignorance as to the nature of spirit, and as to the more occult powers of the universe —the higher spirits are probably acquainted, and even familiar with, the laws of spirit. Before their eyes the mysteries of the elementary bodies lie open, as the cup of a flower, with its coronal and its stamens, lies open before ours. We see only the outlines, forms, and relations of things as they appear outwardly; the more lofty spirits, in virtue of their higher faculties, of which we cannot even form a conception, see and understand the internal nature and structure of things.

But hold! Whither do my thoughts venture in their bold flight? They are endeavouring to break through the limits of their legitimate field of activity, and sacrilegiously to force themselves into the sanctuary of higher powers and spirits. Retreat! Await the hour which thy Creator has appointed, when the all-animating Spirit, the Father of the universe, shall call thee, and perhaps place thee, also, in the rank of the more highly endowed beings.

Oh Lord! Can this be? Shall I be worthy of it? Have my spiritual powers been sufficiently developed? Has my spirit ceased to obey earthly desires, to follow the animal instincts of the body; has it ceased to give itself up to voluptuousness, covetousness, anger, love of revenge, hatred, and malice? Is my spirit free, acting only in accordance with its own laws, *i.e.*, God's laws? Does it live for duty more than for worldly gain? Is it actuated at all times by love, and not by enmity?

Oh Father! Oh Lord God! How my spirit yearns towards Thee! How it longs to escape from the imperfect and to reach the perfect! Could I gain the victory how willingly would I die?

Die! What is death to the spirit? It is but parting from its earthly coil, the body—and from its earthly sister, the soul. Even the latter escapes from its worn out instrument, the body, and withdraws from it its vegetable life.

Death never proceeds from the spirit to the body, for the spirit is life. Death arises from violent disturbance of the spirit's vehicle, the body; or in consequence of the natural forces having completed their circulation in the organism, according to divine rule. They then withdraw from the body, which thus loses light and heat, motion and stimulant; and the natural forces being, as it were, the nourishing oil of the flame of life, this becomes extinct—the human spirit released—is mature!

Oh God! may it be my right, in the solemn hour of my dissolution, to proclaim in exultant tones of joy: I am a power ripened for a better state! Admit me among you, O beings of higher nature, brothers standing on a more exalted level in the scale of creation! I am your brother, for I am immortal!

DEATH IS MY GAIN.

Rock of God ! mine arm doth clasp thee—
Immortality ! I grasp thee—
Night and sorrow may surround me,
   Grief and care my peace invade—
Shall I faint because they wound me ?
   No—I seek thy cooling shade—
Longing after God's own rest
Fills my soul—and makes me blest.

As I reach that mountain height,
Swells my soul with calm delight—
When the cool air, softly kissing,
   Wakes a fresher spring within,
(Feeble image of God's blessing
   After long repented sin,)
Then I feel my course is gained,
Soon my goal shall be attained.

Then, oh then, what tongue can tell
The rapture of my bosom's swell,
When no sorrow more can grieve me !
   When God's mantle wraps me round,
Never more alone to leave me,
   Every chain of sin unbound,
All my soul is happiness,
Freedom all my being's bliss.

(1 *Cor.* xv. 31.)

THE human body with which we are invested on earth, is but the transparent veil of the soul, and we should ever hold in mind this relation between soul and body, for this conception is not only true in itself, but is fruitful of important conclusions bearing upon life.

The Deity willed that the spirit of man should be capable of placing itself in communication with the non-spiritual existences, therefore it was enveloped in a refined earthly material, every part of which is vivified by the spirit. Through means of a tissue of nerves, so delicate as scarcely to be perceptible to the naked eye, and which interpenetrate the entire body, the soul holds command over the latter. Through the body the soul receives impressions from without which tend to its improvement, and it gradually learns to avail itself of the body as an instrument of action upon the outward world. If the bodily veil be rent in twain, if the instrument be destroyed, the spirit loses its power over its former habitation, which becomes as foreign to it as all other earthly matter. This estrangement between soul and body is called death.

The body is a transparent covering of the soul. In all movements and changes, in repose as in action, we recognize the soul behind the appearances of the body. It is not the body that loves or is angered; it is the soul that speaks in thundering accents through the instrumentality of the voice, and which smiles in the merry glance of the eye; it is the shame felt by the soul that suffuses the cheek with blushes; it is the soul's courage, terror, longing, or suffering that is shown in the various expressions of its outward covering. For when the soul is separated from the delicate and mobile covering which we call body—what becomes of the latter? It sinks down and lies like a discarded garment. It grows rigid like a marble statue, and we can hardly believe that these dead ashes have ever been animated by a higher essence.

It is not either the body that we love or hate in others, but the soul which is concealed behind its veil. It is the soul's loveliness that charms us; its wisdom, or its virtue which inspires us with respect; its degeneracy that awakens our indignation. In the presence of the soul-abandoned corpse, all love and hatred cease, for our friend or our foe has disappeared, and his discarded covering makes no more impression on us than any other dead matter.

Natural as it is that no one should love the body of another, but on the contrary, the soul that beams forth from it, as natural is it that each man should love the body in which his own soul is clothed. He seeks to protect and improve it, because the soul requires a worthy and efficient instrument; he endeavours to adorn and beautify it, because the innate and constant yearning of the soul for perfection and distinction involuntarily passes over to that which is most intimately connected with it. The soul even strives, in the feeling of its own unworthiness, to cover its own failings by the beauty of its earthly veil; it tries to draw the folds of this more closely around itself, in order that it may not be seen in its ugliness —and of such persons we say that they present a false appearance.

The necessity that each soul should be clad in a veil of flesh, is one of the eternal ordinances of the Deity. Hence the deep and strong love of the soul for its body; hence that clinging to life which it is almost impossible to overcome.

But what is death? Nothing but the separation of the soul from its earthly covering. What becomes of the covering when discarded? Does it vanish from

God's creation? No, it moulders into dust and ashes, and mingles with the rest of the earth, out of whose nourishing elements it was originally built up. It does not go out of creation, but remains in it available for other purposes. But what becomes of the unveiled soul? Does that vanish from God's creation? Oh, no! How could it be possible that the nobler element should cease to exist, when the baser one is imperishable? Are we to believe that it has been removed from the infinitude of created beings, because it has thrown off the veil through which alone it could reveal its presence to our senses? Nay, it lives! For even the dust in which it once enveloped itself is still in existence. It lives! For God is Creator, not annihilator! It lives! For the All-wise cannot have repented of the exalted purpose for which He called it into being.

And is the throwing off of this earthly veil so very painful? It is true the natural love of life which the Creator has implanted in us, makes us recoil from the thought of parting from our earthly covering; but the strength of the human spirit can conquer the terrors of nature. How many noble men have not met death in the cause of God, fatherland, faith, or friends! *They* felt no fear of death. How many poor, weak, degenerate beings have not, driven by despair, voluntarily sacrificed a life that had become a burden to them!

The dying do not practise hypocrisy, and therefore from their features we may judge what is passing in their minds. This being the case, it would almost appear that a pleasurable feeling must be experienced when the spirit is leaving its mortal coil; for it has been frequently observed that the features of persons who are dying from painful diseases, at the last moment assume an expression of cheerful repose, and that even around the lips of the corpse a placid smile, left by the spirit in parting, lingers, and seems to say, " Ah, what blessed relief !"

But the imagination of those persons who attach too much importance to the body, and who therefore shudder at the idea that it is to be delivered up to destruction in the earth, makes death more terrible than it is in reality. Giving way to self-delusion, they even at times seem to fancy that the dead dust feels painfully its state in the earth, whereas in fact that which feels has hastened into a higher existence, and the corpse, the discarded veil of the spirit, is nothing more than insensible clay.

Parting from the habitual and pleasant relations of life, the loss of well-known pleasures, and separation from beloved friends on earth, may indeed be painful. But in these cases it is not death itself, but that which we leave behind us, that causes us to mourn. It is our undue attachment to the earthly goods which have only been lent to us, and were never intended to be our lasting possessions, that occasions the grief which we experience. It is therefore an imperfection of the soul, a want of true wisdom, which entails suffering, as does every fault. Yea, even the love we bear our friends may be reprehensible. Can we expect that the Deity will take our obstinate attachments into consideration, and alter His higher purposes to suit our views? And in what does the parting from our beloved in death differ from every other parting, even from the "good-night" we wish our friends before we go to sleep?

Death may indeed be fearful to those who have entirely, or in great measure, neglected their immortal soul in this life, who—like the animals thoughtless of the future beyond the grave—have only taken heed for the well-being and enjoyment of their bodies; who have oppressed their fellow-men, or slandered and deceived them, in order to gain for themselves more honours, more riches, and more enjoyment; to whom it seems preposterous to restrain their sensual desires, their animal instincts, in order to strengthen the power of their souls; who call it folly to sacrifice earthly pleasures for the sake of virtue; who consider it silly enthusiasm to work for the good of others, when no thanks are to be reaped, or when persecution and great sacrifices must be encountered.

When the moment has come for such persons to throw off the earthly coil, the body they so much love, for which alone they think God has created them; when they are to part from the dust, for which alone they lived, to which they sacrificed all things, for which they committed so much injustice—to them indeed death must be terrible. For poor, unworthy, miserable, imperfect are their neglected souls, which have lost the sweet innocence of which they could boast in childhood, and which are now loaded with the burden of many sins. As they sowed in life, so they have reaped. For the eternal future of their spirits they never sowed.

Even when in the full enjoyment of health, the unrighteous man cannot at times help blushing at his own depravity. In the midst of his evil-doing he is obliged to confess to himself that he is acting in a manner which he cannot justify either to God or to man. But his soul, though feeling what is right, is conquered by the power of his sensual being, to which long habit has given the mastery. But when the power of the senses declines with the strength of the body, when self-delusion is no longer possible, and the soul recognizes itself in all its hideousness—then what must be his state? With what feelings must *he* look to the future, who has lost *all* upon earth, and who has nothing to hope from eternity?

How different the condition of the wise and noble spirit, which knows its duties and fulfils them, and honours the high purpose for which the omnipotence of God called it into existence. How different the condition of the Christian, who has gained full ascendancy over his lower nature, and ever places the claims of the soul above those of the body; who understands the deep import of the words, to live in Christ.

To him death is a gain. How could it be a loss to him? To him who has made the divine thoughts of Christ his own, neither this earth, nor his own house, nor village, nor city, is his true home. He is conscious that he was not born to be for ever attached to the clod of earth which he cultivates to satisfy his earthly necessities, but to be a citizen of the eternal and infinite realm of God. In his eyes it is not this short life on earth that is the most important, but the life in the entire divine creation. The universe is his Father's house, and God, who dwells therein, is his Father, and every soul in it is bound to him by the ties of brotherhood.

To him death is a gain. For what loss does the soul sustain in death? It only throws off its heavy earthly veil; it only changes its garment; it receives from the Father of love a more beautiful raiment, instead of the cast-off vestment, which its altered circumstances have rendered useless. The soul remains what it was, God remains with it, the divine universe with all the wonders of creation, remain. What does it lose? The friends and relatives whom it loved on earth? Oh, no, they are still in the house of the Father, they are still bound to it by the same ties of brotherhood as before, though they cannot communicate with it any longer through earthly means. Nay, its loved ones are not lost to it. That cannot be lost which is in the hands of God.

To him who knows how to live with Jesus, death is a gain. Or can it be said that this sublunary life is full of roses, and has no thorns? It is true that with the change I lose many pleasures, but then also I shall be placed above many fears and many sorrows. Tears will never be shed by me again, for sweet is the fate of liberated souls!—Is this earthly life so full of unmixed happiness that we should wish it to endure for ever? Why do persons of very advanced age so frequently long for rest, for dissolution, for liberation, for removal into the better life? and why among thousands and thousands of people, is there not one, who, if the choice were given, would begin life over again if its course were to be exactly the same? Well then, what great loss can this life be in reality, when there are so few to whom it has through its whole course brought sufficient happiness to induce them to wish it to remain for ever as it was? Is it not rather a gain for souls, who can with confidence resign themselves to it, to go over into another and a better world? After all what are the terrors of death? Merely the terrors of a childishly timid imagination. The same God, O Soul, that divests thee of one garment, will invest thee with another.

He who knows how to live with Christ, will also know how to die joyfully with Him. (1 Cor. xv. 31.) He dies each time he lifts his thoughts to God and forgets all earthly matters. He dies each time he communes in spirit with his departed loved ones, and feels that he is with them. For in such solemn moments this world is to him as if it were not. He is in the presence of God, in the presence of those he loved. He is what his soul will be when it has been uncoiled from its earthly veil; only not in such great perfection as it will be when it shall be able to communicate with God and the loved friends, in a new vestment, and as it were, through means of more glorious instruments.

Death is my gain; for what is the purpose of my life on earth? Like all mankind, I am destined to live eternally, all nature teaches me this, and therefore, even here below, I am to live for eternity; and all my longing is for a better, higher existence. It is with this in view that I labour to improve myself; it is with this in view that I endeavour to adorn my spirit with every virtue. That which I become through Christ, that is, through following His divine example, that shall I be on yonder side the grave. It is therefore death that leads me to the desired goal. Through it, I reach what I have been ever striving for; through it I become what I was destined to be.

Death is my gain. I exchange a less perfect garment for a more perfect one, exchange a lower seat, in the great paternal house of the universe, for a higher one; I exchange an inferior degree of happiness for a state of bliss, of which my limited earthly faculties can as little form a conception, as the lowly worm in the dust can form a conception of the joys that may vibrate in the bosom of rational man. I proceed from a necessitous state into a world of overflowing plenty, where a drop becomes an ocean, and a spark of light becomes a sun.

Death is my gain. Why should my soul be alarmed at the unknown road along which it has to travel? Is the path that I have to wander here below better known to me? Is not each succeeding hour of my life shrouded to me in impenetrable darkness? Do I know what will happen to me the next moment? Whither I shall go? And yet I live through each of those hours, and each becomes light to me as soon as I live in it.

And equally light will be the hour that succeeds that of death. The unknown road will be made known to me as soon as I enter upon it. Why then should I recoil from it with a shudder? Is it not the same as has been trodden by the dear ones who have gone before me? Why should I not be rejoiced to follow in the path of those souls who will ever be precious to me? Perhaps in the very moment when the earthly veil falls from my spirit, I shall recognize those dear ones, whom I believed so far removed from me, and shall learn that they were always nearer to me than in my earthly state I had any conception of.

Yea, verily, death is my gain! It is closer union with the Father of spirits; it is reunion with my glorified loved ones, for whom my soul is yearning; reunion with those for whom to this day, my wounded heart bleeds, my eyes weep. Reunion! Renewed possession! Renewed life! O ye, whom God's hand directed towards me, and linked to me in His creation! To find you again! To love you again! To be for ever united with beloved and glorified souls! What bliss in this thought! God gave you to me: God, the most exalted love, inspired us with this love, which death cannot destroy, and which binds the mortal, as with invisible bonds, to the inhabitants of the higher world! God does not destroy that which is holy, which is good—for it is His own work! And love is the highest good which souls can acquire in their mutual intercourse. It is because He is Himself Infinite Love, that God has peopled the universe with living souls.

Death is my gain! May this be my last sigh on my bed of death; and may the thought of the love of my Creator, and of the dear ones that have preceded me into another life, be the last that occupies my soul, ere the veil falls from it. When it drops, my spirit shall at once be in those realms of glory which they entered before me.

Therefore, O Christ, O divine Revealer of the Father, be Thou my life, for without Thee, to die were to see my soul enter into destruction! O God-enlightened Teacher, I will think Thy thoughts, I will walk according to Thy divine doctrines. I will contemplate from Thy elevation all earthly matters. With Thy love I will love my brethren, with Thy zeal endeavour to spread joy and happiness around me. With Thy courage I will overcome every obstacle to virtue and will master myself so as to be able to act justly, nobly, divinely. With Thy patience I will bear every ill of life, with Thy wisdom and moderation enjoy its pleasures. With Thy faith I will walk meekly and trustingly in the ways of Providence, and through Thine eyes I will look up to eternity as to my Father's house, and to God as to my Father.

For if Christ be my life, death is my gain.

ETERNAL DESTINY.

PART I.

    Star of day
    Whose laughing ray
Is to cheer our homesteads given—
    Stars of night
    Shining bright,
In the deep blue vault of heaven,—
    Though ye shine
    With peace divine,
Making lovely Earth and Sea,
    Comes the feeling
    O'er me stealing
Still how dark man's life may be.
    Sadly turning
    From the burning
Of your golden glances bright,
    Thus I raise
    My trembling gaze
To the everlasting light,
Which o'er cradle and o'er grave,
O'er the vale where palm-trees wave,
O'er the bloody battle strife,
O'er the joys and tears of life—
Whether fortune smile or frown,
Still unchangeably looks down.
           (*Rom.* xi. 33, 34.)

THE months pass calmly over our heads heedless of our hopes and our sorrows. The seasons vary in unbroken succession. Old things become new, and new ones old, the works of the past perish, in their turn to be forgotten. It is ever the same. Everything has its invariable course assigned to it, its inevitable goal marked out for it. Everything is subject to one great iron rule, the stars of heaven as well as the flowers of the field; the rock as well as the worm that crawls at its foot; the entire nation, as well as the single individuals born into it. Nothing can be otherwise than it is; nothing will ever be otherwise than it is appointed to be. Such is destiny—the eternal!

What is destiny?—How? Everything has been pre-ordained from eternity? No blossom fades, no infant weeps, no rock is precipitated from a mountain, no nation perishes, unless it has been so ordained from the beginning of time? What then of my virtue and my sins? Who is the criminal, who the judge? Is my will also pre-ordained by destiny? Am I nothing more nor less in the great universe than the mote dancing in the sunbeam, not as it wills, but as it must? If everything that happens now has been pre-ordained since the beginning of time, of what avail are my sighs, my wishes, my striving for perfection? Of what avail are my prayers? Were not these prayers also pre-ordained in the eternal councils of destiny? I am, then, but a machine, forming part of the great all; and my supposed free will is but a delusion?

What is eternal destiny? It is the immense, infinite, immoveable universe, in which all things follow each other necessarily as cause and effect. Each effect becomes in its turn the cause of new effects. The tree brings forth seed, and the seed brings forth a tree. My youth having been what it was, I must be what I am. The pre-ordained occurrences of last year have produced those of this year, and had it not been for those of long-forgotten centuries, we should not have witnessed the events of our times. Thus has one thing been linked within another from the beginning of time, and this concatenation extends into the infinite future. There, as in the past, one wheel of the huge world-engine drives the other, one part is indissolubly linked to another. Such is the rule of destiny, and therefore naught can be changed. Just as he who throws a stone into the still waters of the lake knows beforehand the sound that will ensue, and the eddies which will be formed, and which, spreading in ever wider circles, will extend to the distant shores, while in the centre, whence the movement first issued, the waters have already become still again: so might one, acquainted with the nature of all things in the world, know by anticipation, from the movement given to them in the first instance, thousands of years previously, what would be the events and occurrences during thousands of succeeding years. But that would be omniscience, and omniscience is not given to mortal man. Therefore he totters with uncertain step through the great labyrinth of the universe, knowing not what went before, or what is to come after; calling what befalls him, sometimes fortune, sometimes chance, sometimes unavoidable necessity. But the terms chance and accident are merely terms applied to those things the immediate cause of which man is unable to detect. There can be no such thing as chance, as every effect has its cause. Everything is under the rule of necessity; everything has been included in the councils of eternal destiny.

Everything? How? Is then the infinite universe with everything that stirs and moves within it nothing but a machine, a well-constructed clock-work in which nothing can take place but what the constructor has foreseen and pre-arranged? I myself am, then, but a very insignificant part of this world's machine. I am struck with dismay. What am I? Where am I? How alone I stand with my joys and my sorrows in the midst of this cold, rigid organization of the world, amid these dead, will-less beings! Why am I destined to feel and love, when there is nothing that deserves my love? Why hate, when all evil, even vice, is pre-ordained, and follows a law of necessity? Alas, my dearest wishes, my sweetest hopes, abandon me! For what purpose is this juggle carried on? Why should I be made to feel repentance for faults which I was pre-ordained to commit? Why should I hate sin, if eternal destiny has consecrated me to that also?

No, no! It cannot be so! Every feeling within me contradicts this conception of the universe and its laws. My spirit revolts against it. I am distinctly conscious of the freedom of my will; and though my body may be similar to a passive instrument, my spirit is not a machine, it is living; it rules and determines after mature reflection. Nay, the world is not a cold, dead mass, in which everything moves without consciousness, according to eternally pre-ordained laws. The action, the power, and the goodness of a living and loving God animate all things, and spread happiness around. Oh! what would the world be without love, without a Deity, without justice, freedom, and retribution? A gigantic corpse, from which the soul has fled; an unconscious play of things, in which there is no place for the highest and the best, for virtue, love, perfection, but only for their names. A miserable, unmeaning, unsolvable, never-ending riddle; and the most wretched of beings in it, man, with the claims of his reason and the sentiments of his heart!

No; such a conception of destiny is an error of the understanding, arising from a one-sided view of things, which entangles it in self-contradiction, and sets it at variance with everything that we perceive in the outer world, as well as with our inward consciousness.

What is eternal destiny? It is the immense, fixed, endless organization of the world, in which all things follow each other necessarily as cause and effect. Each effect becomes in its turn a cause; therefore, that which takes place to-day is the necessary consequence of the past, and that which I am to-day, is the necessary fruit of what I was in days gone by. I cannot deny this: how, then, shall I avoid those errors of the understanding in which I am again in danger of being involved?

I will take a survey of the various aspects of the universe. When I do this, I perceive in the dead stone, and through all created things up to the highest creature, an infinite number of forces. Everything that is, is in itself a force or agency—that is to say, it acts upon the surrounding matter. Even the dead stone is a force or agency, otherwise it could not act upon the things around it, through its weight, and its cohesion; otherwise it could not act upon our senses, through its colour, its form, or its smell. That which produces no effect upon me is to me non-existent, but that which acts upon me is a force.

The forces present in God's universe are as manifold as they are countless. They form an immense, graduated scale, from the most insignificant entity to the highest. They unite with other forces, and through such union produce new phenomena. What a variety of forces are there not, for instance, in the body which we call a stone! How much greater still is the number and variety in plants; and beyond these again in animals! But there is not only variety in these forces, but also gradations. The vital force of the plant is a higher agency than any that resides in the stone. The plant multiplies itself, has its youth and maturity, and propagates its species. Higher still is the force which we call animal soul; because this latter feels, chooses, judges. Higher still is the force of the human spirit in the beautiful distinctness of its self-consciousness. And forces higher even than this range above us, and are called in the Scriptures, Angels and Archangels.

But all these families and kingdoms of forces in God's creation, are, what they are, by the WILL OF GOD; each has its special sphere of action, its special conditions, its special laws assigned to it, and according to these it must exist and act. Therefore the stone is, and ever remains, a stone, and retains its qualities as such; therefore the roots of the vine and of the thistle seek only such nourishing substances as are in conformity with their nature; therefore the birds of the air live and move otherwise than the fishes in the sea. Every force in nature has received from God its peculiar law, and thus the human spirit has also its own law, which is neither that of the animal, the plant, nor the stone.

In conformity with these special laws of their nature is the action of all created things upon each other. They unite and separate, attract and repel each other, seek and avoid each other, and thus arise the teeming life and ceaseless movement in the universe. The mutual conflict between the various forces constitutes the life of the universe.

As none of the forces, which in their totality constitute the universe, can act otherwise than the sphere of action assigned to them and the laws laid down for them by God will admit of, their action is the necessary consequence of these laws. And when the forces came into being, the will of God, the great and eternal Constructor of the worlds, foresaw all the effects they were to produce. This was the *eternal pre-ordination* of that which was to be.

But when God from the beginning willed the existence of the world, He willed it in His infinite wisdom. Therefore the conflict of the forces created no confusion, but progressive development; not internecine destruction, but a great and wonderful life, comprising all and in which each serves the other. Such was, such is, and such will ever be, the great order of the universe, in which stars and grains of dust move in their appointed circles, in which the humblest grasses and mosses bloom and die away as do entire nations.

And when God in His infinite wisdom created the order of the universe, and created it for infinitely exalted ends, He created it also in the fulness of His love. He, the All-good One, willed that the whole should be infinitely harmonious, and that all the sentient forces in it should enjoy happiness. Therefore we see provision made even for the happiness of the humblest insect; and for the spirit of man He provided far higher bliss. But the insect is bereft of its joy, and feels pain, as soon as it violates the laws of its nature; and in like manner the spirit of man forfeits the higher joys provided for it, when it fails to fulfil the law of its being. And this law is, that it should become perfect, as its Father in Heaven is perfect; consequently, that it should maintain the more exalted position assigned to it, and rule the lower forces, and not allow itself to be ruled by them. The spirit is bound to hold in abeyance the animal forces that reside in its body, to subdue the impure desires of the latter, and to look up to God and to the spiritual world to which it belongs. The spirit's law is conscience, yearning after perfection, abhorrence of all evil, and indestructible desire for freedom. If man allow his spirit to be conquered in its conflicts with the animal and plant-like parts of his nature, he becomes wretched and contemptible in his own eyes. For in the order of the universe, everything is a concatenation of necessary consequences. Sin and imperfection give birth to suffering.

Man is consequently not pre-ordained to be the victim of sin and corruption, but to be made happy through his perfections. If he firmly wills it he can attain this perfection in all the relations of life. He may know beforehand, that when he feels sorrow or suffering there is something in himself which is not as it ought to be. The sorrow and suffering are in themselves his guides to happiness. This is his *destiny!*

Whatever fate may befall us, *we are consequently independent of it, in as far as we are what we ought to be.* Our dear ones may die, but we are not made unhappy by this, unless we forget that they and we are members of the spiritual world; that, as spirits, they cannot be lost to us; and that we ought not to allow ourselves to be attached to the perishable clay in the grave, as though it were imperishable. The death of the body was necessary in accordance with the laws that rule that which is earthly; our grief is the necessary consequence of our too great attachment to that which pertains to earth. This is destiny! *But all things pre-ordained by God are beneficent,* they strengthen our powers; by gentleness they lure, or by terrible earnestness they force the spirit to rise from that which is earthly and perishable to the knowledge and love of the imperishable, from the animal to the spiritual which constitutes our true dignity. Wars and battles, famine and misery, disease, robbery, and arson, come within the rules of destiny. But what are they? Nothing more than the destruction of what is perishable. They point towards that which is imperishable, eternal; that is, to that inward happiness of which nothing can deprive us. Thy despair at the misfortunes which befall thee, was it comprised in the doom of thy destiny? Yes, because it is a necessary consequence of thine own imperfection. The peace of mind which the sage enjoys in spite of every misfortune, is an equally necessary consequence of his greatness of mind, and of the conquering power of his soul.

The more virtuous and the more self-possessed the human spirit be, the more invulnerable it is, the more independent of destiny. God is raised above destiny because He is the All-Holy One. The more holy our inward being, the nearer we stand to God; and the nearer we are to God, the higher we are lifted above the power of destiny.

Thus the apparent contradictions are dissolved into beautiful harmonies; and from out of the darkness comes forth light. Everything must work for our good, everything must be on our side, because God is on our side. The pre-ordinations of the Lord are wise, just, and beneficent. Their end is not to make us slaves without a will of our own, but to give freedom to our spirits; they work with our spirits in order to raise them above fate. Oh! what unbounded riches in the wisdom and knowledge of God! How impenetrable are His judgments, and how inscrutable His ways!

ETERNAL DESTINY.

PART II.

From forth the darkness, deep and vast,
By Destiny our lot is cast—
Round all of earth her net she draws,
And the world owns her guiding laws.

But One there is, enthroned on high,
Beneath whose feet sits Destiny,
Who binds together flesh and soul,
And holds e'en Fate in His control.

For Destiny is but God's slave—
He rules—His grace alone can save;
And mortals strive their game to make,
For Destiny—that priceless stake.

And Jesus leads the spirit choir
Whose souls from dust to God aspire.
He Fate under subjection lays,
Who unto God his soul can raise.

(*Isaiah* lv. 8, 9.)

INDIVIDUAL sages who lived and taught in remote antiquity, and subsequently entire nations, observed the rule of destiny in the course of human affairs, and all hearts trembled before the dread power thus recognized. Philosophic minds among the heathens endeavoured to solve the fearful riddle. They called the eternal, inexorable power, to which everything was subject, which nothing could resist, blind fate. On it, they believed, depended the lot of the meanest worm, as that of the most exalted man, and of every nation. Nay, even all the deities, with which the imagination of mortals then peopled earth and Heaven, were, in their opinion, subject to this universal law; even the mightiest of the gods were not beyond its power.

This belief in an all-ruling fate could not fail to arise among men who had not yet learnt to distinguish clearly between the world of matter and the world of spirit; but who were, on the contrary, so steeped in the material, that physical and moral well-being were to them identical. Beauty, power, riches, honours, were their highest goods. For these they lived; and as they recognized no deeper import in life, the value of their existence rose and sank in their eyes in proportion to the amount of these earthly advantages which fell to their lot. The fate which robbed them of these, could therefore rob them of all. But very few individuals had any intuitive perception of a higher good, of which even the most relentless fate could not deprive man without his own consent. Still fewer had the courage to raise themselves above the power of fate through their own magnanimity of soul. Those, however, who did so, awakened at that period already the surprise and reverence of their fellow-men by the heroism of their virtues; nay, the world was even inclined to place them among the gods.

The views of the Christians regarding this point are, however, very different from those of the heathens. Jesus led the human race back from the errors of the imagination and the understanding, into the paths of eternal truth. He revealed to us the only God as the most perfect of all beings, and as the Father of spirits, whom we are to worship in spirit, and not with offerings and such like. He revealed to us that the whole purpose of man's existence is not hedged in between the cradle and the grave, and He allowed us to cast a glance into the mysteries of eternity. He taught us to hold light the life on this earth, because this is not the true sphere of our happiness. "In my Father's house," said Jesus, "there are many mansions." He taught us to distinguish between the value of earthly and of heavenly or spiritual things. "If ye have but wherewithal to clothe and to feed your bodies," said Jesus, "then be content. Lay not up treasures for yourselves on earth, but in Heaven, and seek before all things the kingdom of God. Be perfect, as your Father in Heaven is perfect. For what availeth it a man if he gain the whole world, and he suffer damage in his soul?" He taught that the soul ought to have the mastery over the body, and pointed out the majesty of the spirit, and its superiority over every good this earth can afford. He showed, in his own life, how a man may rise above his fate, and render it powerless to affect him. He proved that the pre-ordained course of things may indeed interfere with our earthly concerns, but that it is powerless to destroy our inward peace, or the bliss of our spirits.

Destiny or fate is consequently the Divine law to which the material world only is subject. Bodily health and disease, life and death, the improvement or the decline in our earthly position, the increase or decrease of the consideration in which we are held, of our influence, or our power, the rise or fall of nations, victory or defeat on the field of battle—all these, as things earthly, are subject to the law of destiny that rules all terrestrial matters.

But spirits are subject to a very different law. They do not participate in the fate of that which pertains to earth. Their essence is freedom, their law virtue, their end likeness to God. The fate of the material world only regards them in as far as they are connected with matter. The less self-dependent they are, the more they incline to earthly things, the more they mix themselves up with the sublunary world, the more also they come under the law of destiny. He who places himself under a strange master, must submit to his yoke. He who resigns his freedom and his self-control, must be content to be treated as a slave. Therefore, only he who places his happiness in outward things, is really unhappy; therefore, only the follower of Christ, the true sage, is really happy. To them that love God, all things (even the apparently most terrible) work for good.

Spirits are subject to a very different law from that which governs material things; therefore they suffer when they submit to a foreign yoke. In so doing they fall from their original dignity, they become unfaithful to their calling; they desire to be, not exalted spirits, but superior animals. Yet God still loves them. The law of destiny becomes their chastening rod, and drives them back to self-knowledge, urges them to lay hold on higher things. And through fearful disasters and misfortunes the voice of God speaks to them, saying,—" My thoughts are not your thoughts, neither are your ways my ways; for as the Heavens are higher than the earth, so are my ways higher than your ways, and my thoughts than your thoughts." (Isaiah lv. 8, 9.)

We cannot, indeed, entirely dissever the bonds

which bind us to earth. Our place in the scale of spirits is still so low, that we must of necessity live in immediate and close contact with the inferior beings of the universe. But it depends upon ourselves to rise to a higher rank in the scale. To help us to do so Jesus the Messiah was sent. He came to deliver us from the powers of darkness and the bonds of death, which hold in subjection all that is earthly. He came to help us reconquer our lost liberty. But His redeeming life will be of no avail to those who cannot deny themselves, who cannot renounce the world, who cannot, like Him, live a righteous, innocent, and unselfish life. His atoning death will prove of no avail to those who do not possess spiritual freedom and magnanimity of soul sufficient to wish to please God rather than man, and to die as the Saviour died.

We cannot entirely emancipate ourselves from earthly things; but we must not allow ourselves to be mastered by our love for these, but maintain our freedom in regard to them. We are obliged and bound to seek food for our bodies, but we are equally bound not to attach great importance to the gratification of our palates. We ought to dress with propriety; but we must not allow ourselves to be so far conquered by a taste for outward show, as to feel unhappy because we may no longer be able to appear in costly raiment. Purple, velvet, and silk, are, after all, not far different from the winding-sheet in which a corpse is clothed. We ought to labour to improve our pecuniary means, in order that we ourselves, as well as those who belong to us, may be raised above dependence upon the caprice of others, and that we may be able to contribute the more to the furtherance of the public welfare; but we must not seek our greatest happiness in the accumulation of riches, or pride ourselves upon possessing more than others; and then, should our circumstances ever be reduced, this will cause us no shame and no great unhappiness. We ought not to despise the good opinion of others, nor be indifferent to the influence we may exercise over them; but we ought never to seek consideration or influence except through our merits and our virtues. For only in as far as the public consideration in which a man is held, is at the same time accompanied by, and has sprung from, public confidence, can it become a means of doing much good. But to thirst for consideration for its own sake only, to wish for power merely for the sake of possessing it, is to mistake the path leading to the goal for the goal itself, to mistake the means for the end, the instrument for the work it is meant to fashion. To stand high or low in this world's estimation, to enjoy rank and titles, or to have neither, is a matter of indifference to the immortal spirit, which knows that its true dignity resides within itself, and depends upon nothing outward; and that, not the distinction which is bestowed by man, but the worth which the spirit owes to its own efforts, is indestructible.

We cannot and must not disdain the pleasures and joys of life. They tend to refresh and enliven our whole being. But we must not cling to them with such passion, that when they pass away we feel as though we must pass away with them. We must love the objects of our affection, friends, parents, or children, with such tenderness as is natural to refined souls. But we ought not to forget that it is not their body that we love—this will grow old and die—but their spirit. We should ever bear in mind that their last hour on earth will and must come, but that all-ruling destiny cannot separate the spirit from the spirit, but only the body from the body. He who founds his highest happiness on the life-breath of a mortal, founds it on a frail thing indeed. He who does not regard the universe as his heavenly Father's house, who does not recognize the spirit as the object of his love, who does not see in immortality the guarantee of his happiness, let him beware of tender affection, if he would not love that which would destroy him, if he would not be the victim of a fearful destiny. For what he loves must one day become dust and ashes.

Raise yourselves above dust and ashes, ye chosen of God, ye followers of Christ! Enjoy the goods of this world, as sweet, fleeting, transient gifts, but lay up your treasures in Heaven! Pluck the blooming rose, but forget not that to-morrow it will be withered and faded. Live *with* what is earthly, not *in* it, but in yourselves. Accept of every pleasure, but do not give yourselves up to it. Despise neither honours, nor dignities, nor riches, but do not sacrifice to them even the least of your higher duties; let the gifts of fortune be to you mere accidental advantages, for they cannot for ever belong to you, and you belong still less to them. He who acknowledges no master but himself, his virtues, and his God, is master of all things; he is further removed than other men from the sorrows of this earth, and over him destiny holds no sway. He may be poor, despised, persecuted; he may lose his fortune, his comforts, his friends, the consideration in which he was held by others; but his inward contentment, his holy pride in his own worth, he need never lose. He is raised above fate. It is not to the world he owes his inward peace and happiness, and the world cannot rob him of them.

But to whom am I saying this? Who recognizes the eternal truth of Jesus's words, " But seek ye first the kingdom of God, and His righteousness, and all these things shall be added unto you?" (Matt. vi. 33.) Oh! they have eyes and see not, they have ears and hear not! The great majority of men are absorbed in their earthly needs, and have no conception of higher wants. They believe in God, but bear no love to that which is Divine; they pray to God, but are the slaves of their own passions. They honour virtue, yet act viciously. They believe in immortality, yet give themselves entirely up to this world. They desire happiness, yet fly from it. They cannot gainsay the truth, yet cling to the delusions of their senses. They claim to be men, and superior beings, yet are content to remain nothing more than animals. They complain of the cruelty of fate, yet will not raise themselves above it by magnanimity of soul. They remain miserable, unhappy, in conflict with everything that surrounds them, and with themselves. They seek a means of escape, and find it not. The voice of God is loud in their hearts, yet they refuse to follow it. They deserve their misery, for it is their own choice. Therefore saith the Lord, "Your thoughts are not my thoughts, neither are your ways my ways. For as the Heavens (and all spiritual things) are higher than the earth, (and all that is earthly,) so are my ways higher than your ways, and my thoughts than your thoughts."

But to whom do I recall this? To the nations? Ah! behold their misery! This misery is the proof of their errors. How petty are the aims of all, or at least the greater number of the individuals who constitute the nations! What fruits can we expect from such seed? What concord is there among them when the common danger is past? Where is their friendship when their self-interest is touched? Where is their patriotism when their individual advantage is at stake? Where is their moderation in prosperity? Why do they cherish in their own hearts that arrogance which they dislike so much in others? Why do they complain of that pride in others which they do not overcome in themselves? Why do they boast of the reverence they feel for the rights of nations, and yet attack these whenever it can be done without danger to themselves? Why do they praise honesty, and yet seek to overreach others? Ah! they have witnessed the effects of disunion, arrogance, and injustice; they have heard the warnings of universal history, but their hearts are hardened. They had Moses and the prophets, but they preferred to believe in their own falsities and follies. In the hour of need they raised aloft the banner of virtue to save themselves from destruction, but when the danger was over they deserted the sacred banner to prepare for themselves new misery. Thus let it be. Your fate is sealed. You cannot escape your destiny, for you have brought it upon yourselves. "My thoughts are not your thoughts," saith the Lord, "neither are my ways your ways; but as the Heavens are higher than the earth, so are my ways higher than your ways, and my thoughts than yours."

Among thousands, however, there may perhaps be one who recognizes God's thoughts and ways in the decrees of destiny; there may be one to whom his inward being, the consciousness of innocence, and the peace of God, are of more value than all outward goods; one who has given himself entirely to Christ, who acknowledges Him, not in the performances of church ceremonies, but in mind and heart, in willing and acting, in self-abnegation and self-control. Ah! thou only one among thousands, thou art the happiest, because thee no destiny can assail. Thou art raised above every earthly fate.

Oh! I also, I also, will strive for this peace, will seek to attain this height! I will be thy brother, Jesus! Saviour! Thou didst enjoy Divine happiness though the world reviled Thee. Thy persecutors were seated upon thrones, and yet were slaves of their brutal passions; but Thou wert a prince of life, a conqueror of death, and the power of destiny could not terrify Thee. The cross on Golgotha was thy trophy of victory; the crown of thorns was Thy crown of triumph.

I will strive in spirit to reach thy elevation, and the power of God will be mighty in me in spite of my weakness. I will accomplish it, I will be sole master of myself, I will control my feelings and my tendencies, so that I allow myself nothing but what is right, true, and useful; so that I accept whatever the earth offers me that is beautiful and good, but without forfeiting in return my peace or the mastery over myself; so that my inward freedom be not restrained by any outward fetters; so that I may be rich even in poverty, and exalted even though of lowly estate; so that I may belong to Thee, O Jesus, and to all pure and noble spirits. I must, I will accomplish this! O Spirit of God, strengthen my determination! Amen! I shall succeed. Amen.

THE DESTINATION OF MAN.

Let the song of victory sound,
  Christ for us has won the day,
(Us, who to the grave were bound,)
  And chased the night of death away.
Nobly hath the work been wrought,
And for us the victory bought.

With what a noontide brightness, Lord,
  Are His promises displayed;
How shines the truth of Heaven's word
  Man's soul is immortal made,
And before God's awful throne,
Virtue shall receive the crown.

Sing not solemn dirges sadly
  By the graves where good men lie;
For their spirits, brother, gladly
  Wander in infinity—
Christ for all hath victory gained,
And the tyrant, death, enchained.

(2 *Cor.* iv. 17, 18.)

JESUS CHRIST, our Lord, revealed to us in His own life on earth, as in a mirror, what we are, and what we ought to be. I recognize in Him what I ought to be. From the hour of his birth in the humble manger, until that of His glorification after His descent into the tomb, His life was a solemn indication of what the Deity wills that man should be. In obscurity and lowliness He was born, that we might learn that neither family descent nor rank, neither riches nor pomp, invest man with a nobility that has any worth in the sight of God. He died poor; a stranger lent the site for the interment of His body, that we might learn that our destination on earth is not to lay up vain treasures and to attach ourselves to the things that are seen, but to strive after those things which are not seen. Nowhere do the Holy Scriptures tell us, that in the course of His life Jesus advanced in worldly honours and riches; but they do tell us that with years He increased in wisdom, and in knowledge of things divine. His beneficent life-task was to render men happy; He came to redeem mortals from falsehood and sin, and His spirit embraced in its love and mercy not only His cotemporaries, but all those who should be born thousands of years after Him. And He as little neglected the least means of doing good as the greatest. He healed the blind and the lame, and succoured the helpless. All this took place that we might learn that our task in life is not only to attend to our business vocations, to take care that our families increase in rank and riches, but to grow perfect in every virtue, to improve in wisdom and in knowledge of God. For the good of mankind He met death, died wholly resigned to the will of God; His spirit rose above the most galling indignities—above the severest mental pangs which ingratitude and treachery could inflict—above the most cruel physical sufferings, when, exhausted by hunger, thirst, and ill-treatment, He sank down bleeding on the way to Golgotha; or when nailed to the cross, and jeered at by the multitude, He wrestled with death. But glorious was His triumph beyond the tomb; and all this was in order that we might learn, that not earthly well-being, not the enjoyment of the pleasures of this world, are the purposes of our life; that neither want nor suffering ought to deaden in us our love of the Divine, but that whatever fate befall us, the eye of the spirit ought to be directed towards eternity, where the palm of victory and of glory awaits us when the death-struggle is over. "For," say the Holy Scriptures, "our light affliction, which is but for a moment, worketh for us a far more exceeding and eternal weight of glory; while we look not at the things which are seen, but at the things which are not seen: for the things which are seen are temporal; but the things which are not seen are eternal." (2 Cor. iv. 17, 18.)

The day of victory of Him who has arisen from the dead, reminds me of my future day of victory, of my higher destination.

But what is the destination of man? As yet, the idea is not quite clear to me. To many, I know, the purpose of life is a riddle, and more especially to those who look at the things which are seen. Are we here that we may enjoy happiness and well-being in connexion with virtuous sentiments? ask many. But how few persons enjoy unmixed happiness in a world where each hour brings an alternation of pleasure and pain; where one moment we are called to share the sorrows of others, the next we are made to groan under physical suffering, or to yield up our dearest wishes? Or how can the happiness that flows from virtuous sentiments and acts be ours, when each day we rise, like Peter, with the noblest resolves, and yet end it with laments over our own weakness?

What is the purpose for which God called me into

being? Am I born merely to be the plaything of an hour, to fill for unknown ends a brief existence, extending only from the cradle to the grave, or to serve the purposes of other beings to me unknown, who may be amused at my mirth or my tears? Shall I sink down and fade away for ever, in old age, like the flowers of the garden, like the tree of the forest, like the lion in the desert, or like an ephemeral insect? How can I reconcile such an idea as this with the conception of the infinite perfection of God? Why do I bear within me a lively consciousness of being in myself an end, not a means,—a consciousness which makes me feel that I exist for my own sake, and that I am, as it were, a central point of the universe which I behold around me? Why do I see before me high aims to attain which would be impossible in this short existence, while other creatures have no more qualities than are necessary to sustain their earthly life, to provide themselves with food, and to avoid pain and danger?

Thus, even our unaided reason points to contradictions which would necessarily arise, were we to suppose that our destination is comprised within the narrow limits of this life.

But we know that man is spirit, and that the body is ashes, and only a vestment and instrument used by the spirit in this temporal existence, for the enjoyment of what is earthly. The body, or the animal envelope of our spirits, changes as years accumulate on our heads; the spirit increases in knowledge, but nevertheless feels that it is still the same that it has been since the first awakening of consciousness. The body clings tenaciously to the earth from which it came; the spirit never finds rest on earth, is never content with what it has attained, but when one wish is satisfied longs for the fulfilment of another, and again another, and so on without end.

The spirit, therefore, is the most essential and the enduring part of man; that which is unseen and eternal constitutes its life, not that which is seen, or which is perishable; its origin is divine, it springs not from earth. And as the body will one day return to its mother-earth, so will the spirit return to the Divine bosom whence it emanated.

If my spirit be the essential part of me, then, when I speak of the destination of man, the question can only be as to the purpose for which his spirit was created; about the body there can be no question. This is only a subordinate power existing for the sake of the spirit. And, again, if there be a question of the spirit, it can only be as to its vocation during an infinitely prolonged existence. But how can I know what ends the Deity has in view for it after the hour of death in this world? So far my eye does not reach. And yet the voices of nature, of reason, and of revelation proclaim with wonderful harmony what I shall be hereafter, and what I am to hope for.

What is the lichen on the rock, the oak-tree on the mountain side, the eagle in the air, intended to be? Nothing more or less than what they are, and what alone they can be, in accordance with the peculiar powers or forces implanted in them by the Creator: moss, oak, and eagle! Thus also the spirit, which conceives of God, shall become that which, in accordance with the special powers implanted in it, it may, through the infinite periods of its existence, raise itself to be, viz., a being who, through endless self-improvement, is ever drawing nearer to God; an essence higher than a thousand other subordinate forces that live and act in this world, and living and acting independently of these, but understanding them and governing them, and growing without cessation in knowledge which will reveal to it the greatness of God and the grandeur of creation, in ever clearer and more enrapturing light. This is the eternal, the all-important glory that awaits us; *i.e.*, those among us who look, not at the things which are seen, but at the things which are not seen. This is the object of the vague yearnings within our souls; this is the meaning of that commandment of the glorified Saviour, wherein He disclosed the true destination of man, "Be ye perfect, as your Father in Heaven is perfect." (Matt. v. 48.)

To become like unto God is then my destination—to let my spirit grow in the Divine likeness through infinite progression. The truth of this, first revealed to me through Jesus, is confirmed by my reason and by my experience of life on earth. For even the things of this world all impel me in that direction. All things encourage the spirit to extend its mastery over that which is merely sensual, and to hold this in contempt—to elevate itself above the chances of outward circumstances and of fate. To do this is to grow in likeness to God. For in wisdom and knowledge, as in supreme happiness-diffusing influence on the universe, and in perfect independence of fate, God is infinitely great and exalted. Life on earth is given to train the spirit for its sublime destination; but this training is not completed here, but will continue without ceasing in far distant spheres of life, while our happiness will increase with our perfection.

All things stimulate the spirit to extend its knowledge and wisdom. Even for this man is born naked and defenceless, that he may exert and develop his mind in efforts for his own sustenance and protection. The animal enters life ready clothed, and provided with natural weapons of defence, and with unconscious instincts to seek the herbage, fruit, or carrion, which it requires for its nourishment, and which it finds at once. Thousands of years have passed since the creation and peopling of this globe. The animals have made no progress in knowledge or wisdom. Not so man, who is ever impelled forwards by the wants, and sufferings, and cravings of his nature. At first he lived in caverns, next in huts built of the boughs of trees, then in well-contrived, comfortable, self-invented dwellings. At first his hands and nails, next rude wooden and stone implements, were his only aids; then he descended into the bowels of the earth, and brought forth thence the numerous metals which doubled his strength, and helped him to subjugate the animals. The tiger was then no longer too strong for him, nor the fox too cunning, nor the eagle too far above him in the air. At first he clung timidly to the spot of earth where he was born; but soon he roamed into other regions, learnt to communicate his thoughts through means of artificial tones, and acquired a knowledge of foreign languages; and next he crossed the wide ocean from one quarter of the globe to another, and by means of written symbols communed with friends dwelling in far distant lands which his own foot had never trodden.

At first he trembled at the thunder of the clouds, and gazed with vague wonder only at the stars of heaven; subsequently the idea of a Deity took birth in him. He sought the Deity; but in the commencement worshipped Him in the thunder, the fire, and the stars. Then he began to conceive that neither of these were God, but only created things, and he prayed to the Unseen—until, when mankind had become capable of receiving it, the full light was given through Jesus Christ.

And thus the human spirit, driven by the necessities of life, progressed without ceasing from invention to invention, from knowledge to knowledge. That which in the present day is known to every youth, would thousands of years ago, have excited the wonder of the most experienced sage. What will mankind be after another six thousand years of progressive knowledge?

Already we know the immeasurable magnitude of the universe, the size and orbits of the heavenly bodies in closest proximity to us, the plains, and mountains, and the light that clothes the moon, the sun, and the distant planets; the wonderful powers of the atmosphere, of light and of innumerable other works of nature. But God, the All-wise, knows all, while the wisest of mortals as yet knows only a drop in the ocean of the universe. To grow like unto God is the destination of the spirit.

Towards this the whole organization of the universe is impelling us. Everything incites us to extend our dominion over the world of sense, and tends to develop the consciousness of our superior dignity as spirits, as feeble images of God. The will of the spirit, and the desires and instincts of the flesh, or of our sensual nature, are in constant conflict. This is the twofold law within us, of which Paul the Apostle speaks. In the flesh originate all tendencies to sin, to pride, to envy, to revenge, to luxury; in the spirit originate our longings after holiness, our yearnings for the divine, the unseen, and stable. In vain the feeble spirit seeks contentment in the temporal; it is ever repelled by the latter, and thrown back upon itself. In vain the spirit, forgetting its dignity and destination, seeks its happiness in the gifts of this life. Beauty and strength perish; fame is overshadowed; luxury creates disease; riches and earthly goods are ever changing hands, and cannot follow us beyond the grave; parents, friends, husbands, wives, children, all die, none remain, nothing on earth can secure to us lasting happiness. All things impel us to turn away from the seen to the unseen!

Sin is spiritual slavery, virtue spiritual freedom. Sin is dominion of the flesh, virtue is dominion of the spirit. In vain the spirit would forget that it is free and ought to govern the desires arising out of its earthly nature; in vain it would be at ease and avoid exertions and conflicts, give itself up to sensual well-being, and seek no higher wisdom than to elude that which is disagreeable, and to secure the enjoyment of that which is exciting, pleasurable, and honourable in ordinary social life; in vain it resists the warnings of conscience; in spite of all, the entire order of the universe, which is but a great school of spirits, incites us again and again to re-assert our dominion over sensual influences, and to hold light all that is of this earth. For every sin is followed by its own peculiar punishment. Deceit is followed by fear of detection, dissoluteness by painful diseases, intemperance by enervation. For the spirit there is neither rest nor peace, until it has conquered all the passions that war against it, until it has learnt to be just, truthful, independent of base prejudices and sensual desires, and has found the highest bliss in the consciousness of virtue. This is being like unto God.

For this purpose, the spirit is further impelled by everything that surrounds it to look at all matters from a proper point of view, and to judge and apply them accordingly; every error of judgment entails suffering. Towards this likeness to God everything impels it until it is not only raised above the enchantment of the senses, but above the power of fate. The various fortunes that befall men are but God's missionaries sent to instruct and improve; they are connected with earthly matters only. When avalanches fall, when nations are subjugated or liberated, when flames devour houses and other property, and war lays countries waste, when illness comes upon us without any fault of our own, and friends breathe their last in our arms—all these events affect us in our earthly connexions only. The more independent the spirit of the Christian is of all earthly things, the more exalted he is above the events connected with them. He may be rich or poor, be living in superfluity or in want, may meet with friendship or with persecution: but in none of these cases is there anything that can impair his love of Christ, of virtue, and of the Deity. The world can give him nothing which he is not willing patiently to resign again. Life itself has not more value in his eyes than duty. He fears not death; and he who fears not death, nor poverty, nor the judgments of men, what power can fate have over him? He is a spirit like God; he bears his happiness, his highest good, within himself, and no fate can destroy it. Like unto a divinity he stands above all the storms of life, fearing them not in the consciousness of his innocence and his righteousness. This is to be like unto God; This is the destination of man!

And to this destination, which I am to reach through endless progress, I ought, I can, and I will draw nearer here on earth already. Jesus walked the earth in human form, and endowed with human qualities; and yet He extended His knowledge of divine things, and He conquered His earthly desires, and rose above His fate. He had friends; He loved the tender-hearted disciple that rested his head on His bosom; nevertheless, His soul did not cling exclusively and passionately to individuals. "All men and women," said He, "are my brothers and sisters." He was not indifferent to the good things of this world; He was present at the marriage-feast in Cana, and did not refuse the costly ointment offered to Him as a gift by a pious, reverent, and grateful heart; nevertheless, He renounced every sensual enjoyment without a sigh; often He had no place to lay His head, and he made no effort to avoid death when duty bade Him give His life for the salvation of sinners. But a day of victory awaits all godlike spirits, and *He* was glorified beyond the grave.

If this be the destination of man, then woe is me, for how often have I not forgotten it! Woe is the world, for what confusion of mind does there not reign therein! Can it be that nature, and reason, and revelation, have ceased to have a meaning, and that Jesus, the Saviour, has not risen from the dead? For I see men busy about all other matters, but not thinking of those things which are not seen. They sacrifice pleasure, health, and life, for the attainment of other things, but not to improve in spirit, to grow in likeness to God. They pride themselves upon their cleverness; the one claims to excel the other herein; each is anxious to turn time and circumstances cunningly to his own advantage; but who is there that aspires towards that magnanimity of spirit that enables a man to rise above fate, above time and circumstances, above hope and fear?

Alas! and when I look at the mass of the people, what spiritual darkness do I behold! A deep yearning for divine things there is in all hearts; to all religion is something sacred, the eyes of all are turned to heaven, all seek to penetrate the mysterious depths of eternity; but what a melancholy idea they form of their destination, what an unworthy conception of the Majesty of God! They believe that they can purchase their rise in the scale of beings with senseless prayers and church ceremonies, while living as slaves of their animal nature. Here on earth they would lead a life of luxury, and for their fate in the next world they would rely on the intercession of saints, or on the merits of Jesus Christ. Thus, they think, they will obtain their glorification. They would fain enjoy their heaven here below, believing that their good deeds and their prayers are quite worthy of a heavenly reward. They do good merely for the sake of the recompense, and avoid evil merely from fear of punishment. Their conception of Heaven is that of an ever-enduring life

M

of sensual enjoyment. And all these errors are disseminated by the help of unprincipled persons, who allow themselves to be called priests of the Almighty God, and teachers of the doctrines of Jesus; and magistrates see the deplorable ignorance of the people, and look on with indifference, neglecting their duty to introduce better educational institutions, so that the knowledge of Divine things might be spread even among the humblest classes. Is it possible that mankind has so completely forgotten its high destination, that not even a vague and dreamlike remembrance of it survives? Is not Christ risen, who preached,—"Be perfect, as your Father in Heaven is perfect!" But if we do not despair of our destination, and have not lost our belief in the truth of God, why do we live as though there were no eternity? Why do we form to ourselves an image of the Highest Being, far less noble and exalted than we would form of a human being who was described to us as just, and incorruptible, and wise?

Jesus, they honour Thee with their lips, but their hearts are estranged from Thee. They make themselves preachers of Thy holy word, not because they desire to follow Thee, but in order to secure to themselves the comforts of life! They make themselves dependent upon outward circumstances, upon narrow-minded prejudices, and petty desires; they, who as eternal spirits ought to be exalted, as Thou wert once, above the unalterable laws that rule all earthly matters! Not all do this it is true!—Yet the number of Thy true confessors and followers is, alas! but very small.

Jesus, my Divine example in life, in suffering, and in death, I celebrate to-day in my heart the festival of

Thy victory and glorification—may it be also the festival of the victory of my spirit over all sensual influences. I recognize the purpose for which I was created, and the thought of it fills me with holy rapture. As Thou camest forth from the grave, so will I come forth from my errors, and enter into a higher spiritual life; so will I come forth from the slavery of my passions, and enjoy liberty and mastery over myself. And not content with doing this, I will endeavour to awaken others also to a recognition of their exalted destination; I will strive to make my fellow men feel their sublime vocation; I will praise thy greatness, O Father in Heaven, in my home, in the circle of those with whom Thou hast linked me together here on earth; and by my sentiments, words, and deeds, I will endeavour to prove and to make acceptable to all the truth, that amid the things which we see is not our lasting home, but amid the things which we do not see in the abodes of Eternity. That neither riches, nor rank, nor fame, nor other fleeting goods of this life, but self-improvement, growth in likeness to God, ought to be the great object of every spirit, in order that " we may be perfect, as our Father in Heaven is perfect." Amen.

IMMORTALITY.

How shall I know myself for joy, the change how understand,
When God Himself shall take me hence, to His own better land?
What different names the things will bear, which once I deemed Divine,
When in that bright and blessed home God's glories round me shine!

As there is but One Lord of all, one God who reigns in Heaven,
So unto all created things one life alone is given—
And through Creation's wide domain for death we find no place,
The law of change prevails for all—extinction none can trace—
I know my soul shall ever dwell, when freed from earthly stains,
Where in eternal Majesty, Christ, my Redeemer, reigns.

(*Mark* xvi. 1—14.)

The festival of the Resurrection of Jesus, after His death on the cross, may be considered as also celebrated by us in joyful commemoration of our own immortality. His Resurrection from the grave reminds us of the great transformation which our souls also shall one day undergo. The soul is not dust like the body, and never can become dust. As all the powers of the universe created by the Almighty are eternally active, so also will my spirit remain eternally active. Jesus, our example in life, is also our example in death, and His Resurrection is an indication of what we have to expect after death.

There are three great ideas bearing upon the most sacred interests of man, and compared with which all others sink into utter insignificance; three ideas which the mind of man alone, of all God's known creatures, can comprehend, and which form the most sacred treasures of all souls—without which indeed man would cease to be man. These are: the conception of an all-ruling Deity—the belief in the possibility of drawing nearer to God by growing in perfection—the hope in eternity.

He who treasures in his mind these three sacred ideas, follows in the footsteps of Jesus; he is in the way of salvation; he will ever enjoy that peace of soul which is a foretaste of the heavenly bliss that awaits us hereafter.

If the thought of the imperishable nature of the soul and the infinite goodness of God were at all times vividly present to men's minds, we should witness less levity, less vanity, and less heartlessness, and we should experience less fear and awe of death.

Therefore will I this day endeavour to fill my mind with the glorious thought: There is a God, and I am His work, and am for ever indestructible! I will meditate upon my higher destination, upon the more exalted existence which is in store for me, and gladden myself with the hope which Jesus has given me, and which God Himself has implanted, not only in the heart of the Christian, but in that of every human being that treads the earth.

I am born for eternity. Christ has given me the assurance thereof. A day will come when I shall no longer belong to this, but to another world, in which I shall enjoy a higher or a lower degree of happiness, according as my soul has prepared itself in this earthly life for the future existence. (John v. 28; 2 Cor. v. 10.)

I am called to eternal life. This body, in which I

am now clothed, has been borrowed from the earth, and will return to earth. But that which is incorruptible cannot perish, cries a voice to me from the Holy Scriptures. My spirit will enter into new relations, and clad, as it were, in nobler raiment, it will be susceptible of nobler enjoyments. It is in vain for us to search into, and ponder upon, what may be the real nature of these wonderful changes. It is folly to wish to have a knowledge of the state of the soul after death. Can human weakness penetrate the secrets of the Infinite Power? Can human blindness scan the nameless depths of Infinite Wisdom? How could that be made clear to us for which human language has no words, and for which the things of this earth offer no analogy? Even St. Paul deprecated such vain endeavours of inquisitive minds, and to explain that which takes place after death he has but obscure images. (1 Cor. xv. 35, 44.)

Let it be enough for every Christian that he has acquired the tranquillizing conviction that a life awaits him, which from the beginning of time was preordained for him. There God will wipe away all tears from our eyes, and there shall be no more death, neither sorrow nor weeping, neither shall there be any more pain; for the former things are passed away. (Rev. xxi. 4.)

Only a few minutes before His death Jesus, the Saviour of the world, gave the sweet hope of immortality to the criminal crucified by His side. With dying voice Jesus said, "To-day thou shalt be with me in Paradise."

God revealed to *all* mortals alike the eternal and imperishable nature of the human spirit. All nations of the earth believe in the continued existence of their souls after death, though the one people has not received the blessed intelligence from the other. But the Deity has so organized the laws of human reason, that as soon as the mind has acquired a certain power of thought, it is spontaneously impelled to believe in the infinite future that awaits it.

All religions therefore hold out this consolation, and even the heathen, when weeping over the corpse of one he loves, does not fail to lift his tearful eyes to the home beyond the grave. This universal agreement, this universal belief, is God's voice within us!

How, indeed, should the abhorrent thought of eternal annihilation enter the mind of man, when all nature, the entire creation of God, bears witness to the contrary? Nothing that is in the world can ever be lost out of it. The grain of dust which you trample under foot was once part of a rock. The rock has ceased to exist, but its constituent parts are still present. And if the most insignificant of things endures for ever, though in time it may undergo a thousand changes of condition and combination, can we believe that the noblest and most exalted of created beings known to us, the spirit of man, should be an exception? When we see that the grain of dust will remain in the universe as long as the universe itself endures, can we believe that the soul of man, which alone can conceive of God and immortality, will last but for a few brief moments?

Two things are recognized in the domain of creation, ever distinct from each other, viz.,—dead matter, and certain hidden forces which unite and vivify the particles of that matter. These flowers which owe nothing to the tending hand of man, spring from the earth. The plant, it is true, draws nourishment from water, earth, air, and light, but not every particle of earth or every ray of light becomes a plant. There is a secret power present, which causes the grass to be grass, and the oak to be an oak, and nothing else. This secret power, which may, so to say, be regarded as the soul of the plants, knows how to draw towards each the nourishment most suited for it. Through means of this invisible, inexplicable power, the flowers have become flowers.

What sayest thou now,—is it the dead substances which, in combining, generate a mysterious force? or is it the secret kingdom of the forces that play with the dead matter, and give it manifold forms, life, movement, and enjoyment? If dead matter cannot disappear from the universe, thinkest thou that the forces, the higher and nobler elements, can cease to exist? When the plant is abandoned by its indwelling force, and it withers and returns to dust, has the power that once vivified it vanished from the universe? Nay, thou dost not perceive it, but it is still active under other conditions.

The same is the case as regards the human spirit, which is an infinitely higher and more wonderful power, so much so, indeed, that none of the other forces with which we are acquainted can be compared with it. And who can be unreasonable enough to believe that our bodies, composed of earthly matter, have produced the spirits within them—that when the body returns to dust the spirit must also perish? Is it not the spirit that takes care of, nourishes, and protects the body; that directs its movements, and arbitrarily uses it as its instrument?

Verily, those only can be insane enough to doubt immortality, who feel that their lives have not been such as to deserve it, or who have reason to fear it. But they endeavour in vain to delude themselves, to destroy their own reason! A voice within them cries aloud, Thy soul cannot perish! It must continue to exist, and must appear before the judgment-seat! Sinner, sinner, there is a God; and as true as there is a God, thou art immortal, and thy deeds will follow thee into eternity.

The human soul, that spark from the infinite ocean of Divine light, that sublime power, which holds dominion over plants, minerals, and animals, which can raise itself to Heaven, which calculates the movements of the spheres, and which, through an inward revelation, has become conscious of its Divine origin—this spirit, whose thoughts fly across mountains and seas, and penetrate to the throne of the Almighty, this spirit is a self-dependent essence. It exists for itself, and for naught else, nor as part of anything. It creates, as it were, a little world for itself. It is connected with the rest of creation through its senses only, while observing the many changes that take place round it, and developing new power through them. If the human spirit were not created for itself alone, if it existed for the sake of other things, it would lose its value and cease to be, as soon as these other things, of which it formed a part, disappeared. The spirit does not exist on account of the body, on account of the dust vivified by it, on account of this mere instrument, but the body exists on account of the spirit. It is the animating and guiding principle of the body.

And the spirit's wonderful consciousness of its self-dependence, the firm conviction which it possesses that it exists for its own sake solely, and not as part of other things, is the Divine guarantee of its immortality. In like manner the most exalted of spirits, the Deity, the Creator, is not a part of the universe, is not part of aught else, but is self-existent and eternal. Yea, he who doubts the immortality of his own soul, may also, in such moments of fearful mental aberration, doubt Thy existence, O God!

If we observe the unreasoning brutes with their blind instincts, and their capabilities, we perceive that all the powers with which the Creator has so wonderfully endowed them, are necessary for, and conducive to, the support of life, and the attainment of such objects as they may have in life.

Now, were the human spirit created merely for this fleeting life on earth, it would not have required the many and superior faculties which the hand of God has bestowed on it. Had it received, like the rest of the animals, blind instincts to guide it, these would have sufficed in its case also to provide nourishment and support for the body it animates.

But of what use are the glorious faculties of our minds? Why are we, by a wonderful concatenation of circumstances, forced into improving these faculties? Why should we possess a knowledge of God, if this God, before whose throne our spirits worship, is not our eternal Father? Why did the hand of the All-merciful God implant in our hearts this undying yearning for continuous life, if it were meant never to be satisfied? Were the immortality of the soul a delusion, would not man, with his superior knowledge and qualities, be far more to be pitied than the humblest of animals? The latter knows not of death; it takes no care for the coming hour. Why has God, the All-wise, endowed us with the faculty of anticipating the future? Sceptic, wouldst thou dare to utter the blasphemous answer, " that we may be the more unhappy?" Are we then to suppose that God has gloriously manifested His wisdom in stones, in plants, and in animals; but that in man He has failed utterly? The animals attain, through means of their inferior capabilities, as great contentment, and as high a degree of perfection, as their nature is capable of; but man, with his far higher faculties, does not attain to anything approaching the perfection of which his nature is susceptible. This life therefore does not suffice for the fulfilment and attainment of our destination. We bear within us the germ of a perfection of infinite growth, and therefore infinitude must have been a condition of our creation, or the world is a chaos, and the wisdom of God is at variance with itself—a thought that none but a madman can entertain.

Thou believest in a God, and yet, O rash and insensate man! thou wouldst in thy aberration deny the manifestations of His wisdom in the wonderfully organized universe. Every star, every blade of grass, thine own conscience, all the events of thy life, all the nations of the earth, proclaim it in a thousand tongues, He is! He is!

And if there be a God, and He be an all-perfect and all-holy Being, how durst thou doubt His justice?

He who does not believe in the immortality of the soul, and in a retributive justice dwelling above the stars, he believes in an imperfect God, he believes that man's mind conceives a higher justice than the acts of the Most Holy One manifest.

For how can it be reconciled with Divine justice that excellent men and women, that pious Christians, who have suffered the direst misfortunes on earth for the sake of virtue, and without any fault of their own, should suffer thus, if there were no future compensation of supreme bliss for what they have here endured; that bad men, that heartless tyrants, should spend their days amid pomp and pleasure, and be allowed unpunished to inflict upon their innocent fellow-men, upon individuals, families, and whole nations, intolerable evils and misfortunes? If there be no supreme judge and no retributive justice in the universe, what mortal here on earth would venture to follow the dictates of virtue?

True, it is said, that virtue is its own reward—alas! not always. How many have not sacrificed every joy of life for righteousness' sake, and died under great suffering, faithful to the last to the divine laws! No; it is as little an unfailing rule on earth that virtue brings its own reward, as it is that vice always brings its own punishment. But patient Christians, as well as shameless sinners, have an intuitive belief in another world, and that eternal retribution dwells above the stars!

Yea, above the stars dwells the eternal Judge, meting out retributive justice. Weep not, suffering friend of virtue; despair not, persecuted and forsaken innocence; the day of thy triumph will come. Bear thy cross courageously to the grave as did Jesus; like Him, thou shalt live eternally.

We are immortal! not for ever shall we be the prey of death. Oh, ye poor orphans, why do you lament so disconsolately by the grave of your father, your mother? Oh, father! oh, mother! why pine so at the death of your child? It has but preceded you into a better world. You are immortal, and you will find your lost treasure again—God has willed it so. Your fate in regard to this was eternally pre-ordained when the plan of the world was laid. God will also call you away; you will one day be happy in the blessed regions, while others will be weeping for you on earth.

We are immortal!—Sinner, well mayst thou turn pale! The soul of that man, too, is immortal whom thou didst persecute with thy hatred and thy slanderous tongue; immortal is also the starving wretch whom thou didst refuse to help, that thou mightest have the more to spend on thine own luxuries; immortal the soul of the innocent girl seduced by thee, and thus robbed by thee of her every joy in life; and immortal, like thine own, O proud man! is the soul of thy fellow-man whom thou tramplest under foot as thou dost the worm in the dust.

We are immortal!—O Christian, O meek follower of Jesus, the souls of those also are immortal on whom thou hast bestowed thy good gifts. They will bear witness in thy favour before God. The tears which thou hast wiped from the eyes of sufferers will be transmuted into happiness for thee. The children, whom with pious heart thou art educating for eternity, will never be torn away from thee. They will be hereafter as they are here, the souls most closely akin to thine own.

We are immortal! God, my God! nameless, merciful, wise and just God, in this hope is comprised all my earthly happiness. In Thy world there is no death, only life! And that which we call death is only transformation. Thy entire universe is life. Thou Thyself art Life! How, then, could I be in Thee, and cease to exist? Thou hast not called me into existence for this short dream of life on earth—thou chosest for me eternity, and Jesus who has risen from the dead, shows me in His holy teachings the way to reach it. (Col. iii. 2.)

Oh, what inexpressible joy takes possession of my soul! what rapture quickens the pulsations of my heart, at the thought of eternal existence! Sorrows of life, hours of suffering, what are ye?—passing shadows that leave no trace behind them. Warnings from God to follow the holy teachings of Christ. Warnings from my heavenly Father to remind me that I am called to eternal life.

Oh, my Father, I will cling closely to Thee! Through Thy Will I am immortal, and penetrated by Thy Holy Spirit, I will endeavour to make myself worthy of immortality. I will throw off my faults like defiling dust; I will devote myself to God; for I am immortal. With longing heart I strive to raise myself up to Thee, O eternal Father! Receive me and mine into Thy glory! Amen.

WHY MUST THE FUTURE LIFE BE HIDDEN FROM US?

> Yes, I believe; but clothed in dust,
> How weak is still the strongest trust,
> How oft my wavering faith hath failed,
> And wished its hope to sight revealed!
>
> For me, thou Life by which I live,
> Oh, let Thy Spirit witness give—
> Death is not death—'tis leaving earth,
> For nature's second, nobler birth.
>
> When once this transient life shall fail,
> Thy hand shall draw away the veil—
> The veil that dims to mortal eye
> The vision of Eternity.
>
> (2 *Cor.* v. 7.)

How often, when meditating on the future destiny of the soul, do not mortals say, " If we but knew how we shall fare in that future life! If we had but some slight indication of what will be the state of the spirit after the death of the body! If we had but some little knowledge of the abode into which the spirit will pass, some shadowy insight into its destination there, some faint prefigurement of its joys and sorrows in Eternity!"

Such wishes and questionings are pardonable. They do not, however, so much manifest the soul's noble longing for knowledge as they betray common curiosity and impatience. For the desire for knowledge will easily be satisfied with the conviction that the day will infallibly come when we shall know and experience it all, and that it will come as soon as it is good for us. But curiosity will not rest content with this; it wishes for knowledge merely to satisfy its craving; it is like the inquisitive child, who, though certain that at a given time it will receive a gift from its tender parents, yet uselessly endeavours before the time comes to divine what the gift will be.

Therefore human folly has ever been busy endeavouring to discover by subtle investigation the secrets of eternity. Therefore there have come into existence as many notions and fancies regarding the future life, as there have been persons who have allowed their imaginations free play respecting the subject. Among the Jews as among the Turks, among the heathens as among the Christians, the most contradictory ideas prevail, about the state of our immortal spirits after death—ideas which are often highly unworthy of the greatness and majesty of God.

Some believe that in the next world the soul will live in a state of sensual bliss, in the midst of lovely groves and gardens, where are spread richly-decked boards, at which they may feast whenever they please. Others believe that the soul sleeps in the grave until the great day of judgment shall come, when the dead shall arise and stand forth to receive their reward. Others, again, believe that, until the last day of the world, the souls will wander about partly under the earth, partly near the entrance to hell, partly in the air, partly in the vicinity of heaven; and that they have the power to reveal themselves to living men at certain times, particularly during the night, in the form of ghosts, and thus to create terror for no reason or purpose. Others, again, think that the spirits of the departed roam about in some paradise, where their greatest happiness consists in remembering and recounting the deeds performed by them in their former existence. Others teach that before the soul is admitted into paradise, or the place of eternal joy, it must undergo a period of probation, during which it will be cleansed of all the earthly wishes, and cares, and impurities that may still cling to it, in order that it may ultimately enjoy unmixed bliss.

In vain, however, has human curiosity endeavoured to force open the gates of eternity, in order to discover that which lies beyond. It has never succeeded. The darkness in which God has wrapped the land of the future remains impenetrable; and of the dead, not one has yet come back to unveil to inquisitive man the secrets of the world of spirits.

Foolish speculations on this subject have never led to any useful or beneficent result. Men have tortured themselves with their own dreams. They have created for themselves terrific images, which have no existence except in their own heated brains. They have peopled their imaginations with ghosts, or supposed visible spirits, which in their timidity they fancy they see and hear everywhere. They have spread in consequence, not the realm of wisdom, but the realm of superstition; not the kingdom of God, but the kingdom of error and of heathenish fables. They have been less intent upon becoming like unto Jesus in feeling and actions, than upon disputations about their fancies and opinions. They have hoped more from long and formal prayers, from sacrifices and outward discipline, from fastings and purifications, than from following the example of Jesus in virtuous sentiments and works of love. Finally, they have placed the value and essence of Christianity more in certain dogmas and in faith, than in doing those things that are pleasing to God, as they are enjoined to do by Jesus in His Sermon on the Mount, and by the Apostles in all their speeches and epistles. In vain St. James cries to them—" What doth it profit, my brethren, though a man say he hath faith, and have not works? Can faith save him?" In vain thou criest to them, O Jesus Christ; " Not every one that saith unto me, Lord, Lord, shall enter into the kingdom of Heaven; but he that doeth the will of my Father who is in Heaven." They persist in their melancholy conceit; superstitious ceremonies, formal prayers, outward religious observances are to them more than the call of Jesus, more than the warning love of Christ.

Let me then sedulously avoid all mere curiosity on this solemn subject; let me shun all notions and suppositions as to the state of departed souls, which may induce superstitious and irrational fears, and lead me to have recourse to unmeaning ceremonies. On earth there is for me but *one* great Revealer of Divine and heavenly things, and this is Jesus Christ, the Son of God, the Saviour of the world. He alone is my light, my loadstar in the darkness; and all else that human beings, be they ever so wise and holy, would reveal to me concerning eternal life, is only human conceptions, only their special views.

But Jesus, who dwelleth ever in Eternity, who was

there in the beginning, and will be there evermore, Jesus has assured me that my soul is immortal, yet He shed no light upon its state in the next life. He taught us that the soul of man, after its liberation from the body, would be removed into a higher and a happier sphere which God had prepared for it from the beginning; therefore He said to His companion on the cross,—" To-day thou shalt be with me in paradise." He taught that our spirits must prepare here on earth for Eternity; that here already they belong to the great kingdom of God; that this kingdom of God does not consist in outward signs, but is *within us*, in the virtuous and perfect mind. " The kingdom of God," said He, " is within you." (Luke xvii. 21.) He taught that according as each mortal in this life makes himself worthy of higher perfection and of a more blissful state, so will it be meted out to him hereafter. There every one will be judged by his words, his thoughts, and his deeds, and receive the reward he merits. (Matt. xxv. 34—46.)

With these explanations as to what we have to look forward to in Eternity, the disciples of Christ must be satisfied. They know the value of eternal life, and to them the promises concerning it must bring joy. Here, on earth, " we walk by faith, not by sight !"

And why should I not be satisfied with the revelations given in the Holy Scriptures? Why should not that which Jesus has promised be sufficient to tranquillize me? Why should I rather listen to the promptings of my restless curiosity, than to the wisdom of my Divine Redeemer and Comforter?

Had the Deity thought it good for mankind that we should be able to look into Eternity, and to penetrate its secrets, the power of doing so would have been bestowed upon us. But the Omniscient would not that it should be so; and we may therefore conclude that the faculty of following the spirits along their path in Eternity would not be conducive to our happiness and well-being. It is withheld from us until the important hour when we shall ourselves become denizens of Eternity.

Thy inquisitive desire to solve the mysteries of the future world is therefore culpable, is unworthy of thy profession as a Christian, proves a want of trust in the wisdom and fatherly love of God. Be assured, that the knowledge of that which the Lord conceals from thee would render thee unhappy. Are there not in like manner many things which mortal parents conceal from their children in infancy, but which are communicated to them when they reach a riper age? Too early a disclosure of these matters might be injurious to the welfare of the entire family, or be hurtful to the children themselves. Who would blame the wisdom and prudence of these anxious parents, who in this very withholding of knowledge give a proof of their affection for their children? Will not the child himself in later years thank his parents for their reticence?

And the same is the case with man in regard to God! We also shall one day, when death breaks the dark seal of the mystery, recognize the wisdom of the all-loving Father, and stammer forth our thanks. We also shall smile at the futility of our endeavours, at the childishness of our fancies, respecting the eternal future. We also shall then repent with justice of our want of trust in the eternal Wisdom and Mercy.

However incapable we may be, while dwelling here

in the dust and with our limited faculties, of understanding the councils and the exalted ends of the Most High, it is much easier for us to divine why the hand of God has veiled to our eyes the face of eternity, than it is to lift this veil even in the least degree.

The less we know with certainty that which awaits us after this life, the purer, the more unselfish will our virtue be on earth.

What is Christian virtue? Wherein consists the holiness which Jesus demands of us? In self-improvement, self-bestowed blessedness. Christian duty, as Christ understood it, must have no other end than itself; it must not be a means to secure this or that advantage; it must not be a mere measure of prudence.

What value is there in that virtue which makes me give alms to the poor, in order that I may gain honour among men—which makes me avoid enmities in order that my life may be more easy—which leads me to afford help, that I may be helped in my turn—that induces me to perform acts of public utility, that I may win popularity—that makes me act honestly in order to gain confidence—that makes me amiable in manner in order that I may be praised—that makes me show friendship to those who may show me friendship in return? Is this virtue as Jesus understood it? Nay, it is but prudence! It is a calculation how to gain great advantages by means of small sacrifices. "For if ye love them which love you, what reward have ye? And if ye salute your brethren only, what do you more than others?" No; "ye must be perfect, as your Father in Heaven is perfect;" that is to say, your goodness must be without selfishness, you must not debase your virtue into a mere measure of prudent calculation, you must expect no higher reward than is comprised in that virtue itself.

He who does not love it for its own sake, oh! he can never have known it! A child who is only obedient when he is promised a reward, is not a wise or good child, but a calculating and selfish one.

God is perfect, because He is God, and in His own perfection He finds the highest bliss. God is perfect not in order to gain outward advantages; and He is merciful, gracious and beneficent, not in order that weak man, a poor worm in the dust, should worship Him. And in *this* spirit Jesus tells us to be perfect, as our Father in Heaven is perfect.

We are to improve ourselves, to become holy through the practice of every virtue, not in order to receive some other reward, but because in this improvement and sanctification is comprised the happiness of the spirit. The most virtuous and the wisest man is the happiest, simply because he is the most perfect. That which he was here below, that his spirit will remain on entering eternity; and his reward in that better life is, that he is allowed ever to approach nearer to the Divine perfection, ever to grow in likeness to God.

If any one avoid evil from fear of punishment, he is prudent, but not virtuous. If any one refrain from stealing from fear of chains and prison, shall we therefore call him pious? Who can assure me that he would not steal if there were no chains, no prison? If any one refrain from sin through fear of hell, is he therefore righteous? Or, when any one does good in this life in the hope that he will be richly rewarded in the next, is he therefore a saint, in the spirit of Jesus?

If he had no hope, or only a vacillating hope of future reward, would he act equally well? And if not, is his selfish virtue other than a well-calculated means to purchase a great good for a small outlay; to gain, at the price of a small sacrifice of a few minutes' duration, an eternity of bliss?

Nay, it is a beneficent arrangement that earthly eyes should not be able to penetrate eternity. Our virtue on earth is thereby rendered so much the more pure and unselfish, because, ignorant as to what is to follow, we are thrown entirely upon ourselves.

But suppose a revelation of the future world should be made to us, should we be able to comprehend it? How is it possible that, bound in the fetters of earth as we are, and with faculties proportionately limited, we should have the power of comprehending the supernatural? How can the sensual embrace the spiritual? All descriptions would be insufficient to enlighten us, because we lack means of comparison.

If a traveller from our part of the globe visited the savages of the Pacific, and attempted to describe to them the comforts of life and the mental superiority enjoyed by man in our regions, how would he make himself understood, as no conception of the kind exists in the mind of the savage? If a man blessed with sight were to describe to a man born blind the beauties of a landscape, the sublime forms of the lofty mountains at the foot of which roll majestic streams, and around whose summits are gathered clouds glowing in the golden rays of the setting sun, in what words would he represent to the blind man, who knows not what light is, the wonderful beauties of creation? The blind man would remain, as before, in darkness, without the power of comprehending what the other attempted to convey to him; but greater sadness would take possession of him at the thought that he was excluded from so much happiness that fell to the share of others.

Well, then, what are we mortals more than persons born blind, as regards the glories of the future existence that awaits us? Those glories can only be seen by earth-freed spirits, and were one of these to appear to us, and to describe the greatness, the goodness, the majesty of the Creator, as they are manifested in those blessed realms, and the condition of the souls that have thrown off the bonds of flesh, should we be able to comprehend what he told us? Should we not be overwhelmed with sadness at the thought that other creatures of God were so infinitely more perfect and more blessed than we? Should we not think the joys which God has bestowed upon us here below very insignificant in comparison with those He has in store for us? Oh, let us rest assured, that it was with a wise hand that the eternal God veiled the glories of eternity from the eyes of those who, being here on earth, cannot yet be allowed to partake of them; for to behold them would but make us less happy than we are now, when the joys that we do feel are the greatest that we know.

Were we allowed to have a glimpse of the bliss of future worlds, our impatience to attain it would embitter our life upon earth. How soon, and how easily, may not the barriers of life be overleapt! How many thousand sufferers would not in moments of impatience, forgetful of their duties, determine to leave this world!

But it is God's will that we should work out our destination on earth, as far as it is to be fulfilled here; that we should not voluntarily and capriciously put an end to our earthly career, but that we should pursue it to its furthest goal.

Therefore, He placed as guardians before the closed gates of eternity, fear and anxious doubt, and the awful stillness of death, and impenetrable darkness.

These guardians drive back the human race, that it may pursue to the end its appointed path on earth.

In spite of all the discomforts of life, in spite of our impatient longing to be reunited with the friends who have gone before us to our eternal home, the terrors that surround the portals of eternity repel us, and we continue our earthly journey with calmer spirits.

Were it not for that darkness and terror, should we not be like wearied mariners, who, after a long voyage on the stormy seas, behold at a short distance the shores of their beloved country? They see the calm and secure haven, where wind and tempest no longer threaten destruction; they already discover the verdant trees and the peaceful cottages; their hearts yearn towards their homes; their eyes are suffused with tears of mingled joy and sadness at the long-missed sight. They tremble. Every minute before they reach the shore seems a year. Ah! they recognize already their wives, their brothers, their parents, their children, their beloved maidens waiting for them there. They see their arms opened to receive them, and hear from afar the longing cries of affection. What prevents them from flying at once into those arms, to weep out their joy on those bosoms, in which the heart beats so tenderly for them? "Oh home!

oh joy! which we have so long missed!" all exclaim. They forget the helm of the ship, the waves of the sea, the rocks, the surf around them; they forget the treasures which they have gathered together on the long and wearisome voyage—they throw themselves into the sea, to reach the sooner the shores of their home.

Such would be the lot of mortals, did not the dark ocean separate them, for their own good, from their heavenly home.

But not for ever, O my God! does it separate me from the dearly beloved beings who are awaiting me there! I shall one day behold these shores of my better fatherland; I shall at length see them again, those loved ones, to whom my heart clings so tenderly; and shall rest among them after the dangers and hardships that I have undergone on my voyage across the stormy waters of life.

Yes; be comforted, O spirit, God has prepared thy haven of rest! God has kept a home open for thee, where thou wilt find with delight what thou hast lost here. Thou wilt not be alone, thy loved ones are already awaiting thee. They beckon to thee with the palm of victory which thou art to fight for here below. Up then, my soul, fight out the battle! Raise thyself, through the aid of Jesus' Holy Word, in the Holy Spirit of Jesus to that perfection, through which alone thou canst become a denizen of that better land, a partaker of that more blissful Eternity! It is the Lord that cries to thee, "Be faithful unto death, and I will give thee the crown of life."

A JOY IN THE HOUR OF DEATH.

I know, I know, in whom I trust,
And bow me humbly in the dust,
  My Saviour, God, and Lord, to Thee.
If from my sins I may be freed,
If I may hope Thy help in need,
  Oh, then must Heaven my portion be!

And when my last sleep draweth near,
Then dare I, without doubt or fear,
  To the beloved One look on high.
And none who knew me here, and loved,
Will e'er repent, or stand unmoved,
  Beside the grave in which I lie.

(*Rev.* xiv. 13.)

ONE thing after another fades and dies away: herbs of the field, animals, and man. We come, we look around us, and depart again from this world. Whether we are to depart in the bloom of youth, or in the fulness of years—who can say? And in the end it is of little consequence—for of what importance are a few days, a few years more or less? That which is past is as if it had never been. The dust of the infant and the dust of the old man rest side by side in the grave, and there is now no difference between them. Another generation moves above them, which knows naught of them, makes no mention of them, lives on, but is soon to be laid low by their side.

We are all aware of this, and we dread the moment,

but in vain. Whether it be on the field of battle, or on the bed of sickness, or in the midst of our relatives, or in a lonely prison, it matters little; it is sure to come.

To delude ourselves in regard to it, and never to look forward to that moment, is as senseless as it is to be ever tormenting ourselves with thoughts of death, and thus embittering all enjoyment in life. But it is wise to keep in store, for that solemn and dreaded moment, a joy that will turn all bitterness to sweetness.

Many persons, it is true, do think of this, but they do not always make a good choice. They are frequently very one-sided in their selection of that which is to comfort them in the hour of dissolution.

There are many who toil anxiously their whole life through to amass money, in order that they may leave their children a respectable fortune, or at least a competence. That is undoubtedly very praiseworthy. It must certainly be a great comfort to them in their last hour, when parting from those dear ones, to think that they are provided for, though no one may be there to watch over them. That they are not quite forsaken, are not quite without means, will not be beggars, or be hustled about as troublesome beings; that they are placed in a position to lead an independent and honourable life. Assuredly this is a great comfort. Yet it is but a poor joy. For the good or the evil fortune of our dear ones, after our death, does not rest solely on the money that we may leave them. Their future lot depends far more upon their skill, their knowledge, their virtues, and upon the friendship of their fellow-men, and the blessing of God. All the money in the world cannot make us happy, if our mental disposition be adverse. It is true that a moderate fortune will save our children from too great dependence on the favour and caprice of other men. But it is only he who has educated his children so as to render them happy and contented, independently of money, that can say that he leaves them true riches, which thieves cannot steal, and circumstances not impair, and moth not eat. Finally, if we can find no better comfort in the hour of the last parting from our loved ones, than that we leave them some pecuniary means wherewith to get on in the world, then we have done little indeed! Even the heathens do this! We have only fulfilled a most urgent duty, and gratified our own ambition.

Others store up for the hour of death a joy which they have been hard-hearted enough to deny themselves all their life long. We hear that persons who are dying have forgiven their enemies, and have been sincerely reconciled to them.

True, to be reconciled to enemies is a delight to the soul. And to desire to be so is a proof of a noble disposition, if we have given offence by our pride, our covetousness, or our irrepressible anger. But if we look closely at it, what is a reconciliation with our enemies on the bed of death? In fact, nothing more than a declaration that we wish to make peace with them now that we can no longer injure them. What would you think of the sincerity of the desire for reconciliation of a man who, when thrown into prison, promises peace and good-will, and asks your forgiveness for the past? And are not those who propose reconciliation on their death-bed in the same case? Are all those present whom we have in the course of life offended by word or by deed? Can our will to be reconciled to them make amends for the many painful hours and days we have caused them by our quarrelsome and unamiable disposition? And are we sure they have forgiven us all our trespasses? Why hast thou postponed till the hour of death that which thou wert bound to do every day of thy life, and why makest thou peace then, only when thy enmity can no longer be dangerous? Dost thou think that the wish, forced upon thee by the fear in thy heart, is sufficient to stifle the sighs of those thou hast offended, so that they shall not rise up to Heaven to witness against thee?

Of others, again, we hear that, when disposing of their property by will, they have not been forgetful of the poor—that they have bestowed benevolent gifts on alms-houses, and on other useful public institutions; sometimes, that they have made special arrangements for restoring that which they have acquired by unrighteous means to the rightful owners. This is right. We ought not to depart from this world with the consciousness of having committed a wrong, without taking means to make all the amends in our power. And it is praiseworthy to think of the good of the commonwealth, also, in the disposition we may make of our fortunes after our death. Not only our children, or our blood-relatives are our kindred, all the children of God, all those for whom Jesus died, are so likewise. However, the pleasure which we feel in giving away that which death forbids us any longer to possess must be rather a sad one. Why, O miserly, ungenerous spirit, dost thou not give away in thy lifetime, and thus promote joy and happiness? Then that would have been a merit, which in thy last hour ceases to be one. The poor widow, mentioned in the Gospels, indigent as she was, brought her mite to the treasury. But thou hast been saving that thou mightest increase thy goods, and thou hast only become generous now that the moment has arrived when thou canst no longer thyself enjoy thy riches. Thou, who hast spent thy fortune in splendid entertainments, in pomp and luxury, in tickling thy palate with high-priced delicacies, and hast only begun to think of clothing the naked and feeding the hungry since illness and the approach of death have deprived thee of the power of continuing thy life of revelry and self-indulgence—what merit hast thou? Thou growest more abstemious because thy appetite fails thee, and thou givest away what thou canst no longer use. Verily thy virtue is not great: canst thou hope that it will suffice to sweeten the bitter cup of death?

It is a consolation in the hour of death to see oneself surrounded by friends and dear relatives, and to behold in their grief and tears a gratifying testimony of their affection and tender attachment. But does this suffice to take away all the bitterness of the last moment? Who is not saddened by the sight of death? It is impossible to witness without emotion the last sigh of even a perfect stranger. Can we then regard it as a merit in ourselves, as a proof of our inward worth, that those who have been accustomed to live with us for long years, with whom we have entertained relations of the closest intimacy, should weep at our death? Would it not be more gratifying to know in our last hour that those also with whom we have never, or at least but rarely, held personal intercourse, will grieve when they hear of our departure? That the whole community will lament and say, "We have lost an upright fellow-citizen, a supporter of the poor and afflicted, an active promoter of every good undertaking, a pleasant companion, a philanthropist in the fullest sense of the word?"

Truly, one of the greatest joys that can be ours at the moment of death, is the consciousness, that in quitting the world we leave behind us a memory respected by all who knew us; while, on the other hand, there can be no greater pain than to have the conviction that many survive who wish that they had never known us, or had never been brought into closer connexion with us.

That sweetest of comforts, that none who survived Him regretted having known Him, was enjoyed in death by Jesus Christ. He died the death of supreme self-sacrifice for the happiness of all souls; He died the death of inexpressible love, even for the ungrateful, who still misjudged Him. He died, but even His persecutors admired Him; even His judges declared, "We see no evil in Him." A deluded people, in a storm of wild passion, put Him to death—but Jerusalem wept. After the lapse of a few days His enemies were seized with an avenging panic, and thousands who had turned away from Him again sought refuge with Him. Even to this day, after very nearly two thousand years, the race redeemed by Him grieves at the memory of His sufferings and His death. Verily, this is to die in God! This is to be followed by the blessings of one's works long after death.

"Blessed are the dead which die in the Lord from henceforth: Yea, saith the Spirit, that they may rest from their labours; and their works do follow them." (Rev. xiv. 13.)

And this—yea, none but this—is the last earthly joy that every wise man and woman, every true Christian, ought to store up for the hour of death. With such consciousness it is sweet to fall asleep. But what is meant by dying in the Lord? It means to die in the spirit and in the holiness of Jesus Christ. But what is meant by dying in Jesus? It means to die, not merely believing in God and in Jesus, (for the devils also believe and tremble,) but to be one with Jesus. And how can we die in Jesus, if we have not lived in Jesus? What is meant by living in Jesus? It means to live and act in His faith, in His spirit, and according to His example; to live and to act as He would have lived, thought, and acted, had He been in our place.

Only he who has lived in the Lord can die in the Lord. Only he who dies in the Lord can be called blessed. He rests from his labours—he rests, not from his pleasures, not from his endeavours after riches, honours, and admiration, or after pomp and splendour, but from his labours for the good and happiness of others. And he may be called blessed, for his works do follow him.

They follow him to the hour of his death, and the remembrance of them is then his last consolation. He departs joyfully with the happy thought: of all that survive me, there is not one who repents having known me, or having been brought into closer or more distant connexion with me. I leave no one behind me who rejoices at my being removed from the ranks of the living, because my existence has been oppressive and hateful to him. No; I leave a circle of friends to not one of whom I have wilfully done an injury, even though I may have done them no good. I have effected in my life as much as was in my power. I often asked myself, when about to act or speak, Would Jesus have acted, have thought, have spoken thus, had He been in like circumstances? I have lived in the Lord, and therefore I die in the Lord. My Saviour lives, and I also shall live. Blessed is he who dies thus, for his works do follow him.

They follow him to the grave. Oh! what funeral pomp can be compared to the remembrance of our virtues by those we leave behind us; to the tears of affection with which our friends dwell upon our goodness; to the respect with which our fellow-citizens cherish our memory; to the emotion with which even strangers exclaim, Truly this man may be called blessed in death, for his meritorious works follow him! yea, they follow him, and will be turned into blessings for his children and his children's children. His name, which lives in the remembrance of his fellow-citizens, is the best recommendation for the relatives he leaves behind him. The world is willing to reward a deceased father and mother by conferring benefits on their children. In these the parents are honoured! Woe to him who has nothing to leave his beloved ones but money and money's worth! Riches vanish, but an honourable name, acquired through the possession of great virtues, is a sacred treasure, which neither the flames of war, nor the cunning of dissemblers, nor the injustice of the great, nor the violence of the ruthless, can destroy. When the mind of the dying can dwell complacently on this thought, they enjoy in death unutterable bliss; for they are conscious that "their works do follow them." They follow them into the better life beyond the grave. Far above the stars, and—let every sinner tremble at the thought, and every righteous man rejoice—above the stars dwells Retributive Justice. The God of justice lives, and I shall live with Him. What I have done to the least of Jesus' brethren and mine, I have done to Him. God will requite me! The heartfelt thanks of the sufferers whom I have comforted will be echoed in Heaven. The glistening tears of joy or emotion which a feeling heart sheds on hearing of good deeds done by me unostentatiously and disinterestedly, are reflected in Heaven; the deep-felt but unobtrusive praise—unheard and unsought for by me on earth—with which my companions mention the philanthropic institutions, or other works of public utility, which I have founded, will be heard by me in Heaven. Ah! what rapture must fill the heart of the dying man when he can say to himself, " Far from leaving behind me any one who is likely to curse my memory, I may confidently hope that many will remember me with affection!"

I shall one day die!—this is beyond a doubt. But shall I, in the hour of death, feel that ineffable joy which sweetens the bitterness of parting? Ought I not to wish that it may be so? Is there anything I dread so much as the hour of dissolution? And why not, then, endeavour to lay up such store of gladness for it as may lie in my power? Ah! " blessed are they who die in the Lord !"

How, if the next night were to be my last? or the next month? (Who knows when the hour may come, when God shall call him from his works?) Should I, in that case, taste the last and sweetest of all earthly joys?

If I were doomed to die this instant, could I lay my head on my death-bed pillow with the consciousness that I leave no one behind me in the world who has reason to repent of having been connected with me in any way? Is there no one who, by word, deed, or example, I have led into sin? No one who needs blush in secret when remembering me? Is there no one whom I have injured in the estimation of his fellow-citizens by envious gossip, by rash judgment, or by reckless sarcasm? Is there no one who is vexed when he hears my name, because I have maliciously injured his good repute through love of disparagement? Is there no one from whom I have unjustly taken, and perhaps still keep back, what was his by right? Who has perhaps failed to demand it of me, because I have so cunningly managed that he did not know who was his despoiler? Shall I leave to my heirs property so unrighteously acquired, and to which no blessing can attach? Is there no one whose life I have embittered by my caprices, by my discontented, quarrelsome, domineering disposition? Is there no one who may one day lament that I have not attended more carefully to his education? Is there no one whom I have offended, and whose forgiveness I ought to seek? Is there no one who has injured me, and whom I still hate, or with whom I am still at variance?

I shall die one day—that is beyond a doubt. But

shall I die in the Lord? Have I lived in the Lord? Ah! I must veil my face from Thee, O Searcher of hearts, O Omniscient God, O most Holy Avenger! For I feel, when examining myself, that I am not quite blameless. I have still to repair much evil that I have done. I have still to make amends for many things which it behoves me not to forget. I have not always lived in Thee, my Saviour, and therefore I could not now die joyfully in Thee. It would have been easy for me to confer some little pleasure on each one of my acquaintances, and to render them some service, had I availed myself of every favourable opportunity, and yet I have rarely done so. Alas! I may have frequently done the contrary. Ah! I hardly dare to think of it.

Yet, hear my promise, O Omnipresent God! I will think of it; I will improve, I will make reparation, I will redeem what I have neglected, I will live in Jesus, that I may one day, blessed in death, fall asleep in the Lord, with the consciousness that I leave no one behind me who has cause to regret having known me. I may therefore apply to myself also the heavenly words: "Blessed are the dead which die in the Lord from henceforth: Yea, saith the Spirit, that they may rest from their labours; and their works do follow them!"

THOUGHTS AT THE GRAVES OF THOSE WE LOVE.

Vital spark of heavenly flame,
Quit, oh quit this mortal frame:
Trembling, hoping, ling'ring, flying;
Oh, the pain, the bliss of dying!
Cease, fond nature, cease thy strife,
And let me languish into life.

Hark! they whisper; angels say,
Sister spirit, come away.
What is this absorbs me quite?
Steals my senses, shuts my sight,
Drowns my spirit, draws my breath?
Tell me, my soul, can this be death?

The world recedes; it disappears!
Heav'n opens on my eyes! my ears
   With sounds seraphic ring:
Lend, lend your wings! I mount! I fly!
O Grave! where is thy victory?
  O Death! where is thy sting?

(Luke xxiii. 46.)

GLADLY do I turn my thoughts to you, O beloved ones, who have gone before me into a better world! O ye never-to-be-forgotten objects of my heart's devotion, my longing for you is so great, that it seems to lift me above the dust in which I still dwell! It is you who, with angel hands, as it were, bind closer the ties that unite the here and the hereafter, who strew roses on the bed of death on which I shall one day be stretched, and who rob dissolution itself of all its terrors. To think of you, to hope for reunion with you, is to add to my happiness here below, and is one of the sweetest duties of my heart's religion.

I know that in remote times, when the Heathens saw the Christians praying at the graves of those they loved, and even in our day, when Christianity reminds its votaries of God and of Eternity, the religion of Christ was, and is still called, a severe and saddening worship, incapable of inspiring cheerfulness, contentment, or joy in life; and that, in consequence, many have turned away from it. But these contemners of Christianity have not been sufficiently acquainted with it, or have judged it according to the dark views and melancholy dispositions of individual preachers, who loved to inspire their hearers with dread by the pictures which they drew of the terrors of the judgment, and the sufferings of the condemned, and by the idea which they gave of eternity. These men preached a Godhead as prone to anger, as inexorable, and as revengeful as themselves.

Nevertheless, the God of Christianity is the God of love and gladness, for He is the Father of the beings He has created. The religion of Jesus is a religion of love and joy, for it encourages innocent cheerfulness, moderate enjoyment of the gifts of the Father, and contentment with our lot; its object is perfection and happiness; and even death, so much dreaded by all creatures, the Christian religion disarms of its terrors, making it appear as an angel of love and joy, which comes not to destroy existence, but to lift it into a higher sphere. The infidel, the man who scoffs at Christianity may tremble at death, but to the Christian sage it comes as a friendly messenger from God; and for this reason Christians are pleased at times to contemplate death. To them the thought is not fraught with melancholy, but with exquisite pleasure, because, by raising expectations of a higher bliss in the future it makes the present the more delightful. For joy is always purest and most lively when, instead of contemplating its melancholy end, we can look forward to its uninterrupted continuation. And such is the hope of the Christian.

Although on approaching the graves of our dear ones, or when communing in spirit with them, a feeling of sadness may steal over us, this sadness is not unhappiness, but a sweet uplifting of the soul by a rapturous yearning towards those that have gone before us. Know ye not that bliss can have its sadness, and silent joy its tears? If ye will call this feeling pain, oh! then it is a sweet pain, in which there is greater enjoyment than noisy mirth reveals. Know ye not that when a delicate and refined soul is most penetrated by joy it is most attuned to melancholy, and that this feeling in its turn is followed by serene composure and tranquil happiness?

When a father or a mother sinks down by the grave of a lost darling, or when the sight of the trifles which the dear departed one was fond of in life, calls forth his memory in livelier colours; when a gentle and affectionate child treasures up, as a sacred relic after the death of father or mother, some object that has belonged to either; when husband or wife, separated from the loved partner of life, and cherishing the remembrance of their mutual love and their happy marriage, places great store upon some ring, or some letters traced by the dear hand as a token of the affection that united them in life, and a symbol of the indissoluble union of their souls; when lovers early parted, or when friends, brothers, sisters, remember in solitude and retirement the dear ones they have lost; when, with many a deep-drawn sigh, their lips whisper the cherished name; when their tears falling on the grave bear witness to their undying affection: Is it pain and anguish which they experience, or a sad but heavenly satisfaction? If no gratification is mixed up with these tears and sighs, why, then, do we mortals, who are so prone to shun everything that is painful, so often indulge in such sorrow?

No, no; there is nothing painful in the thought of you, O my departed ones! Where there is true love there is also true happiness. Here in my imperfect state I still cling to you with unchanging devotion; here in the dust I still remember you with unaltered affection. Ah! and may I not hope that you in your glorified state, though much more perfect than I am, still remember with affection my faithful, loving heart? Would your happiness be heightened were you not allowed to love in return those that love you? Would He, whose name is Love, who binds magnetically together distant worlds and stars, and who has bestowed affection as the sweetest of His gifts on all sentient beings under the sun; would He have ordained it so, that the better life beyond the grave should commence with the annihilation of that true love which is the universal law of creation? No, no; faithful souls, in time and in eternity, commune lovingly with each other, and join hands above the grave. I have not forgotten you, and ye are cognizant of my love; ye behold the tears, and hear the sighs with which my heart affectionately calls to you. Ye are aware of my undying tenderness, and ye respond to it according to the sublime conditions of your higher existence.

Flow freely, tears of sadness; bleed again and again, old and deep wounds of my faithful heart! Ah! those who have departed from me were truly worthy of such homage. Ye are, as it were, the sacred and only offerings which I can now bring them. It is a sweet pleasure to me to think that they to whom these offerings are made see them and appreciate them. Flow, O tears! open again, O bleeding wounds of my heart! With the blood that gushes forth from these wounds vanishes gradually all that is most sensuous in me, and I cease to cling so tenaciously to the empty vanities of life. With this blood also flows out many of my worst passions which incline me to attach to the joys or sorrows of this life more value than they deserve. In thinking of the glorified spirits my own spirit is purified, and calm contentment spreads through my heart. It is only where faith in God and immortality fail, and man in his blindness believes that with death all ends, that this contentment can never be felt, and that sorrow for lost loved ones assumes the form of dark despair. In those cases the tears of hopeless grief become a solemn accusation of cruelty against the Highest Being, and seem to declare that man is nobler and more full of love than the All-animating and All-uniting Deity who is enthroned above the stars.

It is folly indeed for the mourner, when thinking of the departed, to figure to himself only their earthly form, in all the loveliness with which it was invested in life, and then to contrast it with what it is, as it lies cold and inanimate in the grave,—to think of their former tender affection for him, which now finds no voice; their former joyous disposition, and the delight they took in the things of this earth, which they have now lost for ever, as though it were their bodies that had entertained this affection for him, as though it were their earthly ashes that had experienced these feelings of delight! Why, even in the animal, it is not that which it has drawn from the earth, it is not its flesh and blood that experience pleasure, but a something higher that dwells in it.

They who mourn over the dead because they are no longer able to enjoy those pleasures of life which were dear to them here below, may be likened to a child that mourns over the departure of a friend of maturer age, who has left him to hasten into the arms of affectionate parents, or of a loving bride, or to accept some post of honour. The child deplores that his friend can no longer take part in his sports, but in reality, instead of grieving for his absent friend, he is weeping over the abandoned toys that are laid aside as useless. Ought we to feel pity for that which is utterly dead, and which is incapable of suffering? But such is the state of the body, the mortal coil of the soul, the left-off garment of the departed friend.

Does it not sometimes happen in our sorrow, that, giving ourselves up to strange delusions and to mistaken pity, we lament over the fate of the body, the outward form, while we entirely forget the soul that animated it? For if we thought of the spirit, how could we weep over it as dead when we know that it lives?

Frequently also it is the commiseration we feel with

the sufferings our beloved ones underwent in their last illness, or in the very hour of death, that causes our tears to flow. In these cases our feelings seem more justifiable; yet, upon reflection, we shall find that here also we are deluded by our senses and our imagination. I cannot believe that death, *i.e.*, the departure of the soul from the body, is in itself painful. At all events, it cannot be more so than the illness which causes death, and yet the most dangerous maladies are generally attended by the least suffering, however terrible they may be to witness. For how often has it not been asserted by those that have recovered from such illnesses, that when they were nearest death they suffered very little, and were but partially conscious? We also know that in distressing complaints the patient grows more and more composed as the moment of dissolution draws nearer, and that in many cases of slow disease or of decay of the vital powers from old age, death approaches so gently, that it seems in truth but a falling asleep. Consequently, we have a right to conclude that dying is in itself not painful, (for if it were it would be so in every case,) or at all events, that it is not more so than the illness that precedes it, for otherwise death would not bring with it that increased composure, that painless stupor, which is so much like sleep. Now, if you do not weep and despairingly lament over those who have recovered from a severe illness because of the sufferings they endured in its course, why do you thus mourn for those whom the gentle hand of death has released from their sufferings? Were not the pain and the illness the same whether the patient recovered or whether he died? Yes, say you; but the patient who recovers finds in the renewed joys of life compensation for his past sufferings! Ah! and the glorified soul of the departed, does that not find far greater compensation in the higher sphere to which it is removed? Is God just to those who remain on earth, and unjust to all the other beings that people His universe—unjust towards those whom He calls to Himself with fatherly love, when their time on earth is completed? In like manner as Christ, when dying on the cross, lifted up His voice and cried, " Father, into Thy hands I commend my spirit!" so will I, on the receipt of intelligence of the dissolution of friends, or when standing by the death-bed of those I love, lift up my voice and cry, Father, into Thy hands I commend their spirit! Thou art their God—as here on earth, so also beyond the grave; Thou wert their God before they knew Thee; Thou didst love them before they loved Thee.

He who fears not death feels it not, nor does he experience the awe that takes possession of the living at the sight of it. Children who know naught of death, die quietly without anticipating it. To them, it is but the end of their illness. They may possibly die in cramps and convulsions; but these are no more than a fearful play of the muscles, which, though painful for the bystanders to witness, is not felt by the dying child. For instance, what can be more distressing to behold than epileptic fits? Yet it is well known that persons who labour under this disease do not suffer, and, indeed, are hardly conscious of being subject to the fits, though while in them, they utter groans as if in pain, and their features are fearfully distorted.

Only those that fear death feel it, or rather feel

when it is drawing nigh. The uneasy conscience trembles at the thought of the judgment. The approach of death awakens in the heart the dark despair of a too tardy remorse. There is something inexpressibly fearful in the thought of being unable—at the very moment when life and all its joys are about to fail us—to say, " Father, into Thy hands I commend my spirit!"

Yet we should be mistaken were we always to attribute either the apparent nervous apprehension, or the calm composure of the dying, to the character of the life they have led in this world; for experience teaches that the most loveable and innocent children frequently die under what seems great uneasiness; while on the contrary, the greatest sinners have breathed their last with unalterable outward composure. What we witness when standing at the bedside of the dying is, as a general rule, merely the effects of the malady on the body and its vital powers. What is going on in the spirit of him who is about to depart, while apparently sunk in a state of stupor, who shall say? Those who have seen ruthless criminals led out to die by the hand of the executioner, in the full vigour of life, will know that such persons frequently meet their death with great apparent composure. But is it possible to believe that this outward calm is the consequence of inward peace?

Even good and pious people are, in many cases, rendered uneasy at the thought of their dissolution, merely because they allow their imagination too much scope and endeavour to picture to themselves what they will feel in their last moments. They shudder at the thought of having to exchange all that is dear and familiar to them on earth for the unknown and unfamiliar. But this anxiety would soon vanish, were they sufficiently acquainted with the wisdom of God, as it is revealed throughout the entire system of nature. They would then see that what they look upon as unknown is in reality quite familiar to them, and that what they so much dread ought rather to awaken feelings of pleasure. They would know that the new life they are to enter is only another and more glorious gift of their heavenly Father, than that which He bestows when He calls us into this earthly existence. Hast thou not full confidence in the Providence of thy all-loving and all-seeing Father in Heaven? Why, then, dost thou tremble? Does the child tremble at the thought of the Christmas gift it is to receive from its parents, though what this may be is quite unknown to it? The better lot that God has prepared for us is like a kind and fatherly gift, to which we ought to look forward with pleasure and joyful trust. When a human being enters as an infant into this life, which he has never seen or felt; when his loving mother presses him for the first time with a warm welcome to her bosom; when the father bends joyfully and tenderly over the new-comer and blesses him, does the child shrink back in fear from the unknown and the unfamiliar? How kindly, with how many tender caresses, is he not greeted by all! How gradually he becomes acquainted with the new things that surround him! Now, picture to yourselves that man had, previously to his appearance on this earth, lived in another world and under far more perfect conditions; do you conceive that even in that case he would find the things of this life so very strange? And in the life to which death is the introduction, we may be assured, the welcome we shall meet with will not be less kind and loving than that with which we were received here; perhaps, indeed, the former will far surpass the latter. For in yon life preparations have already been made for our happiness: there are dear ones there awaiting our coming.

Why should I doubt this—and doubt it merely because it is not known to me? Had not God made preparations for my reception on earth, and provision for my happiness here before I was born? Who thought of me before I came? Who measured out my joys to me before I had a heart to feel them? Who meted out my sufferings, before I knew what tears were? Was it not my eternal, all-loving Father? Well, and He who thought of me before I was, before I knew Him—will He forget me now that *I am?* Will He forsake me now that I love Him in return, and have learnt to call Him Father? Will He leave me unprovided for now that I worship Him, and with wondering awe adore Him in His creation?

Ah, no! Father in Heaven, Thou wilt not, Thou canst not do this! Thou canst not, Thou wilt not abandon the spirits whom Thou hast created, when they have but just attained the consciousness of Thy existence and of their own! Thou wert their God before they existed; Thou art their God as long as they dwell in this world; and Thou wilt be their God when they enter into the higher existence which Thou hast prepared for them from the beginning of the world! With rapture, with a presentiment of unutterable joy, I think of the hereafter, where I shall find thee, my God, and where I shall again meet all the dear ones whom thou didst bestow on me here on earth! Ah! what a moment that will be, when I shall feel myself transferred to heaven! What bliss to be re-united with all the loved ones, whom Thou, O Father, hast bound to me by the ties of affection! With lips tremulous with joy, I shall one day utter the prayer, "Father, into Thy hands I commend my spirit." Amen.

THE THOUGHT OF ETERNITY.

> Oh, hope of Immortality,
> Let all my soul be filled with thee,—
>   Teach me the ways of holiness,
>   And when I fail, sustain and bless.
> Oh, God-like gift—by God designed—
> Thee do I ever bear in mind—
>   Why should sad thoughts my heart oppress?
>
> And when to full perfection brought,
>   Then shall I see and know aright
> God's mercy, passing human thought.
>   Rejoicing, shall I bless the sight.
> From doubts which made me tremble here,
> The shadowing veil shall disappear,
>   And all be glory and delight.
>
> (1 *Tim.* vi. 12.)

PERHAPS there is not one of the many sacred subjects of reflection presented to the mind by the religion of Jesus Christ, which so strongly rivets the attention as the doctrine and hope of the immortality of the soul. For the love of life, and the desire for its continuance, is deeply implanted in the human breast. However full of tribulation this earthly life may be, mortal man does not willingly yield it up. However loudly the pious hypocrite may proclaim this lovely world of God's to be a land of misery and a vale of tears, he does not the less desire to abide in it, and he recoils with a shudder from that death, which he so often extols as his deliverer from the wretchedness of this life. Up to the moment when they breathe their last sigh the dying still hope to live; this hope often accompanies the criminal to the very steps of the scaffold, and solaces the condemned in his dark prison cell.

It is this love of life that inspires all mortals with a secret horror of death, which at the same time fills them with faith in the continued existence of their soul after the dissolution of the body. In this love, by which the wisdom of the Creator has bound us as with almost indissoluble ties to life here on earth, He has also revealed to our minds their sublime destination. All peoples, when once awakened from the stupor of mere animal life, embrace with ardour the idea of a life beyond the grave. All religions, even those of savage tribes, teach that the soul enters into a state of bliss, or appears before the judgment-seat, in a future life. But the Christian has a more confident hope than others. He has, in addition to the revelation of God through human reason, the revelation of God through His Son Jesus Christ. In like manner as Jesus conquered death, so shall we also conquer death, and change the perishable for the imperishable.

Even the most frivolous mind cannot laugh away the thought of eternity. Even the most lukewarm Christian, who lives in this world as though he were to dwell in it for ever, cannot always escape from thoughts of the grave. Even the reprobate who, abandoned to his own passions, follies, and vices, exerts all his wits, and brings forth every possible argument, to disprove the existence of an avenging God in the universe, and to throw discredit on the belief in the immortality of that part of his own being that thinks, and wills, and works so wonderfully in the body—even he is sometimes involuntarily, in the midst of his dissipation, compelled to think of God and eternity. The thought forces itself upon him as an indestructible and eternal truth. He thinks and shudders. "The devils also believe and tremble!" says St. James (ii. 19).

There are three testimonies in favour of the truth that man was not created for this short life alone, and that he belongs not only to earth, but also to a higher existence—the world of spirits, which no frivolity, no wit, no power of argument, can destroy. And these testimonies, which are found among all nations of the world, are: the universal belief in a God, the universal presence of a conscience, or an inward judge in man, and the universal faith in eternity. These intuitive ideas are indeed the educators and the preservers of the human race.

In truth, what would the world be without these three great ideas? Where would be the power capable of curbing and taming man, in the frenzy of passion the most destructive of animals, were these three great ideas to vanish from the world? Picture to yourself the human race, with its wild, all-consuming desires, left to itself, without faith in God, without the feeling of right and wrong, and without the conception of a continued existence after death. What safety would there be for life or property? Would an oath be respected? Would law have power to bind? Would an army inspire fear? Would innocence be held sacred? Would tears have power to move? No; all the horrors of hell would be perpetrated under the heavens. Violence, cunning, and cruelty would reign supreme. Assassination would precipitate ruler and subject alike into the grave. The earth would soon be converted into a depopulated waste, similar to what it was before it was trodden by the foot of man.

If the thought of eternity can produce so powerful, so magical an effect, even on the savage, what influence must it not exercise over the Christian, who, having received the revelation of Jesus, and being admitted into His kingdom, has little to hope on earth, but everything to look forward to in eternity? What must it be to the Christian who can say with Christ, My kingdom is not of this world, and not on this earth is my home, but in the eternal dwelling-place of God, in the high heavens, in my Father's house?

And yet (who can deny it?) even in pious Christians the thought of death and of the state of the soul in the future life does not always awaken such feelings as might be expected. Sometimes it depresses the mind too much; sometimes it gives rise to an exaggerated contempt for this earthly existence; sometimes it degenerates into fruitless meditations upon, and inquiries into, the probable condition of the soul after death, and leads to all kinds of delusions; sometimes it embitters our best joys on earth.

Such ought not to be the effects of the thought of eternity. In what manner, then, ought my mind to be occupied with the subject? What effect ought it to produce upon me?

To every Christian the thought of eternity should be as an intimate friend, whose presence is not irksome, however frequently he may visit him, and whose unexpected re-appearance, after long absence, would cause no surprise.

But if it is to be this we must in reality first endeavour to make ourselves quite familiar with it. We must be intimately acquainted with it. We must know what we have to fear or to hope from it. Only an intimate friend is received with a smiling welcome, whether he come often or come seldom.

It is the Christian's duty, therefore, to make the thought of the future life his constant companion, and never to repel it when it approaches. It will never be to him other than a reminder of the eternal, unalterable destination, to which each hour that passes, each step we take, draws us so much nearer.

Besides, we find the thought so frequently in our path, that to evade it is almost impossible. A fresh grave-mound in the churchyard, or a withered flower; the news of a battle in which thousands have fallen, or of the illness of an acquaintance; the walk we take to brace our exhausted system, or our nightly retiring to sleep; the house in which we live, and in which others have died; or the remembrance of parents, husband or wife, children, sisters and brothers, or friends who have gone before us—all these must ever be leading to the thought of the mysterious future beyond the grave.

Well, then, as the thought cannot remain a stranger to us, let us make a familiar friend of it; let us endeavour to correct our ideas of eternity; let us endeavour clearly to define what it will be to us, and in what relation we stand to it.

Not that we ought to allow ourselves to indulge in useless speculations as to the nature of the future life, and the exact conditions to which our souls will there be subject. It is not necessary to do this in order to become familiar with the thought of eternity. Such inquiries can only end in making the wise man feel the limits beyond which humanity cannot reach, the bounds which his reason cannot overstep; while the unwise will be led by them into mental delusions, into groundless suppositions, and be encouraged in visionary tendencies, which may be dangerous to the peace of weak minds, and which, in all cases, must exercise an injurious influence on thought and action, and also on physical health.

Millions of men have dwelt on the mysteries of the future life before thee, O mortal! without succeeding in solving them. For the veil which the hand of God has drawn before that future, is impenetrable. And no ponderings of thine will enable thee to lift it, until God calls thee. Desist, therefore, from senseless attempts to throw light upon the nature of the soul in eternity, upon its local habitation after leaving the body, upon its occupations in the other life. Heed not either the spoken or the written words of those who have woven for themselves a web of visionary delusions regarding these matters which are hidden from human ken; and who, in their foolish presumption, have sometimes even gone so far as to attempt to prove the correctness of their views from the Holy Scriptures. Alas! how can they hope to penetrate the mysteries of eternal life, whose weak mental sight does not even suffice to comprehend the wonderful things of this world, to fathom the mysterious laws of creation, which they behold in action before their eyes each day of their life! How dare they deem themselves wiser than the All-wise, who has, not without good reason, enveloped the future in this beneficent darkness! How dare they venture to measure their strength against the strength of the Lord, whose hand has drawn the curtain before the wonders of eternity!

To become familiar with the thought of eternity, means, to remind ourselves as often as an opportunity occurs, that we are born into everlasting life; that God's inexhaustible fatherly love is infinite, like the existence of our souls; that the hand which has already bestowed on us here on earth so many joys and exquisite gratifications, will not be less generous of its gifts when we have rendered ourselves worthy and capable of still higher enjoyments; that the mercy of the almighty and all-loving Creator, which has from the beginning of time ruled over the measureless universe, and which has also called our souls from nothingness into being, will continue so to rule through all eternity; that if we have firm and unwavering faith in Him, any fate that may befall us, and thus also the change in death, must be for our good, but that we can only feel secure of a happier lot beyond the hour of death when we have fitted ourselves for it; that the only way to make ourselves worthy of it is by growing in goodness during this life, according to the example of the Divine Jesus; that as on earth our happiness increases with our growth in wisdom and virtue, so also will unutterable bliss be our reward in eternity; that by neglecting our souls in this life, and only satisfying those instincts and desires which belong to the body, we condemn ourselves to imperfection and to a grievous and terrible fate after death; that he who neglects his soul here on earth, were he even to gain the whole world, will be the poorest in the world of spirits, where only spiritual treasures, not earthly glories, have any value.

This is what the Holy Scriptures teach us. This is what Jesus, the Saviour, the Judge of the world, teaches, when He says, "And shall come forth ; they that have done good, unto the resurrection of life; and they that have done evil, unto the resurrection of damnation." (St. John v. 29.) "Therefore, my beloved brethren, be ye stedfast, unmoveable, always abounding in the work of the Lord, forasmuch as ye know that your labour is not in vain in the Lord." (1 Cor. xv. 58.)

If we join these considerations to the thought of eternity, it will never occur to us without recalling the necessity of improving our minds and dispositions. Each time our thoughts dwell upon the solemn future, will come the question : " But have I done anything to merit a more glorious existence on the other side of the grave ? Has my soul sanctified itself through Jesus, so that I may look forward joyfully to the lot that awaits me there ?"

For to think of the eternal life hereafter, without at the same time determining to qualify ourselves for it, would be but self-delusion, dead faith. But when it stimulates us to goodness and noble action in this world, it is an angel that leads us on in the ways of Jesus, in the ways of the Lord ; and as we progress in amendment and perfection, it will gradually become more and more to us a thought full of quiet satisfaction, of heavenly calm.

It will then never awaken in us without calling forth also thoughts of the beloved souls with whom we held intercourse on earth, and who have gone before us. We shall then never think of eternity without a rapturous thrill at the remembrance of some departed friend who died in youth, or of parents or children, or of a beloved spouse, or of sisters and brothers. Ah! will the highest, the infinite Love; will God, who is love—God, who united our souls so intimately here on earth—will He part us yonder? Will He sever souls whom He has created for each other, will He separate them in Heaven, where " God shall wipe away all tears from their eyes; and there shall be no more death, neither sorrow, nor crying, neither shall there be any more pain?" (Rev. xxi. 4.)

The thought of eternity will never awaken in us without reminding us of our higher destination. We cannot meditate on our future existence without at the same time thinking of how fleeting and perishable is everything here below. We shall thus be led to contemplate with composure that which previously caused us poignant grief, and to feel more strongly than before that it is folly to give ourselves up to never-ending regret for things which were not given, but only lent to us. For all that we possess, earn, or enjoy on earth, does not belong to us, but to the earth. We are only allowed temporary use thereof. Nothing but the increased perfection of the spirit, to reach which all that we have enjoyed on earth was lent us as a means—nothing but this perfection, this innate nobility of the spirit, can save the spirit, because, as part and parcel of its being, it can never be separated from it, and because it belongs not to the minute points in time and space which we call life and earth, but to eternity.

But though the thought of eternity does and ought to awaken in us the consciousness of the nothingness of life, it ought not to render us indifferent to the beauties and attractions of our present existence. It ought not to fill us with melancholy and sadness, or with contempt of the world; but, on the contrary, to encourage us to a wise and cheerful enjoyment of the blessings that God in His goodness has bestowed upon us. Why, indeed, should we despise a life which we have received from the hand of a loving Creator? Why should we contemn a world which God has created and adorned with countless wonders? Would it not be very blameworthy if the child, impatient to become wise and learned, were to disdain the school in which alone knowledge could be acquired? What inconsistency! you exclaim. But we fall into an equally striking inconsistency when we disdain or fear to enjoy the pleasures of this life, because of our expectations of still greater joys, which God will one day bestow.

O man! small, insignificant plant as thou art, put forth thy buds first, and develop thy leaves and branches, if thou wouldst in time stand forth a perfect tree.

Nay, the thought of eternity does not forbid our enjoying this world and all the good that it brings, but is, on the contrary, calculated to encourage such enjoyment. Instead of repelling us from this life, it ought to bind us closer to it. For here we are to prepare for the future; here on earth, amid happiness and unhappiness, amid flowers and thorns, is the school in which we are to be formed for eternity. How deplorable is the cowardice or the insanity of the self-murderer, who, troubled by earthly cares, with presumptuous hand bursts asunder the bonds which bind him to this life, in the hope that he will meet a happier lot in the other world! Who appointed his lot here below? If he prepared it for himself by his own misdeeds, then how can he hope to be in the next existence a higher, better, more perfect being than he was in this? Or if God sent him misfortunes to try him, why does he withdraw from the guidance of his wise Creator and Father? Does he think that his wilfulness, his pusillanimity, will work a change in the eternal councils of the Allwise? Does he think that he can escape from God and His Divine guardianship?

In full reliance on the guiding hand of his Heavenly Father, and with unalterable faith in the immortality of the spirit, as it has been revealed to all men, the Christian will endeavour to apply to the elevation and purification of his soul whatever may befall him here on earth—whether he gain for himself friends, honours, riches, or meet with hatred, poverty, and shame. He will love this earth as the school in which he is preparing to take his place in a higher rank. He will contemplate without fear the termination of life's journey.

"So when this corruptible shall have put on incorruption, and this mortal shall have put on immortality, then shall be brought to pass the saying that is written: Death is swallowed up in Victory. O death! where is thy sting? O grave! where is thy victory? But thanks be to God, who giveth us the victory through our Lord Jesus!"

When once my spirit, freed from dust,
Shall to my Saviour whom I trust—
  To Thee, my own Messiah—fly,
When once, oh, mother earth! this shell,
In which the immortal soul doth dwell,
  Within thy parent lap shall lie—

What, then, is mine ? What bliss unbounded!
With what bright world am I surrounded?
  What am I ? say, what shall I be ?
What streams of rapture through me flow.
Is't I ? are these my limbs that glow?
  This Godlike splendour, is't for me ?
I am transformed, released from dust—
  Whose throne is there ? Who calls me now ?
Ah ! it is God, in whom I trust—
  Oh, my Messiah, it is Thou !

Oh, Lord, Thy truth, it faileth never.
For life renewed I thank thee ever.
  I shall not to Thy judgment come—
My foe subdued, in chains doth lie—
Death's swallowed up in victory.
  And I, I rest not in the tomb.
Hail, Lord ! All honour, might, are Thine.
  Saviour ! from Thee my life doth spring !
The Angelic choir I haste to join,
  And loudest Hallelujahs sing.

INTERPRETATIONS OF ETERNITY.

FIRST MEDITATION.

GOING IN TO THE FATHER.

> A house of clay Thou buildest me,
>   Wherein my thoughts to treasure,
> And with Thy grace, my God, and Thee,
>   To fill my faltering measure;
> And as I better know Thy ways,
> To exercise my heart in praise,
> And by Thy Spirit led, to prove
> A deeper, and yet deeper love.
>
> Never to die—oh, ne'er to die!
> My heart shall scorn and doubt defy
> To rob it of its glorious faith
> In a new life, surviving death.
> Say I should die—unto Thy side
> Thou, God, wilt be my faithful Guide;
> My soul triumphant sounds the strain—
> Death is not loss—but endless gain.
>
> *(John* xiv. 28.)

ORDINARY people are loth to think of death, and yet there are so many things that remind them of it! They hear deceased persons spoken of, or meet a funeral procession, or learn that an acquaintance has been called away from this world, or their thoughts revert to persons they have loved, whose ashes are reposing in the earth; and in each case there is that which must remind them that no exception to the general laws of nature can be made in their favour. The man who never thinks of the hour of death without a shudder, sleeps away as gently as he who has been longing for dissolution. And yet ordinary people are loth to think of death and the grave. This is very natural. Even were the innate love of life not so intense as it is in every mortal, it would not be surprising that he should recoil from thoughts of death, as they are opposed to everything that is most delightful in life. Death puts an end to our hopes, destroys our favourite plans and projects, cuts us off from our most cherished habits, and with unbending and irresistible power separates us from parents, children, and friends. Alas! it has already torn from us many of life's best jewels.

"And if this be so, why should we, by frequent thoughts of death and the grave, mar the few pleasures we have in life? Let us enjoy while we can, without foolishly embittering our own lot."

Thus say many. Nay, there are many who reproach the Christian religion with being gloomy and austere, because it is ever reminding its followers of the nothingness of life, and of death and judgment.

But, in truth, he who cannot think cheerfully of death has probably never thought cheerfully and rationally of life. To those to whom death is a mysterious, and therefore repugnant image, life itself can be little more than a confused riddle; for they cannot, as yet, have any clear conception of the purpose of their existence. The question as to our being or not being rational creatures, does not so much depend upon what it is pleasant to us to think, as upon what we are by our nature *compelled* to think. But it is religion that solves the enigma of life, and thereby gives us the key to the mystery of death. So far is true Christianity from depressing the spirits and rendering men morose, that, on the contrary, by the views of death which it inculcates, it elevates its wise followers above every grief, and above every fear, and enables them to enjoy the manifold pleasures of life with imperturbable composure, whether their last hour be nigh at hand or far off. If the religion of Jesus in reality do this, what is there to find fault with? Why should we avoid thoughts which will, in spite of all our endeavours, force themselves upon us? There is not a human being who has not sustained some loss in the course of his life; how will he avoid being reminded of this? It is life itself, it is our hearts, that recall to us our painful losses; but it is religion that consoles us, and reconciles us to them, by the exalted views which it imparts of the Divine universe and the Divine mode of action.

Which of your dear ones do you already count among the dead? Perhaps a father who was your guardian angel on earth? Perhaps a mother, who loved you above all others? Perhaps a brother, who walked by your side full of youthful hopes? Perhaps a sister, for whom you felt as if she were your second self? Or if you be father or mother, poor mourners, perhaps it is a child, the sweetest blossom and hope of your lives? Or is it a noble-minded husband, or a gentle, faithful, loving wife? Which of these cherished ones is it that you count among the departed? Whichever it may be, is the memory of this lost one not dear to you, since you shudder at the thought of death when it steals upon you in tranquil hours? Your heart bled at your painful loss, and the wound is not yet healed. Alas! there are wounds that never heal in this life. It is a mistake to think that time cures all wounds. But for those that it cannot cure, the religion of Jesus Christ has a soothing balm.

It is possible that, in some quiet hour of enjoyment, the thought of death and corruption may suddenly fill you with a sensation of horror, and that every fibre of your body may, as it were, revolt against dissolution. Nay, so overwhelmed may you be by the terrible thought, that it may seem to you better that you should never have received life, than to be obliged to yield it up again. But these painful feelings are not caused by the melancholy views inspired by religion, but by your own innate love of life. Christianity, on the contrary, chases away all fear of death, by allowing us to cast a glance into a future beyond the grave, where life, activity, and joy prevail, as they do here.

Do you think that the Saviour, the Light of the world, came in vain to reassure us as to our immortality, and our ultimate destiny? And how does He describe death? He who had more terrible experience of its horrors than any mortal, doomed as He was to die in the full prime of His strength and years, in the possession of unimpaired health, with the consciousness of spotless innocence, and to die the death of a criminal? He called it *going in to the Father!*

And with Him every Christian says, with truth, to die is to go in to the Father, for Jesus' Father is also our Father. The Creator of the Seraphim, as of the lowliest zoophyte, is also our Creator.

What a cheerful conception is not that of our departure from this earth as a going in to the Father!

We ought at all times to speak of our own and our friends' demise in these terms; then death, which the excited imagination of timid men has presented to us under the form of a hideous skeleton, would appear as a friendly spirit, come to help us across the boundaries of life, and to usher us into the Father's presence. In reality, many of the terrors with which death is invested, and of the false notions concerning it which prevail, originate in the erroneous and revolting designations which have been given to it. Thus, sometimes it is called decay and corruption; but we do not decay, nor are we given up to corruption. At other times, to die is to leave the world; but we never leave the world, because this is in itself impossible. At other times, again, death is termed destruction; but we cannot be destroyed. No; to die is to go in to the Father; our souls merely cast off their unsuitable garments to clothe themselves in worthier raiment.

The shudder caused by the images in which we speak of death, is owing to their being borrowed from the condition of the soulless body, and their being consequently false. Every other false conception is in like manner repugnant to us, because of its being at variance with the laws of reason, while imagination endeavours in vain to make that which is unreasonable conceivable.

The condition of the corpse in the grave is not our condition, but merely that of the covering which we have cast off. When we cut our hair with a pair of scissors, is that which is taken off, and which is thrown away, part of ourselves? Nay, how little does this separation affect us! When the warrior loses a limb in battle, and sees it consigned to the earth, does he feel that the condition of this limb forms part of his own state? Nay, the limb decays, but he feels it not. He stills exists, and is conscious of being something quite distinct from that which is capable of corruption.

And what is our earthly coil to us? It is but the worn-out or damaged raiment of the immortal spirit. Why do we not shudder every day of our lives at the decay of our bodies, for, in truth, they do decay daily? According to the observations of profound thinkers and physicians, the body of a man undergoes a total change several times in the course of a moderately long life, so that as youths and maidens we no longer bear the same body, the same flesh and blood, as in childhood; and in old age, again, the body is almost entirely a different one from that possessed in manhood. But we are not aware of these transformations, because they take place through means of imperceptible, natural processes. Is it, then, reasonable to conclude that the final transformation, whereby we are entirely separated from the coarse earthly covering that invests us here, will be perceptible to ourselves? Has any one ever been able to observe, as regards himself, the gentle merging of the waking state into sleep? How many persons have not died with such full consciousness that death was approaching, that they have seemed narrowly to observe themselves during the wonderful transition. There are even instances of their having been able to prognosticate —we know not by what means—the precise moment of their dissolution, and their prognostications have been pretty exactly borne out by the event. But were any of these persons, who so calmly departed, ever known to show signs of pain or aversion while the gradual withdrawal of the soul from the body was taking place? Indeed, even those who have departed amid sufferings caused by the disturbance of the inward functions of the body, ceased to experience pain when the sweet moment of the final disseverance drew nigh.

Away, then, with all repugnant images of death, borrowed from the empty, cast-off garment of the soul, which is resolved again into dust and ashes. This garment is not our real self. Our real self is immortal. All nature, as well as the revelations which we have received through Jesus, whom the Father sent, and who returned to the Father, teaches us this. Without this faith—which is, indeed, more than faith, for it is a beautiful and deep-seated sentiment of the soul, a law of the spirit—God would not be God, the world would be no world, reason would not be reason, and all our thinking and planning would be but the idle dreams of madness.

Before the early inhabitants of the world—then so much nearer the first days of creation than now—knew how to build cities, to manufacture weapons, and to weave clothes for themselves, they were already familiar with the idea of the existence of a supreme, almighty, and beneficent Being, and had the consciousness of their own immortality. And thousands and thousands of years will still pass over this terrestrial globe; every spot on its surface will be changed; where now are deserts, mighty cities may rise in their pride; and cities, in which kings and emperors are now enthroned in pomp and splendour, may be converted into deserts, in which hardly a ruin survives to tell of what has been. But the consciousness of their own immortality, and of the existence of God, is as little likely to change in the generations of men, as the laws of nature, by which the universe is sustained, are likely to be destroyed. If there have at any time been mortals who have doubted, or who have even denied, the immortality of their own souls, such persons have always been looked upon as diseased in mind, or as making a false use of their mental powers by giving themselves up to insane speculations.

Some philosophers have attempted to demonstrate the inextinguishable belief of man in the continuance of his own existence, by words and arguments, in the same manner as self-created conceptions and calculations are demonstrated. But immortality is not a self-created conception, an idea invented by man, as it were, but a blooming forth, or a development of the thinking being; and we can as little prove it in words, as we can prove that we have the consciousness of our present existence. It is enough that we *are*, and that we have the consciousness of our being. Through this consciousness alone is every other idea rendered possible.

But, in reality, men are much less anxious to discover so-called proofs of their immortality (which are, after all, superfluous because of their intuitive belief in it), than they are to ascertain of what nature will be the existence of the spirit hereafter; what will be its fate and its feelings after the separation from the body; what may be that which we call Eternity.

Human curiosity loves to hover round the mysteries of the future state of the soul, and many dreamy visions have been indulged in concerning life hereafter. This curiosity is natural and pardonable. It has its source in our innate love of life, and our consciousness of immortality. But we ought never to forget, that as human creatures, who have but five very imperfect senses, through means of which we can acquire knowledge of the universe, we occupy as yet a very low place in the infinite scale of beings; and that, therefore, it is as impossible for us to form a conception of what our spirit will be, and will know, when placed amid totally different circumstances, as it is for a man born blind to conceive what he would be, and would see, were a new sense—*i.e.*, sight—to be vouchsafed to him, and all the influences of the universe were in consequence to rush in upon him through a hitherto unknown portal of the mind. We must not forget that just as impossible as it is for the human spirit, here on earth, to know itself and its essence, just as impossible is it that it should be able to know what, according to the nature of its essence, it will be when the dark veil is raised which covered it here on earth in the form of a body.

We have received revelations through Jesus whom God sent to the human race, and these revelations are expressed in terms adapted to the powers of comprehension possessed by man. Without being a disembodied spirit already dwelling in Eternity, it is impossible to form correct conceptions of that which lies beyond the hour of transformation. Jesus, however, spoke of death as *a going in to the Father, a union with the Deity.* He gave us the assurance of meeting again in eternity. He promised to the more perfect spirits unutterable bliss, and to sinners stern and just retribution.

Ah! this must suffice for us; it is enough to know God's Omnipotence and Almighty Love on earth, and in this to feel full assurance as to the future, and even heavenly rapture. For this love, so almighty already here on earth, and so clearly manifested each day that passes over us; this love, revealed to us by Jesus, and also by nature, will it cease when the breath and the blood in our bodies cease their action? Would that be a love worthy of the Eternal Being, the Universal Father, towards His creatures, which should be discontinued after the lapse of a few brief moments? No; God, whom I am forced to conceive as Infinite Perfection, whom I worship as such in the smallest as in the greatest of His creations—God is as undeniably an eternal, loving, watchful Father, ever bestowing happiness on His children, as He is in Himself eternal, and as I am a creation of His love: and in our Father's house there are many mansions.

But to what He has called me, whither He will one day transport me, what I shall then be—that I shall never fathom here on earth. But in like manner as we perceive (I can hardly say understand) here on earth already the Majesty of the Loving and Almighty One in His wonderful works, so, also, we can form a vague conception of the future in the present. In the universe, as we perceive it now, we see a reflection of the glory of which we shall once be partakers. In time, we find indications of eternity. The more we study the creations of the Father of the universe as they appear to us on this side the grave, the greater number of signs of eternity do we discover, the greater number of foreshadowings of what the creations of the Lord after death may be.

He who knows God can feel no alarm at the thought of the hour of departure from this earthly existence. And the more we convince ourselves through the study of His works, of the wisdom, the power, and the love of the Father—of how imperishable, how conformable to their end, how perfectly organized, are all His creations, the more inwardly assured we shall feel that His unalterable wisdom, power, and love, diffused throughout the immeasurable universe, will at all times and in all places encompass our spirits, and that wherever they be, they will be of His blessed Kingdom.

He who knows the world, the illimitable, eternal world, does not feel alarm at the departure from this earth, which is but as a grain of sand when compared to the infinite universe. But he has but a very feeble conception of the greatness of God, who believes this earth which we inhabit to be the centre of His glorious creation, round which revolve all the suns and the planets of the universe. Alas! the observations of astronomers make it more than probable, that we and our earth, far from being in the centre of the universe, are placed in the outer circle of innumerable world-systems; and that hence it is, that whereas the rest of creation appears to us in all its sublime regularity and order, the starry heavens, on the contrary, present to our eyes an appearance of confusion—the innumerable worlds, that beam upon us as distant stars, being thinly scattered over the expanse in one direction, and in another densely crowded together. If the star which we inhabit occupied a more elevated or a more depressed position in the choir of glorious spheres, the spectacle presented by the star-bespangled heavens would probably exhibit to our eyes the same wonderful regularity and order that strike us in the rest of creation. Thus, to a person placed in an unfavourable position on the outside of a regularly planted grove, the trees may seem placed without any attention to order or system, and may appear to him to form a confused labyrinth; whereas, if placed in the centre, or any other favourable point of observation, he will instantly perceive the beautiful regularity of the plantations.

He who has any knowledge of the universe, knows that in the great totality of things there is not an atom that does not endure for ever—that the whole is but a wide-spread realm of the most manifold forces. These forces endure, though the phenomena under which they present themselves change. The human spirit is a force in this sense. Its effects, *i.e.*, its thoughts, its wishes, its utterances, change and are perishable; but the spirit itself does not perish with the words it utters. Light is not diminished by the rays emitted by it. It is said that flowers are evanescent, and they are so, because they are but phenomena of eternally present original forces. But though the flowers vanish, the forces, which represent their elementary principle, do not cease to exist in the universe.

And there is one great all-pervading law which I recognize in the universe of God. It is this: *everything is resolved into elements similar to itself.* Water sends up vapours which gather into clouds in the skies; and these fall again as dew and rain, and again form bodies of water. Flowers, animals, the human body, all these having sprung from the earth, and having been nourished with earthly substances, in time return to earth.

Now, just as the unconscious forces or substances, after going through a variety of combinations, return to their original families, so will the self-conscious forces, the rational beings, the spirits who conceive God, return again to their original spiritual family. According to the all-pervading law of God in nature, my body will in death return to earth, but my spirit will soar up to its original home. Is not this universal law of nature a sign from Eternity? Have I understood it correctly? Have I understood rightly what Thou didst mean, O Jesus, my Divine Enlightener, when speaking to Thy beloved disciples of thy approaching death, and endeavouring to prepare them for the heavy trial, Thou saidst: "If ye loved me, ye would rejoice that I have said I go to the Father; for the Father is greater than I!"

Oh! when my time comes and the angel of peace from the better world, whom we call death, kisses me and bears me away from earth, then do not weep, O my beloved ones! for I also shall then have gone in to my Father! Weep not for my cast-off earthly coil, for I also shall have rejoined my original family in my true home, in the beautiful world of blessed, self-conscious spirits. I shall have gone home to the beloved ones, the eternally beloved, the never-forgotten ones, whom I had lost here below, and for whom I so often pined. Weep not, for ye have no reason to weep, as little as I had to grieve for those who went in to glory before me. Yonder are all those to whom my heart cleaved, the costliest jewels of my life; yonder are those to whom the Father bound me by ties of unalterable love; yonder is Jesus, and yonder is God, to whom I come through Jesus! Weep not! to you also will come the happy moment when you shall go in to the Father! Round the lips of your corpse also will hover, to the consolation of those you leave behind, the smile of joyful trust with which you have hastened into the better world! Not here, but yonder, is our home, our true life! Blessed are you and I, for there is no death, only a going in to the Father!

INTERPRETATIONS OF ETERNITY.

SECOND MEDITATION.

THE FUTURE LIFE.

> Father! my heart exults itself in this:
>   That Thou hast not created me for naught!
> Such happiness is mine—with so much bliss
>   Even this transient dream of life is fraught—
> How little is it that mine eyes can see
> Here, oh, my God! or understand of Thee,
> Yet e'en that little is great joy to me.
>
> My life may vanish from this earthly sphere
>   More swiftly than an idle dream of night—
> I know I am immortal—and that *there*
>   Mine eyes shall ope more clearly to the light.
> Thee shall I see, my Father, as Thou art;
> And there my joy, which now is but in part,
> Endless and perfected, shall fill my heart.
>
> (Matthew xxii. 29, 30.)

THE consciousness of the immortality of the soul dates from the beginning of the human race. Therefore, this conviction is found to exist even among the most savage tribes in the most distant countries, whither no ray of revealed religion, or of western or eastern enlightenment, has ever penetrated. Thus, from the beginning of creation, there has been but *one* voice, *one* hope, *one* aspiration, in regard to eternity. And it was the Deity Himself who, in creating self-conscious spirits, implanted in them this intuitive faith. Now, the infinite perfection of God cannot impart delusions. And why should it impart delusions, when it holds in its hand the unbounded realm of realities?

But though perfect agreement exist throughout the human race as to the belief that the higher, self-conscious power that animates the body does not cease to exist when the animal or corporeal life becomes extinct, the notions formed by the nations of the world as to the nature of the future life vary much. For these notions naturally differ according to the degree of mental development, and the amount of experience and of knowledge of God's works possessed by men at various periods and in different parts of the globe. Thus, for instance, in early times, before voyages round the world and scientific observation had proved that our earth is a globe, floating freely in space, and revolving daily on its own axis, and yearly round the sun, it was believed that the dwelling-place of the condemned souls was situated under the earth, and that there they were tortured by means of the flames which were sometimes seen to issue from volcanoes. In the present day every child in our schools knows, that our earth is surrounded on all sides by the heavens, and that it is only one of the smaller bodies which move in regular orbits through infinite space. Before men were enabled by means of the telescope, to determine the magnitudes, distances, and orbits of the stars nearest to our globe, all the celestial lights were believed to be equally distant from us, and beyond these were located the abodes of the blessed, where they were supposed to revel in joys and occupations as sensual as those on earth. In the present day, every child at school also knows that each star is a world, and that the universe is an infinity of worlds.

Every people and every religious sect have thus had notions of their own as to the abodes of the blessed and of the lost spirits, just as at all times the child and the sage entertain very different views of one and the same object.

When Jesus Christ first appeared among the Jewish people and began to teach, He found the professors of the Mosaic religion divided into several sects. For instance, the Essenes, who led a very strict and secluded life, and ascribed the greatest importance to pious actions and abstinence from all sensual gratifications; the Pharisees, who, on the contrary, placed great value on outward religious ceremonies and exacted the most rigid observance of the doctrines and rules laid down by Moses, or handed down by tradition, and who were held in highest estimation among the people; and the Sadducees, who rejected all oral tradition, and denied many of the doctrines taught by the Pharisees, among others, that of the resurrection of the dead. One day, when conversing with Jesus, the Sadducees, either with a view to satisfy their own doubts, or in the hope of confounding Him, supposed certain earthly and social relations to be carried over into the future life, and then put questions regarding them, and expressed the misgivings of their minds on the subject. If a woman marry seven men in this life, whose wife shall she be in eternity? asked they. "Jesus answered and said unto them, Ye do err, not knowing the Scriptures, nor the power of God. For in the resurrection they neither marry, nor are given in marriage, but are as the angels of God in Heaven." (Matt. xxii. 29, 30.)

Similar to these doubts of the Sadducees are the strange reasons which people deduce from every-day life, and with which they disturb their own minds in regard to the condition of the soul after death. The hand which can feel, but cannot hear, might be inclined to deny the rolling of the thunder, because it could not form a conception of it; yet the ear hears the thunder and knows that it exists.

Thus many persons ask, Shall we retain consciousness and memory when we change our body? For if not, though our spirit may continue to exist, this continued existence, without consciousness or memory of the past, will be tantamount to a life as new as if it were then for the first time introduced into the world, and death must in consequence be looked upon as a kind of annihilation.

These doubts, like those of the Sadducees, arise out of the circumstances and events of this earthly life. Comparison is made between the state of the soul after death and its condition during sleep or syncope, when it is unconscious of, or does not remember, what has been done to the body. And this is sufficient to cause uneasiness.

O ye of little faith, let me repeat to you Jesus' words, "Ye do err, not knowing the Scriptures, nor the power of God!"

Can we, with any show of reason, make comparisons between things quite dissimilar, or even diametrically opposed to each other? Or between things, one of which we only know partially, and the other of which we know not at all? Between the spirit still held in earthly bonds, and the self-dependent spirit emancipated from these? How the spirit acts on the body we know only in part; how it will appear when in the enjoyment of full freedom, and unfettered by the dust which now clings to it, we know not at all.

Sleep and syncope are therefore poor comparisons as regards the condition of the soul after its separation from the body. It is true we know nothing of what happens to us during sleep or syncope, and we remember naught of what has taken place. This is not, however, owing to the spirit having ceased to exist during the interval, but to the senses having become incapable of receiving outward impressions, and of providing for the thinking power. When we close our eyes, we do not see, but the spirit nevertheless continues its inward life and activity. When sleep or syncope close all the senses, so that no impressions can be conveyed through them, the spirit is not the less alive and active, although it knows naught of what is going on without, in the world of sense. What surprising and wonderful evidence of this is not afforded by so-called sleep-walkers! Or has it not happened to all of us, at one time or another, to awaken out of a deep sleep without having any recollection whatsoever of having dreamt (although our souls must have been active during the interval), because the lively impressions received from without on awaking have thrown back the images of the dream into the shade, until suddenly they are recalled to our mind, and we become convinced that we have had ideas even in sleep?

Thus the soul of the dying man likewise continues to live and to be active; but as his senses are gradually closing, he also becomes unconscious of what is going on in the outer world. The spirit of the dying man does not perceive death because its own life continues as before. It knows naught of the bed of death, of the sorrowing relatives who stand around it, for impressions from the outer world no longer come to it through the extinguished senses. But when the condition begins, in which, separated from the dust, from flesh and blood, and nerves, it lives in its self-dependent purity—then all points of comparison fail us. The force continues its activity, conscious of its being, and God indicates to it the new path it has to follow. The past and the present must be one to the glorified soul—for it saw not death, it remained as before, a self-conscious power. It enters into new combinations. It goes in to the Father. Its lot is, as the revealed word tells us—Glorification.

"Ye know not the power of God!" said Jesus to the sceptical Sadducees. What mortal, indeed, knows the majesty, the boundless nature of this power of God, which is everywhere present in the infinite universe? But so much do we know, that whatever God has ordained in His Kingdom is sublime, magnificent, wonderful, bliss-inspiring, and wise—in that realm there is nothing petty, nothing defective, nothing superfluous, nothing ignoble! And surely the entrance of the soul into the state of original purity, and emancipation from the fetters of earth, will not be less solemn than is, here below even, every impression received of the glory of the Father of the universe.

The emancipation of the soul from its frail earthly

shell is the triumph of the spiritual power over the dead forces of nature. No fine-spun arguments and interpretations will help us here : before the power of God our boldest fancies fail, and the most extensive knowledge seeks in vain the limits of His infinite might. Any picture we may form to ourselves of the state of the emancipated and glorified soul, cannot be otherwise than mean, foolish, derogatory, for it must be borrowed from things that are as little comparable to the glory of the Heavens as a drop of dew is to the wondrous ocean.

Ye know not the power of God; ye know not what career it has opened to the emancipated soul; ye know not in what new raiment this soul may possibly be veiled when it hastens towards Him, towards the Father; ye know not what new views of the universe may burst upon it at the moment of the great change in its condition. In like manner as a world inhabited exclusively by persons born blind, would have no language to express the varied beauties of colour and form, the brightness of the heavens, or the blue tints of distance, so do we lack the faculty to comprehend, and the means to describe, the phenomena of the future life. Indeed, our language and imagery in a great measure contribute to obscure that which might be clear to us even here on earth, and give us confused notions of that which is in itself perfectly simple. Thus the expressions "eternity," and "beyond the grave," are misunderstood by many. People frequently picture to themselves, in connexion with these terms, something quite separate from our time, and existing entirely by itself; something that is, as it were, to come. But eternity does not only belong to the future, it is already here. We are all living in eternity, for we live in God, and God is eternal. The short dream of our terrestrial life, this short section of eternal being, we call *time*. Time is, however, comprised in eternity, just as our globe is comprised in the infinite heavens. Earth and heaven, time and eternity, are one. We are already living in our Father's house here on earth; but we have not reached the higher grades of perfection, and are not yet there where the glory of God can appear to us in full effulgence. Thither we must be conducted by the angel of the better world, whom we call death.

We live, but our beloved ones who have died also live; we stand weeping on this globe floating in infinite space, but our glorified dear ones are, like ourselves, in God's world; we are here—but they are perhaps in an infinitely more beautiful world; we are limited by our bodies—they probably enjoy greater freedom and bliss. Now, what is it to die? It is generally said to be a passing into eternity; but here already we are dwelling in eternity. It is a transition from the finite earthly relations into a higher, more blissful, to us incomprehensible, state; it is a change into a new mansion of the Father of all; it is the exchange from a place in the cradle with a place on the bosom of the Father. How differently does not death now appear to us! It is not annihilation, but completion; not cessation, but continuation. The loved ones whose loss I lament are still in existence; they are living with me at this very time; they are, like myself, dwelling in the great paternal mansion of God; they still belong to me as I to them. We are not separated. No time lies between us; for I, like they, dwell in eternity, rest in the arms of God. As they are ever in my thoughts, so, perhaps, am I in theirs. As I mourn for their loss, perhaps they rejoice in anticipation of our re-union. What to me is still dark, they see clearly. Why do I grieve because I can no longer enjoy their society? During their lifetime I was not discontented because I could not always have them around me. If a journey took them from me, I was not therefore unhappy. And why is it different now? They have gone on a journey. Whether they are living on earth in a far distant city, or in some higher world in the infinite universe of God, what difference is there? Are we not still in the same house of the Father, like loving brothers who inhabit separate rooms? Have we therefore ceased to be brothers?

Ah! let us not weep for the dead; their blessed spirits can experience no pain. Perhaps they, being more exalted, more perfect than we, and possessing a clearer knowledge of the fatherly love of God, only feel a kind of tender compassion for our ignorance. Perhaps they were unwilling to die, but were torn from our arms against their desire. God willed it, and the change took place. In their glorified state, they bless the Fatherly Hand that guided them into the higher world, and the love which knew better than they did what was conducive to their happiness. Perhaps the past seems to them as a dream, the recollection of which was hardly worth retaining. The soul, the self-conscious element in the human body, may possibly, when parting from the unconscious earthly elements of that body, retain a remembrance of the past. We know too little of the nature of the spirit to deny this, but perhaps the recollections of its earthly existence are its most insignificant possessions. Here, on earth even, the present is of far more importance to us than our recollections of the past. Much of what we have experienced seems to us hardly worthy of a place in the memory, and we forget it. Many of our experiences indeed we would be glad to obliterate from our minds. The present moment is always the one most fraught with enjoyment, yet we are ever striving towards the future. Can we suppose it to be otherwise with the blessed spirits? Perhaps the memory of their former imperfect state would be humiliating and painful to them amid the lustre of their more perfect condition. If we, who are living at this moment upon the earth, had existed previously somewhere in the great universe, but in a very inferior condition, suppose in that of an animal; would not the memory of this our animal condition be humiliating and repugnant to us, after having attained the status of human beings? Would we regret having lost all knowledge of our former degraded state? And may not the condition of the higher beings be, in comparison to that of man, what ours is in comparison to that of the animals? One remembrance, however, there is, which remains dear to us mortals even at the most advanced age—that is, the remembrance of friends and persons to whom we have been devotedly attached. The old man still recollects with delight the companion of his youth, the friend with whom he passed many a happy hour. He may forget everything else, but objects of his affection he does not forget.

Love is one of the attributes which in some degree

assimilate mortals to the more perfect beings; and this attribute can never be lost, for it belongs to the nature of the spirit. God also loves, but in a far higher sense than we. The entire creation bears witness to this. It is true that the sexual instinct and habit seem to engender some feeling like love in animals also; but in them it is but transitory—it is a shadow that deludes us. But God, who loves infinitely more deeply and more purely than man—God, who has diffused the sentiment of love throughout creation, from its highest degree of perfection down to its almost imperceptible appearance in the mutual attractions of the plants—God who, through love, has bound His creatures to each other and to Himself—would He destroy this love, this divine power in the glorified soul, at the very moment that He called it into a more perfect existence? No; *that which is Divine is eternal!* Imperfect man cannot be more perfect than the higher spirits who stand nearer to the Father than we; and though we mortals may lose the recollection of many things, our love for the objects of our affection we carry with us to the grave. In like manner, though a thousand memories may be lost with the mouldering dust of the body, the memory of God, the memory of the creatures of God whom we love, must accompany the soul into the blessed regions. God did not create spirits, and endow them with a knowledge of Himself, in order to allow them to forget Him again after a brief space. He did not unite souls by the spiritual bonds of love, to separate them again for ever. That which the most cruel human being would recoil from, God, who has stamped the impress of His love on every marvel of the creation, cannot will to do. And therefore, the bond that united us in life, O my beloved! cannot have been dissevered by the death of the body. I still belong to you, though you are living in some other mansion in our heavenly Father's house.

I shall continue to love you until my heart also ceases to beat. And you—nay, you cannot have forgotten me, for God is the God of love, and I must still live in your memory, and in your holy state you must yearn for me! You who, dwelling in a higher world, see the greatness of God in all its wonderful sublimity, you now feel for me a more exalted love than I can feel for you. Alas! mine is still mingled with tears; yours knows only rapturous delight. I lift my eyes with sadness to the stars, seeking the home in which your spirits dwell; you look down with a happy smile upon this planet where I sojourn, lonely in the dust, and in secret breathe forth your names with many a sigh!

The mutual love of souls is eternal, like the souls themselves; eternal, like God and His love! It is true, all earthly ties are dissolved between the living and the departed spirits, but our spiritual brotherhood in God continues, and God is the Father of all. In the better world we shall all be equal, as the angels and the higher powers and forces in the creation are equal.

That which belongs to the body, dies with the body. The spiritual alone endures. The power, the faculty of growing in perfection alone continues. Our relations must be of a different nature in Heaven to what they were on earth, for they must be purified and spiritualized; but how, we cannot imagine. The occupations of the blessed spirits in the next world we are equally incapable of conceiving. Most assuredly they are neither the same as on earth, nor similar to them; and everything that has been said on the subject by presumptuous men, is nothing more than idle dreams. We know not how the spirit works in a disembodied state, nor do we know how, when by the Almighty power of God it is clothed in more beautiful raiment, it will act through this. For who knows the power of God? But this much we do know, and a thrill of happiness passes through the longing soul at the thought: the loved ones who died here on earth still live in a more exalted state. That which has once been present is still present in the universe, and that which has once lived, still lives. For "God is not the God of the dead, but of the living." (Matt. xxii. 32.)

What ecstasy seizes me at this thought, the truth of which is so clear, so simple, but which only now beams upon me in all its fulness! Where am I? On this little planet, the earth, it is true; but with it I float in the infinite universe, and in time eternal! Where am I? With Thee, O Father! O God! Even on this earth I am with Thee, and I behold Thee through the veil of Thy wondrous Creation in like manner as my soul beholds itself through its earthly veil, the body. What a glory diffuses itself over all those earthly relations which Thou hast appointed for me! The starry heavens become more sacred in my eyes—I seem to behold up yonder the mansions of my beloved ones in the house of our Father. The spot on which I dwell on this little earth becomes more holy in my eyes, for it is the entrance to the better world! My toiling and plodding, my cares and my efforts, all become sanctified in my eyes; they are but the exercise of the faculties of the immortal power that dwells within me, and that are preparing it for a higher existence. One thing only is *unholy*, and that is sin—the disobedience of the spirit to its own law, its disobedience to Thy will, O most Holy One!

Away, all love, all impure passions, which would desecrate me here in the sanctuary of my Father!

Cheerfully I will look up to Thee, gladly I will resign myself to Thee, O Creator, abounding in love! O joy! to belong to thee, O wonderful eternity which Christ opened to me! To belong to you, O blessed spirits of my ever-beloved ones, who are beckoning me to follow you into the Holy of Holies!

INTERPRETATIONS OF ETERNITY.

THIRD MEDITATION.

RETRIBUTION.

Stop, sinner—cast thy sins away!
Though vengeance, though the Avenger stay,
He comes to judge—He hath the power,
Shed for your guilt the sorrowing tear—
The day of wrath may soon appear,
Swift as a robber in the night.
Hark! even now the trumpets call—
   The stars already pass away—
They sound—they sound—and trembling all,
   From forth their graves must rise to-day.

When through storm He makes His path—
Call ye the hills to shield from wrath—
"Cover us, hide us," shall ye cry.
God comes to fill His judgment-seat,
The Heavens shall bow beneath His feet,
The earth shall melt with fervent heat,
   The universe in ruins lie.
Yet midst the wreck of worlds undone
   The spirits of the just shall rise—
Their course fulfilled, their victory won,
   And crowned with glory—to the skies.
              (*Matt.* xxv. 31—46.)

IT is when people are deeply distressed and almost inconsolable at the death of some beloved object, that it is most usual to remind them of religion and Christianity. At such moments, even those who have never previously in words expressed any interest in religion, are supposed to entertain Christian feelings and sentiments. And rarely does a sufferer revolt against the supposition. By this very appeal to his own inward religion and its consolations he is made religious. It is comforting to him to have a faith, or to profess one. In secret, most persons like to think of eternity, and of the state of their souls after death; but they rarely speak of these subjects. However, when they do touch upon them, it is not without warmth and true feeling, yet less with the firm voice of conviction, than in the questioning tone of curiosity. And those that mock at the idea, do so with a certain reserve, as though not quite sure that they are right.

Many a man, though possessed of the same ineradicable consciousness of immortality as all other men, nevertheless likes, in conversation, to affect scepticism. Not, however, because he doubts in earnest; but because, by raising objections, he hopes to elicit new proofs in favour of his conviction.

That uneasiness which some people feel at the thought of immortality and the future destiny of the soul, and which almost takes the form of doubt, is owing to their thinking that they must be able to give proofs of that which it is as useless as it is impossible to prove. It is impossible, because most persons understand by proof, a kind of sensual perception and demonstration of futurity, which no one ever could pretend to. Even after death the thinking spirit can have no other test of its immortality than the consciousness that *it exists, and will continue to exist*, and the like consciousness it possesses in this life. But in this as in the future life, this feeling or consciousness is matter of the immediate present; the conviction is not derived from the future, for that has no existence except in idea. When the future has been reached, it is no longer future but present.

To demonstrate that which forms part of our self-consciousness is useless. *I exist!* Of what avail is it to prove it? I am conscious of it without any proof, and for this very reason it cannot be verified. For only because *I am*, is it possible that there can be any such thing as demonstration in the world, as far as I am concerned. *God is!* Of what avail to prove it? My consciousness tells me so, and millions of proofs, for or against, can as little destroy my consciousness of it, as they can destroy the nature of my spirit or the existence of the world. *The immortality of the spirit is a fact.* Of what avail to prove it? This is not an acquired thought, not an opinion, the opposite of which might possibly be demonstrated. It is not a faith which we are at liberty to adopt or to reject— no; it is an intuition, proceeding from the innermost depths of our spiritual nature—it is a necessary part of our consciousness. I acknowledge that it is possible that in many human beings this consciousness has never been clearly developed. It may be that there have been people who neither knew of the existence of God nor of their own immortality, although both formed part of their consciousness. But there are likewise millions of human beings who do not know that they are in health, and yet the sensation of health dwells in them, and in all their members. A man is not ill because, when healthy, he reflects not on health. God and immortality are not blotted out because many human beings have not yet learnt to reflect on their own self-consciousness. Not until we are sick in body do we feel the value of health; and those that are sick in mind meditate most upon the possibility and the nature of a future existence. Instead, however, of being content with the simple and indestructible intuition, this unerring and immediate revelation of God to the human spirit, they seek a standard of measure among things sensuous, to aid them in forming a judgment of what the spirit may be when raised above all sensuous things. They endeavour to embrace the supersensuous with the limited faculty of their imagination, and to fathom the nature of the elementary forces of the universe with ideas borrowed from their varying earthly phenomena or effects.

Thus it is that men learn to doubt that which they have lost sight of by seeking for it in a false direction. Because they cannot bale out the ocean with the hollow of their hand, the ocean becomes to them a thing of doubtful existence. Hence it is that many persons conceive God to be a kind of artificially combined action of dead forces, without self-consciousness, without wisdom, will, or love; and they are thus placed in the degrading necessity of assuming that the human spirit is nobler than God, because that at least possesses the attributes which they deny in Him. Hence it is that many persons, though admitting the immortality of the soul, form a conception of this immortality that makes it nothing more than a kind of extinction; for although they do not deny the eternal existence of the thinking power within them, they do not believe in its personality, nor in any connexion between the present and the future. These deluded minds find in all, even the smallest things in the universe, the most admirable order and adaptation of means to ends; but in regard to the highest and holiest things, they think that disorder and the absence of design are matters of course.

These views are no doubt very convenient in some respects; for, as in accordance with them, there is no connexion between this life and the future, those who hold them may live as is most agreeable to themselves, without a thought of anything further. Cause and effect they perceive on all sides in the universe; but that the present noble or ignoble life of the soul may, as a cause, be followed by its consequences in the future state after death, they refuse to believe.

There are moments, however, when these views prove the reverse of convenient; for instance, when the conscience in its natural might speaks in louder tones than the subtle arguments of the artificially misdirected intellects of the reasoners. Still more inconvenient do they become, when by the force of divinely ordained circumstances beloved friends or relatives are taken away from the sceptics, and nothing is left for them, while gazing gloomily into the eternal future, but to send up the cry of despair: " Has the Creator of the world implanted affection in the heart of man in order to prepare a hell for it? Did He unite souls in the tenderest of bonds, in order, when dissevering these by death, to lacerate every fibre of the loving heart?" This cannot be! Does not all that is good in material nature continue for ever? why, then, should that which is good in spiritual nature die and become extinct?

God and immortality are irrefragable truths! The belief in retribution is a necessary result of this conviction, and it is one of the oldest beliefs entertained by the human race. It was embodied in the heathen religions of antiquity, as it is in those of the present day. All religions teach, in accordance with the deep-seated intuitions of mankind, that there is a heaven and a hell—an abode of bliss for the good, a place of punishment for evil-doers.

Without retribution, the immortality of the spirit loses all meaning, all value; without immortality, the existence of the Deity loses all importance in our eyes. Belief in the one is founded in belief in the other; the one cannot exist without the other—they are indeed identical.

Jesus constantly alluded to retribution as a consequence of the justice of God. He referred His hearers from this life to its continuance after the death of the body, for the solution of all the mysteries and apparent contradictions met with here on earth. Who does not know the beautiful and striking parable of the rich man and Lazarus, which He narrated to His disciples to make clear to them the compensation in Heaven which follows good or evil done, or suffered, in this world? (Luke xvi. 19—31.) Or who does not remember the grand and terrible image in which He depicted the last judgment; the stern Judge of the dead on His throne of glory—before Him the gathered nations, appearing as before a human tribunal—accusation and defence, and finally judgment. (Matthew xxv. 31—46.)

In these similes and parables the Divine teacher revealed the future destiny of our souls, the inevitable consequences of our acts, our dispositions, and our sentiments, of our virtues, and our sins. In each

He expressed the eternal truth: *Retribution awaits you!*

Even the world that now surrounds us is full of indications of eternity. "We see now as through a glass, darkly; but then face to face." (1 Cor. xiii. 12.) And as I see in the dark glass of nature the majesty of God, I divine from the creations which surround the earth the order of the infinite universe; as I apprehend from the constant presence and never-ceasing activity of the unconscious forces of nature, the indestructibility and everlasting existence of the higher powers; as I behold in this momentary existence, called earthly life, but a point of eternity, and know myself and all those who have died before me to be living in this eternity, so also I perceive here below indications of a retribution which reigns throughout eternity, as it does on earth. As surely as the entire creation and our entire life is comprised in the eternal infinite, and as surely as the law of retribution will continue to reign on earth, after I have left it, as it does now; so surely does it already reign over the spirits who dwell not on earth, so surely will it prevail in regard to those who die after me.

In nature, everything that is contrary to law is attended by evil consequences, whereas everything that is in accordance with law is attended with satisfactory consequences. Whatever takes place is followed by its effects which, assuming ever new forms, continue in endless succession, each becoming in its turn a cause. However, we cannot always distinguish the consequences of one thing from those of another, for they cross and intersect each other. But whatever takes place to-day is a consequence of what took place yesterday, as this again is the product of previous days. Nothing can occur to-morrow the foundations of which have not been laid to-day or some previous day; and what we call accident is only the result of some cause hidden beyond our ken in the great crowd of events—the consequence of circumstances which we may have overlooked, but which the Lord of the universe had freighted with their import. In this ever-flowing stream of cause and effect the sceptre of the great Rewarder and Avenger makes itself felt.

If we consider the most insignificant acts of human beings, we shall find that they are followed by their inevitable consequences in like manner as are the acts of nature. There is no difference. Imprudence, good sense, levity, all lead to good or to evil. And can we suppose that such should be the case in respect to natural events, and to every act of man or animal, and that the highest perfection to which the human spirit can attain should alone form an exception to this Divine law? Should virtue, the perfected stature of the immortal soul, alone remain without any consequences in regard to the soul itself? Is it indifferent whether man, made in the Divine image, and endowed with freewill, grow in likeness to God, or in likeness to the brutes? Who can believe this, that knows the earnest lessons which life teaches? What man in his senses can believe it? Who can believe it, that seeks in Jesus the highest truth, and who revolts against the thought that perfect justice should not be one of the attributes of God, the all-perfect Being?

The law of retribution, or of cause and effect, prevails. It rules in regard to dead matter; why not in respect to that which is living? In the human body lives a sublime power which we call spirit, and which is endowed with consciousness, perception, and will. It is the nature of this power to strive for self-development, that is, to strive towards a perfection infinite as all spirit. It bears furthermore within itself the *eternal law,* written by the hand of God, and purified from the overlying dust of sensuousness by Jesus Christ, our Saviour from sin. And according to this law is the striving for perfection regulated.

Can we suppose that the Creator implanted within us for no purpose this fundamental instinct of self-development? Or that the law that regulates this self-development is given for no purpose? Is it a matter of indifference whether we follow it, or whether we deviate from it, whether we grow in likeness to the brutes or in likeness to God?

And if, O man! this be not a matter of indifference; if here also the general law of creation, the endless concatenation of cause and consequence obtains: canst thou believe that the spirit is perfected on earth, and that its perfection has only reference to the life on this little planet? How is it possible to believe in spiritual perfection on earth? Countless numbers have died early from unknown causes, others lose, as they grow old, the use of their worn-out senses, and hardly retain any power over the body, the tool of the soul. Does not this interruption of the onward course towards that perfection, which our inward instincts and all the laws of nature impel us to strive for, indicate that the work is to be continued in a future existence?

But suppose that the goal of perfection could in

truth be reached here on earth; would it be of any avail in regard to this life? Nay, there are numbers of human beings that get very well through this life without virtue, by the aid of cunning and cleverness alone. Look at the beasts of the fields, they know naught of the higher aspirations of the spirit, and yet they live contentedly according to their nature. Ah! it is but too true, the mere earthly life can be carried on without any strength of virtue, but not so the true existence of the soul. Therefore virtue does not exist for the sake of this world alone—it is ever pointing to eternity.

Indeed it not unfrequently occurs, that virtue and mere worldly or animal happiness are diametrically opposed to each other—that virtue, which transports the spirit with joy, causes suffering to the body. Do you think the ennobled spirit will not receive compensation in the course of its eternal existence? It may happen, and it has happened, that human beings have by means of nefarious acts, which they could not think of without blushing, and which in their inmost hearts they abhorred, secured to themselves the most brilliant earthly advantages, such as honours, riches, rank, and power. Why, then, did they blush, and why did they in secret shudder at their own degradation? It may happen, and it has happened, that noble men have felt it their duty to shed their blood and to spend their fortunes in the cause of truth, or to sacrifice life itself for the good of their loved ones, or for the salvation of their country or their people. Why have they made these sacrifices? Why were they unwilling to live a life they deemed unworthy? Why is there something far more exquisite than the mere breath of life? Dost thou think that these sublime characters, with their hearts so full of excellence, have died in vain? Oh! if thou wert right in supposing this, then selfishness would be a virtue, madness reason, and the highest truth a lying contradiction. No; there is a God! And nature and eternity, in which we have our being, are the kingdom of God. And in the realm of the All-Just, the law of retribution rules. The human spirit, which by its own will, and by rising above its animal nature —above ambition, sensuality, envy, gluttony, the love of revenge, and other vicious tendencies—attains to self-dependence, freedom, greatness, will be after death a more *perfect and mature power, a more Divine creature;* and will have made many steps forward in the path that leads to the highest goal which the Eternal Being has marked out in the infinite distances of existence. This spirit will have attained to a higher perfection than millions of other beings, and *this is its heaven!*

And again, if a human creature, endowed with will, perceptions, and peculiar spiritual laws, nevertheless makes himself the slave of sensuality; is cunning, irate, ambitious, gluttonous, covetous, voluptuous, or in other words, lowers himself to the level of an animal possessed of the mere germs of humanity— this spiritual being who has unresistingly allowed the self-conscious power within him to be overcome by the blind forces of nature, will, after the death of the body, be an *immature, impaired, decrepit power.* It has prepared for itself the low position it will hold in the scale of beings, and in the rank of only half-conscious, animal souls. Millions of glorified spirits in the enjoyment of ineffable bliss hover above it. Its state is near to annihilation, *and this is its hell!*

Boast not of thy triumph over innocence, unprincipled seducer; the brutes also are voluptuous. Boast not of thy hoarded, useless treasures, covetous miser, insensible to the wants and tears of thousands of sufferers; the dog also watches greedily over its heap of bones. Boast not of thy cleverness and cunning, selfish villain; of how thou hast managed to conceal thy malignant trickeries, and to thrust out of thy path those who obstructed it; of how thou art able to enjoy the fruits of thy frauds in security and peace; the thievish fox also excels in cunning. Unhappy men, ye must seek your equals among the animals—among the glorified spirits you will not find them. Ye know not nobility of soul; can ye expect that there be for you a Heaven of higher perfection? Ye have not sought for virtue; would ye ask for its reward? Ye do not admit that Jesus died for you; would ye lay claim to a share in the Redemption wrought by Him? Ye have not acknowledged the Most Holy, and He will not acknowledge you. "Verily, I say unto you, Inasmuch as ye did it not unto one of these little ones, ye did it not unto Me." (Matt. xxv. 45.)

As the present day lays the foundation of the history of the morrow, *so does the life of the spirit on earth lay the foundation of its history in eternity.* Improvement and happiness are the objects of the better spirits here on earth; they are their destiny in the next world. It is vain curiosity and hopeless speculation to endeavour to know how and where this destiny will be fulfilled. Sensuous man can only comprehend the things of this earth; to grasp the things of other worlds his senses do not suffice. Or is there any one who has measured the abounding wealth of God? It would be equally idle to speculate upon the local habitation and the mode of punishment of those spirits who have rendered themselves unworthy of a higher destiny and a better world. Jesus speaks of these matters, it is true, but only in parables, representing them under the semblance of human things. And when He compares the deplorable state of the sinner's soul with the agony caused to the human body by fire, the all-consuming element, He avails Himself, with terrible purpose, of an image much in use at that day among the Jews.

Nature, reason, and revelation, thus agree in showing that the death of the body can make no difference in the life of the soul; that between the minute in which the last breath is drawn on the bed of sickness or on the field of battle, and the minute in which, in accordance with the eternal laws of the Creator, we enter, as emancipated, free, self-dependent spirits, into a new world, there must necessarily be a moral connexion, such as that between cause and effect in the material world.

It is thus the soul's active power of virtue that raises it up to a higher destination; and it is not the loving Deity that condemns us, but our own imperfection and sinfulness. The justice of God is tempered by love and mercy, and therefore the self-condemned may perhaps, after having been purified in the furnace of new and bitter trials, again be allowed to approach the All-Good One. But the more perfect spirits will ever be in advance of them, for the consequences of the neglect of the soul on earth endure eternally.

Retribution is the law of Thy kingdom, O Lord of the Universe! Father and Judge of our spirits! I also shall receive my reward and my punishment. The harvest I am to reap in eternity is sown here upon earth. I shall die—but not cease to exist. Why do I turn pale at the thought? I shall die—in a few years I shall be spoken of as one that has passed away; a few years more, and I shall have been forgotten on earth, as millions have been forgotten before me. But Thou, O Father of spirits! Thou hast not forgotten these millions. They still belong to Thy Creation ; they still live ; they are Thy children ; Thou guidest them to perfection through paths unknown to us, in like manner as on earth Thou gavest them pain and pleasure to serve as their monitors.

I exist, and shall exist, while others are passing heedlessly over my grave. But Thou wilt not forget me. I am Thy child, and shall be so even when I shall be freed from the earthly coil that now encompasses me. Thy child, perhaps Thy unhappy child, lost through my own sinfulness! Sold for earthly lust to the vengeance of sin! Removed far from Thee, and from the bliss of the more perfect spirits, by my neglect of my own soul. Woe unto me, should I have debarred myself from saying when I die, that I am going in to the Father! should my imperfection have raised an eternal barrier between me and my glorified beloved ones in the better world.

I tremble at the thought, that when all earthly joys fade in the hour of death, no hopes from the gardens of the heavenly paradise may spring up to cheer my spirit! Oh, Eternal Father, I also am Thy child! Banish me not from Thy presence! Love me, that I may be blessed! Ah! Thou desirest that I should be blessed, therefore Thou hast sent me so many warnings in life; therefore, also, Thou didst send Thy Son, that I might lay hold of the salvation He offered me. Why have I so long neglected doing so? Is it not I alone that am to blame? Alas! have I not too often been the willing slave of my earthly lusts, of the passions, which I have in common with the brutes? Ah! how little have I hitherto had in common with Jesus! How can I, after a misspent life here, hope for communion with Him hereafter?

Oh, Father, have mercy! Nay, Thou never refusest mercy; but do I ask for it with a contrite heart? How many hours will my earthly career still last? Through Jesus I will devote them to Thee, by endeavouring from this moment forward to purify and perfect my own soul. Amen.

INTERPRETATIONS OF ETERNITY

FOURTH MEDITATION.

REUNION.

He gave it—He hath taken it away—
    He who in grieving us no joy can take.
Patient of evil—He the righteous' stay
    And comfort—unto Him my prayer I make—
Is it not His? all, everything I have?
    Who, then, can have such right to all as He,
Who says, " Enclose thy prey," unto the grave—
" Bring forth," to mothers in their agony?
Reverence is mute—but love in faith is blest.
God loves us, though He rob us of our best.

How can He rob us? He may take again
    What is His own; but is this robbery?
My bitter flowing tears will I restrain—
    He is almighty—naught but dust am I—
Yet me He raises from my anguish sore
    To His own world of deep, unfading bliss,
Where loving hearts shall meet again once more,
    Who have been torn apart by death in this,
What God, the Faithful One, who changeth never,
Has bound together, He will ne'er dissever.

              (*Luke* xxiii. 43.)

BLEED freely, and bleed ever afresh, deep wounds of my heart! Welcome again and again, nameless and holy sorrow which stirs my spirit at the thought of the loved one who has left me. To the living I can speak words of affection, I can devote acts of friendship, I can express my love in tender caresses; but what can I give to the beloved dead, whose ashes repose in the grave? To him I can offer no other tribute than the tears which I shed in remembering him—no signs of affection but my sighs. In my solitary walks, where his cherished image ever accompanies me, my hands are clasped in constantly renewed agony, my streaming eyes are turned silently towards heaven, and from my lips escapes the sigh, " Oh, my God! my God! why was I doomed to lose the loved one of my soul, the light of my days? Alas! why was he so early torn away from my heart? He was happy; why was he not left to enjoy still further happiness? He was devoted to me with tender fidelity; why was he not allowed to reap the reward thereof? Fain would he have clung to life—fain would he have lingered in pain and illness, could he but have remained among us. In vain! The film of death spread over his eyes, and the soul, so full of love, departed from us. Ah! How willingly would I have given my life to re-knit again the bonds which bound him to life. But my prayers were unheard! There was no mercy for me! It was accomplished. The heart ceased to beat. In obedience to the call of the Almighty, the spirit of a new angel left us— hastened along new paths into the regions of eternal glory."

They try to comfort me, saying, " Why dost thou weep, thy beloved is happy? Wouldst thou, were it in thy power, deprive him of the bliss which the eternal Father has vouchsafed to him? He has won the victory; thy grief is of no avail. Call not upon thy glorified loved one, he is happy!"—What feeble consolation! He is happy, the angel who has fled from us! I know he is happy, for I believe in God. Did I not know this I should despair; I should curse my existence in a world so unmerciful, that it has only tears for virtue, only cruel separation for faithful, loving souls; while for heartless vice it has pleasure, and for treacherous infidelity, satisfaction. He is happy, I know it, for I know God and His love. But I—am I happy? For that which the beloved departed spirit has lost he will find boundless compensation in a higher and better life. But what can make amends to me, in this world, for my heart-rending loss? I have still friends, it is true; but he is not among them. I may win new friends, but I shall never again press him to my lacerated heart. In vain I call his name; in vain I pray; in vain I stretch out my arms towards him. Others whom God has left me are dear to my heart; but they cannot take the place of him I have lost. For, in the love of souls, one cannot take the place of another.

Therefore will I not only be faithful to my love through life, but also to my sorrow. It is the sweetest incense which widowed faith can offer on the altar of the dead. It will die with me, when, in the last hour, the yearning aspirations of my heart shall at length be dissolved in the ecstasy of approaching reunion.

Why force such consolation upon me? It will not give me back my lost one. My grief may, perhaps, in time become less poignant, but my love and my longing will remain the same, even though I should hide them from the world. Why, then, try to console me?

Hast thou beheld thy father or thy mother in the narrow coffin—hast thou seen the venerable head resting with closed eyes in the eternal sleep of death? Ah! if so, with what tenderness didst thou not gaze for the last time upon the features of the countenance which had so often beamed upon thee with affection! with what reverence didst thou not touch the stiffened hand, which guided thee so tenderly in youth—which in infancy so willingly lifted thee over every thorn in thy path—which had so often been raised to Heaven in supplication for thee! Hast thou beheld the corpse of thy child in its coffin? Thy sweet child, whom thou didst tend and watch through many anxious days and sorrowful nights! But thy care proved vain. Thy hopes lay strewn like withered leaves over the lovely corpse. The joys which the future had promised died with thy darling. In his face, still lovely in death, thou didst read the tenderness with which his heart beat for thee before its throbbings were stilled. With stifled voice thou didst whisper the last, the eternal good night! You were separated. The heart of father or of mother had to tear itself from the child of its affections, and to resign itself to solitude.

Hast thou seen thy husband or thy wife stretched with pallid cheek on the funeral bier? Thy Heaven on earth, thy better half laid low in death? Then hast thou felt as though thou wert no longer thyself, as though the nobler part of thyself had been taken away. Widow, or widower, didst thou not sob forth: "Why, oh! why have I been left behind? Why cannot I follow thee into thy Heaven?"

Hast thou seen brother, or sister, or friend, or

beloved companion of thy childhood, laid low in death? Hast thou seen the cherished remains borne away from thy home, and with them all the joys that had sprung from the happy relationship? Thou stoodst there like a tree struck by lightning, that has lost its leafy crown, and has been rent asunder in the prime of its strength.

Oh, how bitter is the pain of parting in death! Is then affection a crime, that it must be so cruelly expiated? Why did the Creator give us a heart receptive of love, and endow us with a wealth of tender feelings, if this heart and these feelings are not to be taken into account in this life? Why was the treasured object bestowed upon me, and why was I allowed to bind myself to him by such tender bonds, if these were to be dissevered, and the pain thus rendered ten-fold greater? What had my beloved lost one been guilty of, that he should be doomed to suffer so intensely in his last moments? Why should this angel, when drawing near to the hour of his glorification, be tortured with the pangs of disease? Of what good was it to me to witness his patient suffering? These are fearful, cruel enigmas, which I cannot solve! But they render my grief more intense; they increase my sense of misery to an unutterable degree. I see how wretched is the lot of man—I see that the mercy of the eternal Father is no more.—O my God, Thy mercy! Ah! forgive, forgive the injustice which the despair of the moment inspired! No, Thy mercy never ceases! Even on the bed of death Thou wert the Father of the sufferer. Thou didst not inflict greater pain than he could bear, and his severest agonies Thou didst mercifully assuage by unconsciouness. He was perhaps less aware of his physical state than I supposed. My tender anxiety, my imagination filled with terrors, impressed me with exaggerated notions of the pangs which he endured. Perhaps I suffered even more than he, for what is the anguish of the body compared with that of the soul? Great is my distress, O Father! But greater still my faith in Thy wise guidance and in Thy unbounded love. Thou, O Lord, didst give me my soul's beloved; and Thou, O Lord, hast taken him away.

But why hast Thou taken him away? Wherein had I offended? Was my love for him too great? Was I unworthy of my tranquil happiness? Can we love too much? Yes, Father, I acknowledge it; *we love too much when we cling so passionately to some object in this world, as though it were to belong to us for ever.* Did I not know that here on earth human beings meet but for a little while? Did I not know that either he, the object of my affection, must leave this world before me, or I before him? The first time we grasp a new friend's hand, we ought to think of the parting pressure we may have to give to that same hand, and to remember that the hour of separation is ever nearer than we anticipate; this will prevent our friendship from becoming too ardent. When father and mother impress the first rapturous kiss on the soft cheek of the new-born babe, let them remember that this sweet plant of God is entrusted to their care for a few hours, a few weeks, or a few years, only. Then they will each day be prepared to give back the precious nursling when the Lord demands it. Woe to them if they deceive themselves, if their passionate fondness refuse to believe in the possibility of separation, and they mock at the warnings of reason! *Then the loss becomes a punishment, and the anguish so much the more poignant, because it is a consequence of their own want of reflection.*

Yes, Heavenly Father, I acknowledge how earnestly Thou dost ever admonish our souls not to give themselves up with too great devotion even to the noblest pleasures here below. We are not to abide here. Our life on earth is to be but the beginning of our life in Heaven. Here we are but to lay the foundations of the holy and beautiful things, which are to be completed in the true home of our spirits. We must ever keep in mind that each good we may enjoy on earth is but a loan, not a possession; that nothing is our own but our virtue; and that everything is in Thy power, O Father, not in ours. When we forget this, we begin also to forget our own destination; and we may then be thankful for some serious warning, that rouses us out of our dreams and delusions, and, as it were, calls out to us: " Here you cannot abide; here all is fleeting! think of elevating your minds by truth, of ennobling your souls by fulfilling the word of Jesus. The most virtuous is the most happy, only to the holy belongs the holiest, here and hereafter."

I will therefore try to be composed. I will listen to the voice of religion, to the voice of truth—indeed, were I to refuse to listen to it, would I not have to expiate my immoderate passion by severer suffering? If my misfortune fail to make me wiser, should I not deserve to be awakened to a sense of my duty by still greater misfortunes? I will no longer give myself up to the unavailing melancholy that renders me incapable of fulfilling my duties towards my God and towards my fellow-men. I will banish from my mind all gloomy images, and will cease to torment myself with questionings as to whether I had done enough for the dear departed one, or whether I had not neglected some kindness that might have been shown him either during health or illness. If this has been the case, it was the will of Providence that it should be so. How can man with his limited insight and power hope to escape errors and shortcomings?

God willed the death of him for whom I have wept so much; he was ripe for the better world. Before I drew the breath of life, before my lost one was born, God had fixed his last hour. The germ of his destiny began to unfold from the first moment he beheld the light of the world, and the appointed events of his life commenced their influence. He was still smiling cheerfully in the circle of his relatives, when he began to die, and the angel of death was hovering over him. His death, and the very hour at which it took place, were the consequence of a moment long past and unknown to him. All the skill of the physician, all my tending, could not have added one span to his life. The bright light was to be extinguished. In all probability the treatment by the physician, my care, and my prayers were also included in the pre-ordained concatenation of events. God's providence had taken these also into account, and permitted part of their activity to take effect, but only the useful part. And when the life of the dear one was ripe for the sickle, all human skill and care proved unavailing. But God's will was carried out. And shall I dare to complain? Am I wiser than Divine Providence? Kinder than the Creator? I loved the dear one who has gone to rest; but God also loved him. What God doeth is well done. He separated a beloved soul from me. My tears flow.

God separated! Nay, God of Love, Thou dost not separate souls Thou hast once united! Who says that my glorified friend is lost to me? That which is with God cannot be lost. And am I not in God's hand, and my beloved likewise? Am I not in my Father's house, and my beloved also? I live, but thou also, O cherished soul, art living! I think of thee with a sad, yearning heart; canst thou have ceased to think of me? Can love be extinguished when God is love?

Thou rejoicest to-day in thy more perfect state in the better world! While my tears are flowing thou mayest be exulting in new-born bliss. While I stammer forth thy earthly name with trembling lips, thou mayest be awaiting my approaching arrival with joyful anticipation. O glorified spirit, God's love has perhaps vouchsafed to thee a happiness which in my mortal state I am incapable of conceiving! Thou seest me in my lonely sorrow, thou lovest me, hoverest around me, guidest me! Perhaps thou art one of the guardian angels who carry out the Lord's behests in regard to me.

Nay, we are not separated. The Divine universe is but one. This earth forms part of the Divine edifice; the present hour forms part of eternity. I enjoy it here on earth, and thou enjoyest it in happier regions. We still belong to each other, although thou hast gone in earlier to the Father, by whom I, also, shall one day be called. And of what great importance is it whether we be summoned to enter the Holy of Holies an hour earlier or an hour later? I am not yet called because I have still much of my Father's work to do on earth. His holy will be done. I know that for me, also, unutterable felicity is in store, when I shall have completed my course. Whether it be in this year or in another, what matters it? What is the longest duration of man's career? A fleeting morning dream. When it is passed, and the hour strikes—oh! then to meet again, to stand face to face again with thee, shall be the reward of my faithful, glorified spirit. To be reunited to thee! To see Thee again! Oh, thought full of heavenly rapture! To meet thee again, absent angel, whose loss I am ever lamenting! What a moment will that be in the paradise of the better world! As human beings, we should cling to each other with tears of unspeakable joy; as glorified spirits, we shall bow down in grateful adoration of God, and be dissolved in bliss.

Reunion! But can it be possible? On what do I ground the sweet hope? Whence does it come to me?

O Thou, whose wisdom has so often lifted my soul to God, whose word has never deceived me, whose promises have ever been wonderfully fulfilled—Jesus Christ, eternal Son of the living Father, sent to comfort suffering humanity, Thou hast inspired me with this hope and trust. When on the Cross, thou spakest to Thy fellow-sufferer, "Verily I say unto thee, To-day shalt thou be with me in paradise," (Luke xxiii. 43,) Thou didst speak words of rapturous hope to all sorrowing souls.

He, for whom I am weeping here in the dust, has not been taken from me for ever. We shall be reunited; God's voice has promised it. Even in material nature I perceive a wonderful striving of dissevered forces towards reunion. Those elements which belong together will, in spite of all man's efforts to separate them, always find the means of reuniting. I see throughout creation that among the living organisms as well as in inanimate matter, certain beings and certain things are in closer affinity to each other than others, and are ever mutually attracting one another and amalgamating. Throughout God's great kingdom there is a division and a connexion of things, as in families; they adhere to each other, they always find each other again. Were it not for this fundamental principle in creation, the world would be a chaos, an endless confusion of forces and phenomena; there would be no separation and no combination. But light ever blends with light, earth with earth. Watery particles rise up from ocean, lakes, and rivers, but return again from the skies as rain or dew. Each thing finds its like. I am astounded at the effects even of the elective affinities in lifeless matter, in which like always seeks and amalgamates irresistibly with like, while it rejects whatever is foreign to it. And what we call elective affinity and sympathy in the material world, is love in the spiritual realm. God Himself is the highest power of Love, hence the neversatisfied yearning of the spirit for union with Him, for happiness in Him, for perfection.

And if this Divine law of attraction and reunion rules on earth, and in the high heavens, as far as my eye can penetrate the various families or galaxies of stars—where every planet has its satellite, where every sun belongs to a special system of planets—can we suppose that it rules less in the world of the higher spirits, where that which in lifeless things is but a vague impulse, is raised and ennobled into a conscious sentiment?—in that world where dwells God, the source of all love, where His laws and His works are but the results of love?

It is true, the form in which the beloved being became dear to me on earth, rests in the grave. But in reality it was not this perishable form that I loved, but the imperishable spirit; and the veil that surrounded the lovely soul was only dear to me because of its connexion with the angel spirit whom it concealed. The veil has fallen, but the angel lives! But shall I meet him again? If so, how shall I recognize him, since he has lost that outer form in which alone I knew him.

Why these questions so full of doubt? Poor mortal, hast thou measured the power of God? By what means do the elementary bodies in creation find and recognize each other?

When bright-eyed spring awakes, millions of plants stand forth in the full bloom of their loveliness, and each species sends forth through the air its golden pollen to the others of its kind. Without this pollen fructification is impossible. These blossoms are often separated by considerable distances, and yet the pollen, the almost invisible dust, finds the flower for which it is intended. Among millions of flowers it floats as if attracted by some magic power towards that one only which is of similar nature to itself. Here in this earthly part of creation is a miracle which I witness every year. And is this miracle of the Almighty not an indication of the things of eternity? That infinite power of God which guides the fructifying pollen from afar to the only flower that awaits it, can it fail in the realm of higher beings, more closely akin to the Godhead? Oh, yes; there is reunion after death! That which God has united is united for ever. Therefore, O beloved spirit! beloved through eternity! we can never be parted. Thou in Heaven, and I on earth, belong to each other for ever. Be happy in the higher regions where thou dwellest. I shall one day be with you in paradise. Why then, should I weep? We are both living in the great house of our Father. To me thy absence is pain, it is true; but I could not, would not, wish that thou shouldst again wander with me here on earth among the living. Even had I the power to call thee down again from thy blissful habitation, I would not do so. For thou hast fought the good fight; thou hast won the victory; it is not for thee to return to me, but for me to hasten to thee. I know the way that will lead me to thee without fail—it is the path of earnest dutifulness, the sincere Christian spirit with which I fulfil God's behests on earth—it is the way to God Himself. Sin and vice only, can separate me from God and thee.

My anguish was great at thy death, but great is now the joy of my soul. Thou, O blessed spirit, art my beloved still, and thou drawest me with hallowed bonds after thee into the better world. Through the love of spirits, Heaven and earth are made akin. Some of my dear ones are with God. What a Heavenly thought is not this!

Father in Heaven, my Father and Father of the glorified souls that belong to me! As in the cruel hour of parting I raised my hands to Thee in anxious supplication, and with streaming eyes I prayed—" Oh, leave me my beloved !"—in like manner, Father, I now raise my hands to Thee, with exultant satisfaction, crying,—"Thanks that Thou didst call away my precious one!" His death has, indeed, deeply shaken my whole being, but it has made me nobler, holier, more religious. I feel myself drawn nearer to Thee; I feel more alienated from earth and all its belongings, and will never again give myself up to these with immoderate ardour; a bond is established between me and Eternity, which can never be destroyed. I no longer live on earth only; I live, also, in Heaven with Thee, and the dear one whom Thou gavest me, and whom Thou didst take away.

There was a time when the thought of death and the grave overwhelmed me and made me shudder. How could I, indeed, love death and the grave, when to me they were only the great gulf that threatened to swallow up my happiness! Then the earth was still a Heaven to me, and Thy Heaven, O God, a sacred desert, in which I thought of myself as a stranger, whom no one there knew or loved. And I feared death, and recoiled from the unknown land.

Now it is the goal of my longings; there is my haven of rest, my home, all that I most treasure! There are the companions of my heart, of my life! And when I feel most happy among my friends on earth, the thought comes to me: in heaven thou wilt be happier still! When gloom settles on earthly things, I say to myself, Yonder all will be clear and unclouded.

Through Jesus Christ I will render myself worthy of the bliss Thou hast prepared for me from the beginning of time. O Father, I will do Thy bidding! I will live a life of love and devotion to my fellow-men, so that I may hereafter, in my glorified state, enjoy Thy love. Amen. Help me, O Lord Jesus, Light of my soul! Amen.

INTERPRETATIONS OF ETERNITY.

FIFTH MEDITATION.

REUNION.

When o'er my cold and narrow bed,
The last fond parting tear is shed
  By sorrowing friendship, broken-hearted,
In that blest life shall I rejoice,
Where round me sounds each dear one's voice,
  Where God again unites the parted.

What we begin in weakness here,
Shall rise to full perfection there—
  Perfect! Eternal!—*One* the word.
The earthly germ of purest love
Can only bloom in Heaven above—
  For there is bliss, and there the Lord.
(*John* xvi. 16—22.)

RISE up, O my soul, from the tumult of this life into thy true freedom; throw off the burden of thy sorrows and expand in the hope of eternal peace; look up from the whirl of pleasure, and contemplate thy higher destination!

For what is this drop of earthly life in which thou at present revellest, when compared to the ocean of infinite glory which will be opened to thy admiring gaze when this short dream is past? What is all the pomp of the earth, all the glitter of golden dust here below, when compared to the splendour that will meet thine eyes at the portals of Eternity? Ah! why waste thy admiration on the poor torch with which thou illuminest thy dwelling? What is it compared to the lustre of the sun, in whose effulgence countless worlds float, drinking in light, and heat, and life?

Yea, Eternity, final goal towards which all are hastening—the sorrowing and the joyful, the king and the beggar, the sage and the fool, the old man and the laughing child—Eternity, that awaits us all, be thou to-day the subject of my thoughts! The very mention of thy name makes my soul feel freer, nobler, purer! Earthly things, which at other times fill me with pleasure, or wound me with their thorns, seem insignificant and contemptible in thy presence. Religion is more attractive, more divine, more exalting, when it awakens in my bosom wonderful presentiments of a future existence. Eternity, at the thought of which levity shudders, sin turns pale, and the sceptic trembles in doubt—Eternity, consummator of all that is begun, retributive judge with sword and palm-branch, all-reconciling, all-equalizing Eternity—thou art the comforter of the sage, the joyful hope of the Christian!

To me also thou shalt bring consolation and hope—consolation, when I weep over my unhappy lot; hope, when amid a cheerful circle of friends I rejoice in life. Consolation, when my views of life become obscured by melancholy; hope, when in the midst of joy and happiness the thought forces itself upon me: everything changes, and what man possesses is taken from him again! Consolation, when the hand of death robs me of my dear ones, when I stand sorrowing by their death-bed, gazing with tearful eyes at their pale, cold, rigid features, which will never again smile sweetly upon me; hope, when one day death beckons me also, and I must part from souls tenderly devoted to me, from affectionate friends and weeping orphans.

O Eternity, my hope and consolation, revealed to me through Jesus Christ, thou storest up for me all the treasures of joy which have fled from me here below! Why, then, should I tremble before thee? Towards thee the storm-wind carries the sweet blossoms, which it here snatches from my wreath of joys. Why, then, tremble at the thought of thee? In thee, and in thee only, can I find again that which I have lost on earth, and that which I shall leave behind me on earth, when I, in my turn, am called away. What deep and rapturous emotion is caused by the thought, that I shall find again what I have lost! That in Eternity I may hope to see again those whom I saw and loved on earth! Oh, my dear, my beloved parents! Oh, affectionate companions of my childhood! Oh, ye who were bound to my heart by ties of blood and tenderness? Oh ye, whom my tears, my silent despair, could not recall to life! Oh ye, who departed sorrowfully from me to go over into the better existence—*I shall find you again! I shall see you again!*

My heart swells with new and heavenly joy—my eyes o'erflow with tears of longing—my spirit, rising on the wings of prayer, guided by the light of religion, approaches the mysterious portals of eternity; it draws nigh unto you in the lovely and distant worlds in which God dwells, and where you abide, in a nobler, happier state than mine. I am still here in the prison-house of earth, ye are free in the higher world! I am still weak and imperfect, now dwelling in sunshine, now in shade; ye revel in the never-clouded brightness of the Deity, of the Angels, and the blessed! Oh, could ye hear the voice of my heart, could ye see the tears with which I yearn for you! I call to you, I sob forth the prayer: Remember in your beatitude the one you left behind, and who will love you evermore! There is a God, *and God will re-unite us.*

We shall see each other again! It is no dream, it is no delusion! Jesus, the sanctifier of the world, Jesus, the revealer of God, has promised it to His followers.

He spake the sweetest of all consolations when, in one of the most trying hours of His life, He foretold to His disciples the tribulations and persecutions they would have to endure; and endeavoured to prepare these men, who clung to Him with childlike simplicity and devotion, for His death, His going in to the Father. "A little while, and ye shall not see me: again, a little while, and ye shall see me, because I go to the Father. Ye now have sorrow; *but I will see you again,* and your heart shall rejoice, and your joy no man taketh from you." (John xvi. 16, 22.)

We shall see each other again! In that fearful hour of death when Christ, bleeding on the Cross, seemed abandoned by God, a malefactor, condemned to the same death as Himself, but full of faith, prayed to Him for comfort, and Jesus gave him the most blessed of all consolations. "Verily," so spake the World-Redeemer, and spake it with dying voice;

"Verily, I say unto thee, To-day shalt thou be with me in paradise!" (Luke xxiii. 43.)

Can I doubt when Jesus speaks, Jesus, the miraculous Heaven-sent Messenger, Jesus, born of God, and who came to enlighten the dark world of spirits in accordance with the will of the Eternal Father? Can I doubt the word of life which He brought to many? In whom could I believe if not in Him? Is there any one who before Him or after Him has proclaimed more sublime and sacred truths? Who has there been before or after Him who, like Him, has taught in such a way that the wisest of living men, and the simplest child, could follow Him as an unerring guide? Who has before Him or since given such an example to the world of holy living? Who has, like Him, taught the human race self-knowledge, and pointed out its true dignity and destination?

We shall see each other again! Jesus hath said it. With deepest fervour my faith embraces this Divine truth, which I hold from Him, and which is in such perfect harmony with God's love and greatness; which affords a sacred key to the thousand dark mysteries of life on earth, and without which I can see naught in creation but saddest contradiction, aimlessness, and confusion.

Thou sayest, O melancholy sceptic, "I cannot conceive how we shall be able to find each other and to recognize each other in that other world! For though the spirit may go into a happier existence, the body, through means of which we know each other here below, remains in the grave, and returns to the dust from whence it came." I admit that dust returns to dust; but it was not dust which was loved by dust—

it was the soul which clung lovingly to another soul. Thou doubtest because thou canst not solve the mysteries of eternity. Thou doubtest because thy limited understanding cannot fathom the depths of God's Omniscience and Omnipotence. Thou doubtest because thou dost not know in what form the spirit is clad after death. He who would know this, he who would embrace and understand the entire order of creation, he must himself be God. This thou art not.

The limitations of thy understanding preclude thee from the highest *knowledge;* but the force of thy reason impels thee to nourish the highest *faith*. And the laws of reason are the voice of the Deity! To resist these laws is to descend to the level of the animals, and is a proof of insanity. Be what thou wert meant to be, what thou art bound to be—a reasonable being, and thou wilt at once find that the most perfect accordance reigns in the universe.

But whatever the cavilling sceptic may say, he can only *assert* that it is possible that death may separate us for ever! But he can prove nothing against the hope that whispers, It is possible that we may meet again on the other side of the grave! His arguments are mere conjectures, inspired by his splenetic mood, or, perhaps, by a vain desire to say something striking. His own feelings must revolt against these weapons, with which, weak as they are, he would endeavour to shake the power of his own faith, and the faith of all nations, civilized or savage. Even in soulless nature, we perceive that kindred forces mutually attract each other in obedience to laws unknown to us. And when dust flies to dust to unite itself with it, how can we suppose that higher organizations, self-conscious beings, should be excluded from the rule of these beneficent laws of attraction? Are our spirits of less importance than the pollen, which escapes from the cup of the flower to seek, among a thousand others, for one of similar nature which it may fructify? Sceptic, explain to me this incomprehensible wonder, and I will explain to thee how self-conscious, self-directing, and living spirits find each other again, and satisfy their yearnings in the regions of eternity.

Was it man who prescribed for man the law of eternal love? Was it man who implanted in his own bosom all the best affections? Was it man who, together with the sentiment of love, created its desire for everlasting duration? Nay, it was God's hand that planted these feelings in our hearts; it was God who inspired the desire of kindred souls for eternal union. And He who bound us together here on earth, for a brief space of time, by such tender ties— He who is Love, Mercy, Goodness—would He dissever again, for no purpose, the bonds which He Himself had woven? He, the Most Blessed, would He inflict upon us woe greater than the most cruel of men could subject us to? He, the All-holy One, would he delude us through means of our holiest feelings, and deceive us in the hour of death? He who bids our hearts to love, would He desire to witness our despair?

Base and terrible thought, flee from me. I believe in the All-perfect God, and with this faith comes the tranquillizing conviction that He will not dissever the sacred ties that bind soul to soul, and which He Himself created. He is all-perfect, and cannot repent of any of His works. How, then, should he repent the noblest of His inspirations and provisions: the mutual love of souls, their happiness, and its duration?

God is! Therefore shall we, who were created for each other, meet again. *He* is the Creator, and He is love! We shall see each other again, we shall belong to each other again; eternity will satisfy the longings of millions of noble souls.

What would immortality be without the immortality of my consciousness, without a continuance of my higher essence. And is it not the power of virtue and love in the soul, which alone gives me any value in my own eyes, and makes the world of any value to me?

Immortality without the consciousness that I have previously existed, without connexion with the past, would not be immortality, but annihilation. Were I to be born again in eternity, without any consciousness of my past existence, my birth would be nothing more than the creation of a new being, who had never until then existed.

No; God is! And sure as He is eternal and all-perfect, I am immortal; and being so, the power of my spirit, my virtue, my love, cannot die with my body. Every nightly slumber on earth is like unto death, and every awakening like the new existence. Each morn when I arise from sleep the remembrance of my previous life, my acquired virtues, my sentiments of friendship, return. Explain to me, O sceptic, what makes this miracle possible every morning; then will I explain how it is possible that kindred souls should recognize each other, and cling to each other, in eternity also.

Were those bonds, which God has knit together, to be dissevered for ever by death; were my faithful love and the hope of sweet reunion to die with my body—oh, then, all that seems to me most glorious in God's world would be disjointed and annihilated! My soul would be robbed of its most precious treasures, of its sweetest joys—all Eternity would be to me like a place of banishment, where my bereaved soul would roam about searching in vain for what it had lost. Oh, in that case, an everlasting grave would be far preferable to an everlasting life, in which love could only weep hopelessly at the remembrance of its losses. Then we should shun love and friendship on earth even more than envy and hatred. Then the greater part of the earthly life of millions and millions of noble human spirits will have been as naught. Oh, then I should implore the eternal Love to root out all affection from my heart. My cry to God would be : Why didst Thou give me a heart, if such wounds were to be inflicted on it? Why didst Thou lead beloved souls towards me, if Thou didst mean to tear them away from me again? Why didst Thou bestow upon me this sentiment of love, this heart full of faith, if it only enables me to feel more deeply my losses, only gives me the capacity for more intense suffering? In vain then is the hope which makes husband or wife die with the name of the beloved spouse on his or her lips, which makes a sister pronounce the name of a dear brother, or a tender mother that of her darling child? Eternity would thus be an infinitely enduring, never-satisfied longing—a never-ceasing lamentation over losses never to be repaired.

Nay, sad sceptic, listen to the words of Jesus who

promises us reunion in eternity! Listen to the voice of reason, which condemns those insane doubts of thine that would throw the world into confusion, and would make thine own life and the whole of creation appear aimless and disjointed! Acknowledge what experience teaches thee each day, what the entire history of the world, what every look at the wide creation teaches thee: *God leaves nothing incomplete which He has created!* He does not begin and then leave unfinished; He is eternal, and eternal is all that He has brought into existence.

One of the most blessed and tranquillizing reasons for the belief in the immortality of the soul, is the inward aspiration after virtue, and the happiness attendant upon this, which the Deity has implanted in us. The goal we thus strive for is seldom reached on earth; the virtuous man is often the most unhappy; therefore, only in Eternity can this thirst for perfection and for happiness be satisfied; but there it must be satisfied, if everything here below is not to be looked upon as aimless, and if virtue itself is not to be deemed a vain delusion.

Every reason for belief in the immortality of the soul, is at the same time a reason for the belief that kindred souls will meet again in eternity. Alas! what manifold sufferings do not noble beings here below endure for the sake of their beloved ones— friend for friend, parents for children. And can we suppose that these tears, these cares, these sacrifices, will remain unrequited? Death robs them of the noblest, the dearest, part of their life; and you suppose that their grief would remain unheeded, forgotten, by the justice of an all-loving Godhead?

No, no; the heart revolts against this thought; reason condemns it; the Divine words spoken by the lips of Jesus contradict it.

Dwell ever with me, sweet and heavenly faith, that I shall one day meet again, in the land where tears never flow, all the dear ones whom I have lost here below. This faith dispels the gloom of life. In its light God and His Creation, life and eternity, appear in more glorious connexion and accordance.

We shall meet again—what matters it how and where? God is there as here, and His will is our bliss. We shall be re-united, O ye ever-beloved souls! it is no dream, no empty delusion, that we shall belong to each other for evermore.

Ah ye! whose lowly graves the green mould of forgetfulness is already overspreading, ye are not forgotten by me. My heart still beats for you as when it responded to yours; my eyes still shed tears at the remembrance of our parting. We are not separated for ever. Perhaps ye remember me in yon happier regions, as I remember you here below. For me this life has no longer any attractions. I have no rest, no joy, but with you; my every wish follows you into the better world. And ye, O ye blessed ones! perhaps ye smile at my grief as glorified spirits smile, knowing how near is the hour of reunion. Ye smile as does the husband, who after long absence from his beloved spouse, draws nigh unknown to her, and while she is still lamenting over the separation.

Ah! when shall I again embrace you? When shall I cease to sigh? When shall I again in intimate and eternal union with you, praise the Lord and Creator for our ineffable bliss? Even the remembrance of our life on this earth will still be dear to us; for here we found each other; here it was that God gave us to each other; here our souls blended with each other!

O God, Thou art love! Why do I continue to weep for the dead? They have gone to Thee, and I shall see the blessed ones again! To those who have faith in Thy fatherly love, even the pain of waiting becomes a sweet enjoyment. Calmly I bide the hour when Thou wilt lead me in to the dear ones. With rapturous delight I look forward to an Eternity of bliss, and with thankfulness I look up to Him who has prepared this happiness for me from the beginning of all things.

INTERPRETATIONS OF ETERNITY.

SIXTH MEDITATION.

REUNION.

Ah, no! The Universe is not a dream;
This life is not a fragment cast aside—
Each is a part of the eternal scheme,
By which a better life to this is tied.
Departed spirits do but soar above—
The lost on earth, the dear ones whom we love,
Wait till we stand, uprisen, by their side.

Oh, blessed promise, which the Saviour gave,
Thou fillest us with rapture, ever-growing,
Thou shinest over every loved one's grave
On which our sorrowing tears are sadly flowing.
Thou guidest our weary souls along the road
That leads us heavenward, through faith, to God,
And to a union which no end is knowing.

(*Revelation* iii. 21.)

THOU art taught by the revelations of Jesus; by the voice of the past, sounding through a thousand years; by the evidences in nature, from the grain of sand to the glittering star; and by thy inward monitor, thy conscience. Thou confessest: *Yes, there is a God!* an almighty, all-holy, all-just Being, who created the universe, and who directs the lifeless forces in it; who, as the eternal Spirit, loves all spirits as His children; who does not repent of what He created in His omniscience; who does not destroy the least grain of sand in His creation, and much less, the nobler energies in it—the human spirits which are capable of conceiving God and honouring Him.

Thou confessest that there is a God, and in so doing thou confessest *that immortality must necessarily be the destiny of our souls!*

But if thy soul be immortal, thou canst not but admit that, in some way or other, consciousness must be retained after death. For not to be aware of thy identity is the same as annihilation. Or not to know that thou art the same that existed previously, and how thou didst exist, is not continuance, but a new beginning—a new creation.

Were we not to be conscious after death of our previous existence, our goodness, our nobility of soul, the sacrifices made by us on earth, would all be useless. For, of what avail would be a reward in the next world, an amelioration in our condition, if that which led to it had been forgotten? Or, why should our sins be judged on high, why should retributive justice be meted out to us in the degradation of our spirits, if we are not aware of how we have merited our punishment, our degradation? Retribution in the next world would be meaningless, rewards and punishments after death might as well be so many acts of injustice, or at least be called so. Virtue here on earth, the improvement of the soul, vice, its degradation, would—if there be no connexion between this life and the next, be almost a matter of indifference. Whoever believes in the perfect justice of God, whoever believes in the absolute holiness of God, must also believe in a *true continuation* of the spirit life ; *i. e.*, in a *continuance without interruption*, in an intimate spiritual connexion between the here and the hereafter.

Such a connexion, however, is impossible, unless the soul retain the consciousness of its previous existence. The soul, when once emancipated from the imperfect earthly coil which often impeded its activity, may perhaps in the next world develop a vigour, of which, in our present state, we can form no conception. Thus, in the dreams of the old man while his body sleeps, memories from his youth, or his early manhood, which in his waking state he had completely forgotten, are often revived with wonderful distinctness.

This belief in the connexion between the future state and the present has not only at all times prevailed among all nations which have emerged from the first stage of barbarism, but Jesus, the Divine Man, also shadowed it forth in that first parable in which He endeavours to impress upon men the coming of a day of retribution. (Matthew xxv. 31—46.) He introduces the righteous, and puts these words into their mouth: " Lord, when saw we Thee ahungered, and fed Thee ? or thirsty, and gave Thee drink ?" Yes ; Jesus who was filled with divine wisdom, and to whom divine revelations were vouchsafed, hath declared to us mortals, not only the undying nature of our souls, but also the uninterrupted continuance of the consciousness of our acts. But this continuance of consciousness is not possible, unless we retain the remembrance also of those persons with whom we have been intimately connected on earth. For the greater number of our actions have had reference to them; they have induced our virtues and our vices; they have been the objects of our love or of our hatred, of our generosity or of our malignity, of our mercy or of our cruelty.

To the earthly understanding which knows only earthly means, it may indeed be difficult to comprehend how and in what way the recognition between those whom God's love bound together in this world by the ties of affection, shall take place in the next. But is it not folly to reject a thing as were it not, merely because with our limited earthly faculties we are unable to conceive or to imagine it? Must not the higher beings, if they be witnesses of our weakness and our conceit, smile at our folly, as we smile at the ignorance of the savage, who refuses to believe in the possibility of men communicating their intimate thoughts to each other in full detail, without being in presence of each other, and without the aid of the voice? He also mocks at any one who tells him: "There are men who possess higher minds and greater cultivation than we; they can communicate and make themselves intelligible to each other, though separated by thousands of miles, though mountains, seas, rivers, and deserts, intervene between them." And when he is told of the art of letter-writing, he takes it for supernatural sorcery.

Is not the relation in which we stand to our future more exalted state, and to our present comprehension of it, very much the same as that in which the savage stands to us?

The belief in the recognition of, and reunion with, our beloved ones of this world in the future existence beyond the grave, is coincident with the belief in true immortality. We cannot separate the one from the other without at once destroying our conception of the perfection and love of God. Therefore, though our ideas of the future life may be very imperfect, and, indeed, they cannot be otherwise, let us remain satisfied with vague foreshadowings of what will be our destiny there. We are but children; let us, then, think of, and believe in, that future existence with childlike simplicity. For that which will take place when the corruptible shall put on incorruption, that no mortal can conceive, no human language express.

Yet the influence of the thought of immortality and of reunion in eternity on the heart, is such, that we cannot but desire frequently to occupy ourselves with it. Our Divine Master did not in vain give us a conception of it. We shall recognize each other, and our deeds shall cleave to us. He distinctly tells us this in His description of the great day of judgment and retribution. "Where have we seen Thee? Where have we had an opportunity of doing good to Thee?" inquire the righteous and the sinners in the parable; and the answer is: "Verily I say unto you, Inasmuch as ye have done it unto one of the least of these my brethren, ye have done it unto me." (Matt. xxv. 40.)

The thought of reunion in eternity has, as I have said, a powerful influence on our moral life. What wonder is it that those who cannot look forward to this reunion otherwise than as a moment of indescribable terror, should try to destroy their own belief in it? What wonder is it that those who cannot dwell on the idea without shuddering, should prefer to exert their intellect to the utmost to find plausible arguments against its truth—should prefer to live in contradiction with their own reason, with their own conceptions of the power, greatness, wisdom, and justice of God, rather than admit this truth?

But not what man wills, not what he chooses, will take place, but what the Eternal God wills, that which He has pre-ordained in the harmonious organization of the universe, that which He has revealed to us by general and unmistakeable intuitions, that which He has declared to us through His holy Word.

Yea, frivolous mother and unprincipled father, ye shall stand face to face again with the children whom ye neglected, whom ye left in such shameful ignorance, that vice sprung up in their hearts as weeds spring up in the uncleansed soil. You will recognize them in their degraded state, and their crimes will rise up in judgment against you, even yon side the grave—for it was your guilty neglect that left their young hearts to go astray.

And thou who here on earth, in thy base selfishness, art a world and a God to thyself; who, entertaining supreme indifference towards thy fellow-men, thinkest only of thyself, and esteemest those fools who labour disinterestedly for others, or perhaps even sacrifice part of their own happiness to secure that of their fellow-creatures: who wilt thou meet in eternity? Thou who never thoughtest of others, but only of thyself, who wilt thou meet to give to thee those thanks that are due to virtue? No one! Thou wilt stand alone in the better world, alone and unloved, a stranger to all who surround thee. No loving soul is there yearning for thy presence. Thou art one of those who have had their reward. For thou didst selfishly stipulate and receive thy payment for whatever good thou mayest have done on earth. When thou gavest alms, when thou didst found charitable institutions, or contribute thy mite to undertakings for the benefit of the commonwealth, it was with a desire to gain favour in the eyes of the world, it was with a view to reaping honours in return. Thou hast passed through life without love, without friendship, because thou believedst all other men to be as selfish and as basely interested as thyself—without love, without friendship, thou shalt enter the ranks of the immortals, and stand alone among the blessed.

We shall meet again in eternity! Tremble, covetous wretch and heartless profligate, who have despoiled the unprotected widow and helpless orphans, or squandered in dissipation the sums which pious forefathers bequeathed for the assistance of the indigent and unfortunate. Know, that every sigh your hard-heartedness has drawn from those you have oppressed, has been heard by the omnipresent God! Know, that the tears which some poor innocent has shed in secret at your injustice, have been seen by an omniscient God! And these sighs will be counted out to you, and the tears measured before you. You will meet again the unhappy victims whom you deceived with impunity here below. In the next world your deeds of darkness will be dragged into broad daylight. Your hypocrisy will be of no avail yonder, where the All-Just One reigns and judges. Delude yourselves on earth, delude others as well; but in the end no delusion can prevail! Proclaim, while here on earth, there is no God, no eternity, no reunion! Even here, the voice of conscience, in serious moments, contradicts the subtle falsehood; even here, your guilty hearts palpitate at the fearful thought; but God is, and yon side the grave is eternity, where judgment, and the spirits of those you have wronged, await you! Your intellectual subtlety, your loud denial, cannot destroy eternal truth.

God, eternity, judgment, and meeting again of spirits! Listen to this, shameless voluptuary; and turn pale at the *possibility*, tremble at the *reality!* Listen to this, deceitful seducer of innocence; listen to this, father of poor abandoned, despised orphans, on whom thou hast bestowed life, poverty, and shame; thou shalt meet them again! Those whom thou hast disowned in this world, those whom here on earth thou madest the companions of wretchedness and despair, shall witness against thee in eternity! Merciless father and seducer, there is a God and a day of retribution; and that day will find thee without consolation. The innocence that fell a victim to thy lusts, and which was by thee given over to perdition and everlasting tears of despair, shall witness against thee!

The thoughts of those who have known each other on earth meeting again in eternity, fills the sinner's heart with dismay; but in vain the soul, conscious of its own guilt, resists the conviction. To the holier spirits only is the thought welcome; only to virtuous minds it brings unutterably sweet hopes. It gives them a vivid sense of the undying nature of nobility of soul, of their own dignity, and of their high destination. It renders life less burdensome to them, and sweetens the hour of death. It strengthens their endeavours to grow in virtue, and their power to overcome evil. They understand the meaning of the sacred words: "He that overcometh, shall not be hurt of the second death." (Rev. ii. 11.)

Righteous old man, who with failing powers art tottering towards the end of thy career, weary, and longing for rest—thou art happy! Thou knowest what awaits thee; thou knowest what thou leavest! What happiness has earth still for thee? Thy senses are blunted; thy spirit can no longer work through them, no longer reveal itself through them with the same power. Thus also in the old fruit-tree, though the wonderful vital force (the soul of the tree) is present in unabated vigour, the delicate vessels and tubes through which the nourishing sap, drawn from the earth, is sent upwards through every branch and twig, have become time-worn and hardened. Therefore, though the branches are still clad in verdure, the leaves are sparse, and the tree bears neither bloom nor fruit.

Thou hast almost become a stranger on earth. The playfellows of thy youth have long since departed, all thy best friends thou hast survived—even the greater number of the faithful companions of thy later years are in the grave. They have gone to rest, and thy dust will soon repose by the side of theirs.

But beyond the grave is thy fatherland; there reunion with all the beloved of thy soul awaits thee; there thou wilt be surrounded by the angels of thy childhood; there thou wilt behold once more the smile of the beings thou lovedst so tenderly here below, but whose eyes thou sawest grow dim in death. Soon thy disenthralled spirit will speed to meet them, exclaiming, with exultant joy: "Blessed am I! I have fought a good fight; blessed be the ineffable love of the eternal Father of spirits!"

We shall meet again! Youth and maiden, righteous children of righteous parents, who lament over the death of father and mother, you will meet them again! The love of these parents was what you valued most on earth. When cares oppressed you, your father's affectionate solicitude soon relieved you of the burden; when sorrow weighed upon you, your tender mother knew how to alleviate it. They have been called away from you, but yet a little while and they will be restored to you.

There is a way that leads to them, often full of thorns, and wearisome to wander, but unfailing. This is the way which Jesus indicated to His beloved disciples that they might find Him again. It is the path of virtue, of holy sentiments, and deeds. Never depart from this heavenly path, never be unfaithful to the memory of your parents.

When your youthful blood glows with unwonted passions; when vice approaches you in seductive garb; when turbulent desires lead you into perilous temptations; when a moment comes in which you feel yourselves wavering between innocence and guilt, between generosity and meanness; when all good resolves seem to abandon you; when even the voice of religion has lost its power over your hearts—oh! then think of the beloved deceased and of your future meeting with them, and you will recover your dignity, and resume your allegiance to virtue!

Remember the beloved ones who have gone before you, and your future reunion with them, when you are praying in the house of God, and when at your daily avocations. Remember them when you are quaffing the cup of pleasure, when you are engaged in the turmoil of business, and when depressed by misfortune—and you will not lose sight of the path that leads to them! Love is an invisible spiritual bond: it reaches across the grave into the happy regions of the better world; it knits together kindred souls on earth and in Heaven, in like manner as the love of God embraces the entire universe, and upholds and blesses it.

Remember the beloved ones and your reunion with them whenever an opportunity offers to perform a noble deed, to do good to an enemy, to rebuke the evil-speaking of a slanderer, to help a poor and suffering family, to originate some undertaking of a generally useful character—you will then fight the good fight for the crown of life, and your guardian angels will rejoice, for eternity is opening its portals to you.

We shall be reunited! Dry your tears, O father or mother, who art weeping for a beloved and promising child, and thou also, lonely widow, sorrowing in solitude; cease to grieve, sister, for thy much regretted brother, or brother for thy sister; friend, mourn no longer for the friend torn from thy bosom. Close all wounds that torture tender hearts! The dead are still alive. We are not parted for ever. Reunion awaits us all!

Divinely revealed truth, be my blessed comfort evermore. I also have lost what I loved. I also, when in solitude, weep for the sweetest joys of my life, which have descended into the grave. Into the grave?—Ah, no; for it was not the clay that I loved, but the soul, which smiled to me through the gentle eyes, and which spoke the words of tenderness that sounded from the eloquent lips. And this soul still lives, for God lives. It still loves, for God loves. Oh, heavenly thought! I am still cherished by my dear ones in the better world, with a purer, nobler, and more tender affection than here in the dust.

Ye love me, O ye dear ones, for whom my tears flow, whom my love follows yon side the grave. Love me, and the grave cannot separate us. How can it separate those whom God united here below in such tender bonds? My sadness is not the fruit of doubt, but of my longing for you. We shall be with each other again in that blessed land, where there is no sorrow and no parting, but only perfection and bliss inexpressible. The Creator made us for each other, and He created us not only for this earthly life, but for eternal existence. In this world He only allowed us, as it were, to catch a glimpse of each other, that we might aspire the more ardently towards our higher goal. He attached our hearts to heaven, not only by the bonds of faith, but likewise by those of love.

Yes; on the other side the grave, not here on earth, is my real fatherland, my true home. Towards the land where my loved ones dwell, turn my tearful eyes; to it ascend my devout thoughts, my sacred vows. Yes; though abiding on earth, I will live for eternity; among mortals, I will live for the immortal ones who have gone before me. If there be a sin cleaving to me, I will cleanse myself of it. If there be an impure desire poisoning my heart, I will banish it forthwith. If there be a wrong that I have committed, I will repair it. If there be a fellow-being whom I have offended, I will seek reconciliation.

We shall, we must, be reunited. Oh, God! I thank Thee for Thy overflowing Grace and Mercy. What return can I make? I feel my poverty, my impotence; but I feel also that through Thee, my God, my Eternal Father, the universe is blest. I will seek solitude, I will fall down before Thee, with mingled tears of sadness and joy, and my sighs and my tears shall glorify Thee in silence!

MEMORIAL FESTIVAL OF OUR TRIUMPH OVER DEATH.

Yes; thou shalt rise again, my dust, more blest
After thy hasty rest.
Undying life to live,
Will He who made thee give.
    Praised be He!

Sown but to bloom again once more, was I.
The Harvest Lord goes by;
He gathers in the sheaves,
Nor thine, nor mine, He leaves—
    Praised be He!

Oh, day of gratitude! Oh, day of bliss!
God's own best day is this,
Which, my short slumber o'er,
From the cold grave once more
    Shall wake me.

How like a dream will it then seem to me—
With Jesus shall I be—
In all His joys I share,
Each weary pilgrim care
    Is past for me.

Oh! to the Holiest, my Redeemer, lead—
Then shall I live indeed
In sanctity, there raise
My voice, His name to praise,
    For evermore!

                    (*Luke* xxiv. 5, 6.)

"*Why seek ye the living among the dead?*" asked the angels of the sorrowing women who came to the sepulchre of the Saviour; "He is not here, but is risen!" (Luke xxiv. 5, 6.)

He is risen! The disciples heard the tidings, and a thrill of awe and joy passed through their souls, and courage revived in the hearts of the timid among them, who, since the death of their Lord, had been roaming about like sheep that have lost their shepherd.

He is risen! The persecutors and murderers of the Messiah heard it, and were terror-stricken. They refused to believe in the miracle. They endeavoured to put it down by audacious falsehood. They asserted that His disciples had stolen away the dead body. But in vain was their clamour! The living Christ appeared before His followers; He appeared in the land of Galilee. He is risen! cried the exultant heavens; and all times, all centuries to come, will repeat the joyful cry.

My soul also rejoices that He is risen. His triumph is my triumph; His victory over death and the grave is also mine; His life is my life. The festival of His wonderful resurrection from the grave and from corruption, is also the memorial feast of my future elevation above the world and death, when the corruptible shall put on incorruption, and the mortal the immortal.

His resurrection completed the work of the Messiah on earth. He had lived, taught, and performed good deeds; the holy seed of God was sown, but the soil was still untilled, the growth of the seed uncertain. Christ was still misjudged by many; the purpose of His coming was not understood, even by His most intimate friends. They hoped that He had come to found an earthly throne; to restore the kingdom of David; to free them from the dominion of Rome; to establish the rule and the power of the Jews over all the nations of the earth. This was their hope. Yet the Messiah had said, " My kingdom is not of this world."

He was doomed to suffering and death, to seal the truth of His doctrine with His blood, to fall a willing victim for the sins of the world, and to bring the sacrificial worship of the Hebrews to an end by His death. He suffered the death of the World-Redeemer. His blood was, as it were, required to make the seeds of godliness germinate, which he had sown in the rough soil of the human heart.

But His work was not finished. With Him died the courage of His first followers.

Their bright dreams of earthly power and splendour were destroyed, and with them also their hopes and prospects.

His death had rendered incomprehensible to them what He had taught and prophesied. The life of the Messiah had become a mystery to them, their own destination a secret. That which had been begun was not completed, but was broken off. Gloomy doubts obscured their souls, as the night of the sepulchre hid the corpse of their Divine Master.

Just then the tidings broke upon them: He is risen! And, lo! a new day dawned upon them. The mystery that clothed His words was at once solved; they comprehended His prophecies; they understood His divinity. Full of holy enthusiasm, they responded to His call. Now, shame and honour, life and death, were as naught to them when compared to the message He had given them to deliver. The seed of God, which He had sown, began to sprout vigorously. His resurrection acted on it like the breath of Spring. Death had vanished; hell was vanquished; humanity was reconciled to God; the heavenly kingdom of spirits founded; He had finished! Thus the festival of the Resurrection of Jesus became the first and most sacred festival of the Christians, and at the same time a memorial feast of their own redemption, through Jesus. Let us keep the feast, said they; let us do it in remembrance of the purification from sin, of which we are made capable, through His word; let us cast away every vicious tendency that desecrates us. For, as a little leaven leaveneth the whole lump, so doth the smallest sin dishonour and desecrate the whole dignity of man. "Therefore, let us keep the feast," cries St. Paul, "not with old leaven, neither with the leaven of malice and wickedness, but with the unleavened bread of sincerity and truth." (1 Cor. v. 8.)

As Jesus finished His task, so will I finish mine. As He completed the redemption of a world from the fetters of sin and error, so will I complete my sanctification through faith in Him and in His Word. If His life be my life, then, also, is His victory my victory, His glorification my glorification—then shall I not taste death. My spirit shall soar triumphantly above the grave and the dust of earth, towards heaven.

I will seek redemption through Jesus, for in no one else is there salvation. To be redeemed through Him, is to become like unto Him; to be pure in mind, and to do good; to be free from every sin, and to live for God alone; to act in my appointed sphere with godlike nobleness of soul without selfishness, without base motives; to recognize in the world of spirits my home, in the Creator of the boundless universe my Father, and my kindred in all created beings like myself, who lie worshipping at His feet; to seek my happiness, not in the dust and in the fleeting things of this earth, but in eternity.

Christ has risen from the dead; He has finished His work. I also shall rise again, and shall complete my work. If I live in the spirit of Jesus, the grave has no terrors for me. The grave can only hold my corpse; my corpse is dust and ashes; dust and ashes in themselves have no life; but the soul is life; therefore my soul cannot die.

Cannot die? Not so! Did not Jesus Himself say, "Fear not those who would kill the body, but those who would kill the soul?" And what is the death of the soul? Sin.

Where there is sin, there the lusts of the body prevail; there reason is silent; there the conscience is stifled; there the activity of the spirit is paralyzed; there is death. Sin is the death of the spirit. In like manner as a dead human body is insensible to all influences that may be brought to bear upon it, so is the spirit when vice has conquered. As the dead body is without strength, so also the spirit loses its power when the brute instincts are triumphant. As the dead body is without a will, so also the spirit loses all freedom, where passions, such as worldly ambition, luxuriousness, voluptuousness, covetousness, and malice, prevail.

Therefore is sin the death of the spirit! And can a spirit, that has not lived a true life on earth, continue to live when its body dies? Does it not sleep the eternal sleep? Will it not be as if it had never existed?

It is from that death that Jesus has rescued us by His doctrine, not from the death of the body. This death we must all die. But when we sanctify ourselves—that is, when we purify ourselves from all vicious tendencies, from all animal and sinful desires—our spirits imbibe eternal life in vigorous draughts. The death of the body is not the death of the soul. If, then, a perfect soul, after the example of Jesus, does not die, of what importance is the decay of our bodies? We live! what matters it that the earthly coil which clings to us, should fall away? We live, and live through the word of Jesus; and we may exclaim with rapture: Where is thy sting, O Death! O hell! where is thy victory? Praised be God, who has given us the victory through our Lord Jesus Christ!

If sin be the death of the soul, then virtue, or likeness to God, must be its life. Every infraction of the divine laws is a death-wound inflicted on the spirit, and every deed pleasant in the sight of God is a quickening of our spiritual life.

And thus I understand when it is said, that the wages of sin are death! When it is said, that Christ saved us from death, by showing us the way of life. Yes; He has saved us from death, by showing us the way of life; by pointing out to us our high destination, and teaching us to know our own dignity; by affording us the surest means to reach perfection: His own example; and by bidding us deny ourselves and our sinful desires, and follow Him. Therefore, using figurative language, He called Himself our way to life.

Christ has risen! He has finished gloriously His Divine Mission; He has conquered death for me, if in my life I do show forth His merits and His holiness, and avoid sin, which is spiritual death.

As Christ had not finished until His task on earth was completed, until the grave and death had been conquered, until His disciples had been consecrated, and He had returned to His Father; so shall I not have finished until I have reached the end of my career. As long as I remain on earth my existence will be a constant wrestling with sin, a constant struggle with death. Not until I have reached the end will it be proved whether my spirit has conquered death and sin, whether I have fought the good fight, whether I have won the promised palm of life. How long shall this struggle still endure? When shall I rejoice in my victory over death and sin?

However long it may be, I will hold fast my faith, and shall not weary. "For he that overcometh," saith the Lord, "shall inherit all things; and I will be his God, and he shall be my son." (Rev. xxi. 7.) And however long my struggle may still endure, the festival of the Messiah's completion of His work shall be to me a reminder of the victory I also must win. Ah! that I might be able each time I celebrate thy victory, O Saviour, to celebrate also my triumph over death and sin!

Blessed are ye, O glorified spirits, who have already overcome! O ye beloved of Jesus! ye saints of God! in solemn silence I will celebrate the memory of your triumph also. Ye have fought the fight; I am still wrestling with sin. Ye are rejoicing, having reached the goal; I am still weeping at my shortcomings.

Blessed are ye, ye have conquered death in Jesus, and with Jesus! The resurrection of the Lord became your resurrection. He has risen; He lives; and ye live with Him.

He lives! He is risen! The heavenly assurance that this gives us, that we also shall rise from the dead, quickens the wounded hearts of the disconsolate mourners who despair at their lost joys. To us also God has promised immortal life; our souls shall not be victims of the grave.

He lives! He is risen! Oh, disconsolate father, why walkest thou so sad and unsympathising among thy fellow-men, seeking the child of whom death has robbed thee? O mother, why dost thou weep on the tomb of thy darling, calling him by his name, and asking the silent and mysterious grave to give him back to thee? Why, O mourners, do ye seek the living among the dead? Those ye love are not there; they are in the bosom of the Father! Celebrate cheerfully the Easter Festival. It is the festival of the Resurrection, and of the remembrance of our victory over death. Father, mother, think of this! There is no wall of separation between life and eternity; there is no real separation from those ye so tenderly loved. Your child lives. Ye also shall live hereafter, for Jesus lives, God lives. There is no death, except through sin.

He lives! He is risen! Unhappy husband, why pinest thou to descend into the silent tomb, where she sleeps who was thy noblest possession on earth, thy all in all? Her dust rests there, it is true. But why seekest thou the living among the dead? The grave is not the home of her spirit, which was born to eternal life. Its home is in the bosom of God. God is with you; how, then, are you separated? She lives, and thou livest, and God embraces you both. Fight out thy fight, O mourner! the apparent separation will not be for long. Celebrate cheerfully the Easter Festival. It is the feast of the Resurrection, and of our own victory over death.

He lives! He is risen! Yet thou, O lonely widow, thou still lamentest with stubborn grief over thy departed husband? Thou, O desolate maiden, askest the grave to give up the loved one whom it tore from thy bleeding heart? Thou, brother, still grievest for the sister who faded in early youth? Thou, sister, weepest bitter tears over a brother gone to rest? Whom seek ye, then, in the grave, my friends? Why seek ye the living among the dead? They are not there; they are with God. Celebrate cheerfully and trustingly the Easter Festival—the festival of the Resurrection, and of our victory over death.

Christ lives! He is risen! I also shall live and be with God. Jesus' Resurrection is my resurrection, because His life is to be my life. We are not the prey of the grave! O ye who have already overcome, and ye who will one day overcome, we are all God's children! Why should we despair?

> O'er earth and time, my soul, mount high,
> O'er death and o'er mortality—
>   Upraise thee, trembling soul.
> Thy Fatherland is there—in Heaven—
> The Resurrection was but given
>   To lead thee to thy goal.
> E'en here, amidst the wreck of death,
> The higher nature gleams beneath.

Dry leaves are all thou look'st on here,
'Tis dust of dust that fills the bier—
　Thy brother's earthly shell.
The fragile shell may broken be,
And waste away; but not o'er thee
　Prevails the grave's dark spell.
Free from the burthen of life's pain,
Thy high reward awaits thee then.

The Father's love thou then wilt see—
His love will comprehended be—
　His foresight wilt thou reach.
Creation's vast unbounded scheme,
The countless myriad worlds that gleam,
　Will all His wisdom teach.
Bright midst the starry host Divine
Shall the new earth and Heaven outshine.

Then, full of joy and reverence deep,
To-day thy resurrection keep
　With Christ—thy life, thy light.
The blessed hope of Heaven regained,
The endless, Godlike life attained,
　In His own holy height.
Was not Christ's coming but for this:
Man to perfect, and win us bliss?

THE TRIUMPH OF HOLINESS.

He left, with honour crowned, His rock-hewn tomb,
And God was reconciled to man.—The gloom,
   The curse, from Mount Sinai has passed by.
Instead of death, He gave us life above;
Instead of wrath, He gave us heavenly love,
   And confidence through His own victory.
He—He alone, fulfilled it in that hour—
The work of grace, of mercy, and of power—
   All praise unto the Resurrection be.
      Death may appear,
      We know no fear,
O Death-Destroyer, for we follow Thee!

Shout, shout aloud to God with joyful voice!
Let the whole universe in praise rejoice,
   The conquest has been gained, the battle's done,
All that was dim and doubtful is made clear,
God's will is spoken so that all may hear,
   He, the Most Holy, has the victory won.
Shall I not, then, with stronger courage bear
The galling weight of earthly grief and care?
   Can what God loveth ever be cast down?
      Raise thine eyes
      Unto the skies,
And know, the Eternal cannot be o'erthrown.

                 (*Rom.* viii. 28.)

AFTER the death of Jesus, His disciples fled in fear and trembling. They sought solitude to weep over the death of their Divine Master, and also concealment from the sanguinary cruelty of the Jews. And in the first bitterness of their sorrow at the loss of their dearly beloved friend, many doubts probably arose in their breast. I seem to hear their complaints: "Jesus, our Divine Master, fell a victim to cruel murderers. How could God forsake the beloved One who called Himself His Son? How could the Most Holy allow the base multitude to point the finger of scorn at the Holy One? Who will venture to be virtuous and just, if virtue and justice lead to the felon's doom, while vice triumphs and prospers? Is there a Judge on high, and yet He is silent? Is there an all-loving God in the universe, and yet He permits the innocent to suffer painfully for deeds of which he has not been guilty? Permits him to suffer without succour, without alleviation, without consolation? Does God dissever the sacred bonds of love which His own hand has woven, and does He leave hearts to bleed to death of wounds which have been nflicted because they trusted in Him?"

But on the third day the strange rumour spread through the land: The crucified has risen! The unjust rulers, the murderers, were seized with terror; but endeavoured to allay their fears by doubts and denial. The friends of Jesus heard the tidings, and, though still doubting, they were filled with gladness. They afterwards beheld their Master like one glorified, and, with feelings of devotional joy and awe, they stammered forth, "My Lord and my God!" (John xx. 28.) Holiness had triumphed.

Jesus had won the great victory; His innocence had triumphed gloriously over all His past sufferings: the Divine character of His revelations was made wonderfully manifest to those who still required such a test. Treachery, persecution, crucifixion, death, and the grave, had proved of no avail. They had only been permitted that they might swell the triumph of the eternal Son. And thus, in this superlative instance also, we behold, as in a great picture, the manifestation of the blissful truth, which the Holy Scriptures hold forth to us to this day: "We know that all things work together for good to them that love God." (Rom. viii. 28.) That which is holy must ultimately be triumphant.

But what is holiness in the spiritual world? I will tell thee. It is immaculate purity! It is that which maintains itself in its native simplicity without any admixture of things which do not belong to it. Therefore, that mind must be called holy in which only the purest virtue dwells, and no passion, no tendency to sin. Consequently, the spirit may be said to be sanctified when it is unstained by anything earthly, when it is not swayed by the influences of the body, but determines and guides itself solely by its indwelling Divine laws. Such a spirit is sure of attaining the highest good; it approaches daily towards perfection. Purity is indestructible, eternal; only that which is mixed, compounded of various elements, is perishable, for it ultimately dissolves again into the elements of which it is composed.

This truth holds good of the living and of the dead. It is a law of nature. Everything in the world which we perceive through our senses is composed of simple substances. As soon as these combine, their purity is alloyed. But when as compound substances, they are destroyed, they immediately return to their primitive purity. Thus, gold is valuable in proportion to its purity. In vain is every attempt to destroy it by fire,

The ashes of burnt wood can never again become wood; but gold, when subjected to the action of fire, only throws off the dross that is mixed with it, and comes out of the crucible purer and more valuable than before. The same is the case with a holy mind when it passes through the purifying fire of earthly tribulation. It throws off the sensuous desire for honours, wealth, and other enjoyments, which may still cling to it, and comes forth purer, and holier, and with intensified consciousness of its own spotlessness.

Holiness wins the victory. The history of all times and all nations proclaims it. Many errors have prevailed since the beginning of the world; but they disappear gradually as men learn to know truth. *No error can endure for ever; while on the other hand, since the·beginning of time no truth has ever perished.* Each truth acquired is handed down from generation to generation as a precious treasure, and one century inherits it from another. No doubt it may at times be obscured by passing errors, as is the sun by passing clouds. But the clouds are no part of the sun, and truth remains ever distinct from error. It has, therefore, each time come forth the more majestically from out of the dark mists of ignorance. Human violence may indeed do much to impede its progress —may silence men's tongues by fear, so that they venture not to declare the truth, and may persecute it even unto death. But it lives on in noble minds though all lips be mute; for though tongues may be restrained, thought cannot be coerced. The spirit is free within the realm of thought. It scorns the impotence of man; and on the grave of many a persecutor, Truth has, with undying energy, once more reared her divine banner.

Holy, as truth, is goodness. The history of the world bears witness to it. The good that has happened on earth has been followed by blessed and lasting consequences. For only that which is good and just is in harmony with nature and with the soul. Evil, on the contrary, is in antagonism with the entire creation. Crime has indeed often been clad in royal purple, and has often trampled on innocence with impunity. But the purple has mouldered away, the crime remained a crime, and from the blood of the persecuted innocence has arisen a triumphant avenger. In vain vice sharpened its murderous axe, and doomed virtue to die in the flames; though trembling cowards burnt incense before the ruthless tyrant, the sinner's pride was soon laid low, and the funeral pile of slandered innocence was changed into a throne of glory.

For this reason the memory of wise and virtuous men has ever been revered even by very remote posterity. They have been the benefactors of entire nations and of generations of men; but being misjudged and scorned either by the ignorance or malice of their contemporaries, they have too frequently been the victims of their own goodness, and of the barbarity of others. But was the cause for which they fought therefore extinguished? No; that which was holy remained ultimately triumphant. With calm consciousness of the good they had bestowed upon the world, the noble spirits of these victims of human oppression rose purified and exultant to Heaven, there to receive a more glorious palm of victory than could be won on earth. What did they lose by being misjudged by the world! In carrying out their virtuous purposes they thought not of the world's applause, but acted spontaneously, urged on by their inward instincts and aspirations. They were consoled by their firm conviction that they were accomplishing that which would tend to increase the happinesss of mankind, and which would never be destroyed. And they did not deceive themselves. For that which is holy ever triumphs; and posterity names with a blessing the men whom their contemporaries condemned.

The remembrance hereof ought to strengthen and elevate our minds, and to inspire us with courage and unswerving determination to act so as to gain the approval of God. In like manner as the wisest and noblest among our predecessors ever moved onward with their eyes fixed upon God, and trusting in the righteousness of their cause, so let us also uphold the cause which we consider good and just, and likely to diffuse happiness, though the base multitude may scoff at us, and accuse us of low and selfish motives, and persecute and ill-treat us; for that which is holy will ultimately gain the victory!

Be Thou my example! O Christ, Friend of man; Thou, who in the great battle with fate didst not allow Thyself to be led away from the Divine path by temptations, or by threats; but didst persevere in love and well-doing, though surrounded by hatred and persecution—be Thou my example in action.

Be Thou also my example in patient suffering, Thou greatest of sufferers, who, when forsaken by all, when betrayed by Thy bosom friend, when Thine enemies rejoiced openly at Thy fall, when Thy most faithful followers fled from before Thee, and the most zealous denied Thee—still remained meek and humble, unshaken in Thy sublime grandeur of soul, in Thy Heavenly virtue.

And be my example, my strengthener in hope, Saviour, risen from the dead, who, in the Majesty of Thy victory, didst annihilate the powers of evil that arose against Thee, blessed the world, gloriously rewarded the devotion of Thy beloved disciples, and beheld the Heavens opening to receive Thee, while the nations of the earth lay worshipping at Thy feet.

That which is holy ever remains triumphant;· therefore be holy. Only that which is impure decays and perishes; therefore avoid all that is impure! Has the voice of God, speaking through the marvels of nature, through human events, and through the holy words of revealed religion, no power over thy heart?

Be holy; that is, be *pure*. Beware not to let sensual influences obtain too great a hold over thy mind, and whatever thou undertakest, let it never be for the sake of earthly reward. Do the good that thou art able to do, or that thou mayest wish to do, without any hope of reaping honours or riches in return. If thou lookest for such return, oh, verily, then thou dost but make virtue the tool of thy baseness, and thou must be counted among those of whom the Saviour said,—"They have their reward!" Love thy fellow-beings; help them with a goodwill whenever thou canst do so; alleviate misery as far as it lies in thy power; speak well of others whenever an opportunity offers; promote useful undertakings even when commenced by others; but do all this, not in order to make thyself beloved in return, not in order to win a reputation, but because thou art convinced that what thou dost is right and good, that the deed is worthy of thee, that through it thou manifestest that perfection which thine own conscience, thy God, and thy Saviour demand of thee. In acting thus, thou wilt keep thyself pure from gross earthly influences, thou wilt sanctify thy mind.

Go forth and arrest the evil that others may be planning; comfort the unhappy whose misfortunes thou canst not prevent; try to promote the interests even of those who may have sought to injure thee; convince thine enemy by thy generous acts towards him, that he has formed an erroneous opinion of thee; but do not these things from fear, but from a sense of duty, from the feeling that a true Christian cannot think and act otherwise. Then thy deed will be free from impure earthly alloy, and will be solely the fruit of the spirit called to immortality and perfection. To do thus is to approach the goal of holiness; and that which is holy is triumphant at last! Therefore persevere without ceasing in thy pure aspirations, and do not allow thyself to be led astray by any apparent disadvantages, by any personal annoyance, by any humiliations which thou mayest be subjected to in consequence. He who is incapable of such strength and elevation of soul, he will remain lost among the crowd of vulgar minds, and will deserve the ruin which he will bring upon himself by his weakness and his vacillation.

All men respect in others that firmness of mind and strength of principle which are proof against every fate; yea, even in bad men, we cannot at times help admiring the extraordinary determination and inflexibility with which they advance towards the end they have marked out for themselves. Only those persons can with truth be called contemptible who have no power over themselves, who are honest to-day, base to-morrow, who are ever vacillating between virtue and vice, sinning and repenting, and who never attain to any kind of self-dependence. We despise them, because in them there is no decided purity of will. One day they set virtue aside for fear of exposing themselves to the malicious observations of senseless worldlings, another day they follow virtue because they think that more honour is to be won in this way than in following sin. But they succumb, for only that which is pure and holy ultimately triumphs in life. They fight no real fight against the power and influences of the senses, for their vacillations testify that they are but helpless tools of their own passions. In none of the circumstances of life do they show any will or spirit of their own; what, then, can remain of them when in death they lose the body, which, with its earthly lusts, ruled them?

Only that which is holy triumphs! Remember, O soul, the majesty of Him who has risen from the dead! When men conspire against thy higher principles, and give thee in return for the good thou hast achieved, not gratitude, but the curse of envy, of jealousy, and malice—remember Him! Adversity is only a test of thy courage, a trial of the strength of thy virtue. It is easy during a lovely summer evening to profess indifference to the inclemency of the weather, or while resting in the lap of peace to boast of the prowess we should give proof of were we to encounter an enemy; but it is in bearing up against storm and rain, and the sudden changes of the temperature, that the strong man shows his hardiness, and it is amid the sanguinary horrors of the battle-field that the hero proves his courage.

He who has made up his mind to act purely and nobly, that is to say, to think, and speak, and act according to his best convictions, must be prepared to encounter many vexatious obstacles to the carrying out of his good intentions. For if all that is good and useful met with no impediments, his arm and his heart would not be required to promote it.

Whoever determines to do his best in life according to his convictions—to be just, fair in all his dealings, truthful, and zealous for the public weal, must be prepared to find numbers of persons endeavouring to oppose him. Many, simply because being of an envious disposition they hate everything that is praiseworthy which they have not themselves projected or accomplished; others, because your efforts may possibly be opposed to some selfish plan of theirs, cherished in secret; some again, because being themselves without any inward worth, they are unable to conceive that others are better than themselves, and therefore attribute base sentiments even to the best of men, and believe that the most upright acts are dictated by selfish motives; again, many will oppose you, not because their intentions are less good than your own, but because their views are totally different, owing to their education, their temperament, their outward circumstances, and experiences of life being different; others, though they may do full justice to the purity of your intentions, will resist you, because they consider you a mere enthusiast.

But if your convictions are well founded, if you have tried them by the test of your conscience, and conceive them to be in accordance with the will of God, and you know them to be *pure* from every admixture of passion—if you firmly believe what you propound to be truth, or what you undertake to be for the benefit of the world, then do not hesitate to remain faithful to yourself! For it is eternally true, that to them that love God, all things work for good. Every obstacle will but stimulate you to greater exertion, and will prevent you from relaxing in your efforts; every contradiction, every objection, will make you reflect, and perhaps turn your attention to points on which you have erred, or on which you might otherwise have gone too far. These impediments will therefore serve to purify your principles from all earthly dross, and render your triumph the more glorious.

And should the storms that assail thee prove too violent and thy courage and thy strength threaten to give way, oh, then, think of Him who is risen! God was with Christ, and God is with every noble soul in its greatest tribulations on earth; God is with thee, because thou seekest Him! It is possible that thou mayest fail; but what wilt thou lose? Perhaps the fame of the moment, perhaps thy earthly life. But of what importance are these? Do these things affect the sublime and immortal essence in thee which we call spirit? Nay, they are but of the earth, earthy, and in every case vanish in death. Remain faithful to thyself to the end! The good man may fail, the good cause never!

That which is holy is triumphant at last. Jesus, Thou who art risen from the dead; Messiah, wonderful, glorified, majestic Victor over life and death, the halo which surrounds Thy grave teaches me to see and to love this great truth. Thou also hast triumphed, and century proclaims it to century with exultant joy; and the human race, blessed through Thee, worship Thee.

Little did Thy contemporaries think, whilst Thou wert living among them humbly and misjudged, that Thy name would become the object of the world's love and reverence. Little did they think, when thou wert preaching the highest and most sacred truths with Divine power and simplicity, that the words spoken by Thee in remote places, to a small band of followers, would resound through hundreds of years from the lips of millions of men, in all languages, in splendid temples and in desert caves, in the palaces of kings and in the hovels of the poor. Little did they think when Thou wert nailed, bleeding, to the cross, between two malefactors, and drew thy last sigh amid the scoffs of the malignant multitude, when the faithful doubted, and Thy beloved ones fled in dismay; little did they think that this cross would become the symbol of Thy God-like services to the human race, and would be raised as such in the burning deserts of the tropics, on the ice-fields of the far north, whither no warm sunbeams ever penetrate, on the shores of unknown seas, and on the cloud-capped summits of high mountains.

But, strengthened by Thy victory, and filled with the Holy Ghost, Thy disciples spread through all parts of the world, and proclaimed to the astonished nations the glad tidings of the kingdom of God. In spite of torture, chains, sword and cross, they completed the great work of the redemption of the world. They fell victims to their zeal, many of them breathed their last under fearful sufferings; but their cause was triumphant!

And I, Jesus Messiah, I will do as they! I will purify myself of every evil tendency, of every weakness; I will stand forth in word and deed as a perfect man, who prizes Thy word and Thy truth above all things. When occasion offers for serving my fellowmen, I will not first selfishly consider what would be to my own advantage, nor timidly give up what duty bids me do, because of the obstacles and the trouble I may have to encounter. In the end I shall succeed. And my reward I carry in my bosom; for that which is holy will triumph!

THE CONNEXION BETWEEN LIFE AND ETERNITY.

When, after a few fleeting hours are past,
   Thy will is fully perfected in me,
My earthly burthen is removed at last,
   And from the chains of sin, my soul set free—
The last sad tear that earth can claim is shed,
And " dust to dust," I rest among the dead—

How shall I to myself, for joy, be known,
   When the dark veil is taken from mine eyes ?
When the bright Angel brotherhood shall own,
   And my glance pierces Heaven's mysteries ?
And what was sacred held from mortal sight,
To the freed spirit is revealed in light.

Here, ere Thou cam'st Thy hidden ways to teach,
   My boasted wisdom was an idle dream—
Of all the countless joys my soul shall reach,
   My searching gaze can scarcely catch a gleam—
Yet I, confiding in Thy truth, believe,
What *Thou* hast promised, *that* shall I receive.

Mercy of God ! without or mark or bound—
   The Heavens have not sufficient tongues to praise,
Nor words of worth enough our thanks to sound
   For that Thou lend'st Thy light to guide our ways.
One single ray from Thee outshineth far
The sun and moon, and every glittering star.
                      (*Revelation* xiv. 13.)

THE year is but a quick succession of brief moments. Who is conscious of the infinitesimal part of life that is comprised within each of these infinitesimal periods of time, and which vanishes even while I am thinking of it? When a year has elapsed, even this longer period, on looking back, seems to us but as a moment. It was here; it is gone; and it will never come again.

The day passes speedily by. Another and another follows, and passes as quickly. The duration of a moment is but that of the twinkling of an eye; and what are weeks, months, and years, other than a succession of such moments, which I comprise under one name?

In all things I find constant changes going on, and yet all, in fact, remain ever the same. Thousands and thousands of years ago, all was as it is now. The mutable is ever comprised in the immutable the fleeting in the enduring. I distinguish minutes, weeks, months. But it is only the human understanding that separates and makes distinctions, and applies different names. In reality, all are one and the same time. What I denominate the seasons, are but the varying positions assumed towards the sun by the globe which I inhabit. Time is immutable.

And though all things seem infinitely varied, nevertheless, one thing is but a consequence of another; and each is intimately connected and identical with all.

All things must, by the closest concatenation, be joined into ONE, for there is but one universe. There are not two universes differing in organization, or opposed to each other. There is but ONE God, whose wisdom and laws originated all existence as a UNITY, as an integral, consisting of many integrant parts.

Now if all things be but parts of a whole, and there be but one Creator of the whole, and each one thing be indestructibly linked to all others; how can you speak of time and eternity as if you were speaking of two distinct universes?

How senseless would it not be to suppose, that the life we enjoy one day is distinct from that of the next, because the days are separated by the shadows of night! Who imagines because in autumn plants wither and return to dust and earth, that with the new spring, when vegetation recommences, a new world, so to say, begins! There is nothing different from what has been; all is again the same as it was, eternally the same.

Dost thou think that when the plant withers, and its dust is dispersed by the wind, the component parts of that which was a plant have been blown out of the universe, and have been reduced to absolute nothingness? Nay, whether united in a plant, or scattered as motes in a sunbeam, they are present and indestructible, irremovable from the universe of God. The hidden power of life, which combined this dust into verdant, blooming plants, also continues apart from the dust, and in winter as in summer, works actively in the seeds, in the universe. When the sun of Spring reproduces the conditions laid down by the Creator, according to which the vital force acts upon the elementary substances around it, this action recommences, and new plants germinate, and put forth buds, and leaves, and blossoms. Thus every new thing is ever a reproduction of the old; ever the same, however new it may appear to the eye of man.

In the universe there is nothing new; and nothing old is annihilated. What we call new and old, are mere distinctions made by our understanding, means to help our feeble powers of conception. In reality there is in nature nothing new and nothing old, for God's creation is eternal. It is only the relations of things to one another that change, and these changes are what we call temporal. Whether a flower withers and dies, and is dissolved into dust and vapour, or whether some world, inhabited by millions of beings, is destroyed and reduced to dust, it is the same thing. Neither the component parts of the flower nor of the world can escape from the universe of God. It is only their relations to each other that have undergone a change. We make a difference between the flower and the world, because relatively to our bodies the one seems to us very small, the other immense; but to the infinite and omnipresent God, nothing is small, and nothing is great. Therefore is the most insignificant worm, and the most powerful of mortals on this earth, of equal importance to Him. His Providence and His Love embrace both alike, as being His creatures.

We must beware not to persuade ourselves into believing that that which we can see with our limited sight, measure with our small standard, and comprehend with our restricted faculties, within our circumscribed sphere of life and space, is exactly such as we conceive it to be. We make distinctions where in nature, strictly speaking, none exist. To us, that which is invisible, and beyond the sphere of our comprehension on earth, is as if it were not. There is nothing whatsoever extant on earth, of which the elementary substances were not previously in the air, in the form of impalpable and invisible particles. The whole globe which we mortals inhabit has been formed out of components of the atmosphere. From the air, water is precipitated; from the air, the plants receive their constituent elements; from the air and the plants, the animals receive theirs, and man his from all. Mountains, forests, oceans, &c., are all, as it were, children of the air, and may again be dissolved into air. All are one.

All are one. Therefore are all things so closely linked together that the single links are often indistinguishable. In the eternal universe there is no yesterday and to-day—these only exist for us mortals, who inhabit the little planet called the earth, which by revolving round the sun causes a fleeting alternation of light and shade, cold and heat, which we call days and seasons. In the eternal universe there is no beginning and no ending, but only a constant play of relations, and this is what we call life; but eternal, as the things themselves, as all God's works, are also their varying relations to each other. Consequently there is an uninterrupted reticulation of life. The particular relations of certain parts may cease, but the substances or forces themselves can never cease to be; and as little can the constant variations of relations, *i. e.* life, cease to be. That which seems to us as a beginning and an ending, as a blooming and fading, as morning and evening—that which we call birth and death, old and young, is only the varying play of the relations of things in the universe, or the life of the creation. That which we call death is therefore in itself a confirmation of life, an act of life, and life itself!

Time and eternity are the same to God. But they are likewise so to me. Why make this distinction? There is but *one* Eternal. After death I shall be in eternity, but I am already in it. After death I shall be with God; but here below already I live, and move, and have my being in God.

However, with that intensified vital action, which we call death, an active process of separation and renewed combination takes place in all my component parts. As in autumn the vital force leaves the withering plant, so in death the spiritual part of my being withdraws from the earthly part. That within me, which I call my real self, and which is capable of conceiving God, enters into combinations with other substances and things in the life-teeming universe. But my discarded body, which returns to dust, also continues in God's universe and enters into other combinations. And I, the God-conscious I, the conceiving and perceiving spirit, I, also like the dust of my body, shall continue through all Eternity.

Am I a different being to-day to what I was yesterday, because I have put on other garments? No; for though I may yesterday have worn an inferior dress, and to-day wear a better one, I am nevertheless the same being. And as little as the raiment which I wear forms part of myself, as little does the body form part of the spirit, which in death puts it off. But the same as I have been while clad in the body, the same shall I be after having entered into other combinations. For I am and remain the same spirit, in like manner as my body remains the same dust.

Consequently, from the brief space of time which we call earthly life, I pass over into the higher or lower, happier or unhappier relations into which I may hereafter enter, a worthy or unworthy spirit, according as I may have proved myself in this world.

And thus are fulfilled the words of Scripture : " Their works do follow them."

"Blessed are the dead which die in the Lord from henceforth; Yea, saith the Spirit, that they may have rest from their labours; and their works do follow them." (Rev. xiv. 13.)

Our works do follow us, because between time and eternity there is an intimate and indissoluble connexion : more intimate indeed than that between the drops of the sea and the sea itself. The whole system of created things is but one; and therefore living in time, I am living in eternity; and living in this world, I am living in the universe, my Father's house, in which I shall live for evermore; for the connexion between the unit and the all, of which it forms an integral part, can never be dissevered.

I know that this indissoluble connexion between time and eternity exists, because, not only is the smallest mote dancing in a sunbeam imperishable, but so likewise is my self-conscious spirit, which aspires towards perfection. Things change yet endure. The circumstances that surround me vary, but I ever remain in the midst of the infinite vital action of the universe. Now, if my soul is imperishable, and ever retains its identity, how can the connexion between to-day and to-morrow, between the here and the hereafter, between time and eternity, ever be interrupted ? I know that the connexion exists, because there is but one God, who has ordained all things, who encompasses all things, who created all things perfect, not as fragments and disjointed parts, but as the intimately connected and closely interwoven parts of a whole, infinitely harmonious in all its causes and effects. And God is my God to-day, as He will be my God when the circumstances of this life no longer surround me, but I shall have entered into other relations and connexions.

Therefore, blessed are the dead who die in the Lord, for their works do follow them. They *follow* them, for in the great concatenation of things there are no missing links, no interruptions. One thing proceeds from another; as in the smallest, so in the greatest; as in earthly, so in moral and spiritual matters. Whether thou risest or thou fallest, thou takest the place thou hast prepared for thyself; nothing that is done can be undone. Thy works do follow thee.

There are degraded human beings, very little removed from the brutes, who lack the energy to develop any of their indwelling spiritual capacities. They aspire to nothing better than to be animals, and to satisfy their animal desires. What they hear said about virtue (conformity to the eternal laws of God) seems to them irrational and absurd, or at least they wish to think it so. To be clad in costly apparel, to recline upon soft couches, to live in grand houses, to feast on dainty viands, to drink the best wines, to enjoy ample pecuniary means, to have the power to oppress others and to tower high above them, to possess much worldly knowledge, to be able to calculate cunningly, and to be irresistible in action—in a word, to be a kind of perfect animal, such is their highest ambition. Of more exalted things they have no conception, so utterly degraded are they. If you tell them that it is their duty to sacrifice all earthly things for the good of their souls, for the acquisition of true nobleness of spirit, they look upon you as insane.

Such men as these (in their innermost hearts they are generally unhappy) are very much inclined, if they cannot deny the Creator, or refuse to see Him in His creation, at least to deny the eternal, all-pervading laws of virtue. They would fain persuade themselves that God takes no heed of our actions, that piety and goodness are inventions of the schools, mere prejudices instilled in childhood, and intended to keep people in due subjection to their rulers. That which is useful they deem expedient, and that which is expedient they consider wise and good. Whatever is for their worldly advantage they pronounce right; what injures them is, in their eyes, wrong; and they hold all means justifiable which enable them to attain their end.

Nevertheless they are dismayed when they perceive that though there are various religions in the world, yet virtue is the same among all nations. There is consequently something stable and unvarying in the human spirit, which relates to its destiny, its mode of thinking and acting, and according to which it judges itself, and is judged by others. Virtue (which is conformity to the will of God) is consequently not a shifting, accidental thing. A pious and righteous man is honoured in all countries, by civilized and uncivilized nations, and he is trusted far more than are shrewd and clever men. On the other hand, a selfish villain, without faith or belief, who puts no restraint upon himself, is detested by all. Thus it is now, and thus it was thousands of years ago. State constitutions, church ceremonies, languages, customs, science, ideas as to what is useful and what is injurious, have altered; but the laws of God in the sphere of the spiritual, the laws and ideas relating to piety and virtue, are as old as the human race itself. Virtue is as indispensable to the immortal spirit as food is to the mortal body. Withdraw all nourishment from the body and it perishes, withdraw virtue from the spirit and it perishes.

If righteousness be but an accidental thing, if it be not in immediate connexion with the nature of the spirit, why is it that even the boldest decriers of virtue are frequently reluctant to commit actual crimes, independently of any fear of punishment in this world? Why is it that there are things which they dare not do? Or why is it that when they do perpetrate bad deeds, they would fain, if they could, conceal them even from themselves?

Virtue is but the perfection of the spirit, its mature development in regard to its destination in the universe. The dying sinner is therefore an immature yet rotting fruit on the great tree of life. Virtue, or perfection of the spirit is, however, nothing more than its self-emancipation from the trammels of the earthly nature connected with it—its emancipation from the animal instincts, its self-government according to its own inward and eternal law of right, and of obedience to God; a rising from animal nature to angelic nature. Virtue is the spirit's self-elevation to glory.

It is not therefore skill in art or handicraft, nor the power of cleverly calculating events, and turning circumstances to account, nor deep learning, nor extensive knowledge, that constitute true greatness of soul, but piety and virtue! That which is useful to the world in which we are at present living, will remain here when we quit it. It was derived from this world, was suited for it, and will remain in it. But the virtue which sacrifices life and all earthly goods to carry out the will of God, the virtue that abstains from the things of this world, is not meant to remain in this world, and is often in antagonism with it: it is not of this earth, earthy, for it is in conflict with all that is earthly, and conquers the power of the world. Virtue, consequently, belongs exclusively to the spirit; and it is the source of those holy works which follow the righteous.

The virtue that denies the world does not belong to the *here*, but to the *hereafter*. It is not born of this earth, but comes from God. Its effects are therefore not limited to this world, but extend through all eternity. All else may be rewarded on earth; but virtue in itself is above all reward. And whatever is done for the sake of reward is not virtue, but an act of earthly expediency. The righteous do not act for the sake of the profit to be derived in this world, their eyes are fixed on eternity. They aspire after perfection, after life in God, and with God. Thus they live, and thus they sleep away in the Lord, without any thought of the pains and pleasures, the praise or blame, of this world. "Blessed are the dead who die in the Lord, for their works do follow them."

It is the hand of the Almighty and Everlasting God that has linked together Time and Eternity; where, then, is the power that can deny or destroy this evident and indisputable connexion?

My heart thrills with pleasure at the thought which Jesus, the holy Revealer of God, has so distinctly expressed! Time and Eternity are one, my here and my hereafter form an uninterrupted whole, as surely as there is but *one* universe, and *one* God, and that my works do follow me.

Blessed! ah, blessed am I, for I will and shall die in the Lord! For who can separate me from the love of God?

Blessed! ah, blessed are they who die in the Lord, for their works do follow them! O my beloved ones who early departed this life, leaving me behind, you are enjoying the happier lot towards which I am still striving; never did I feel so strongly the connexion between life and eternity, as when I stood weeping by the side of your pallid corpses, as when I kissed with burning lips your clay cold cheeks. Ye died in the Lord and are blessed. Ye belonged to God, and therefore He called you to Him. Alas! He knew and saw what I did not. He witnessed how often ye had struggled with yourselves in secret; how repentant ye were when ye had committed even the smallest fault! how trustfully ye looked up to Him! how ye communed with Him in earnest prayer. Now ye have overcome, and your piety, your innocence, your goodness, your love, do follow you. With forgiving tenderness the merciful Judge looked down upon those errors which His children knew not how to avoid. Ye are not the least of those whom He has taken into His fatherly heart, He who allows not even the worst of sinners to be lost.

Why does my soul sorrow for the dead? O ye blessed ones! I also shall one day, and perhaps very soon, throw off my earthly covering, as ye have thrown off yours, and shall, like you, be clad in more glorious raiment. We shall meet again, we shall be re-united. Love, like virtue, is eternal; for God is love. Similar to the connexion between life and eternity is that which exists between loving spirits. I have not entirely lost you, ye dear ones, whom the Lord hath given, and whom He hath taken away. Nay, He hath given you to me, not taken you away; for even to this day we belong to each other. We are all still dwelling in the house of our Father, though in different mansions. I am living in eternity as are ye, only ye have entered into new relations and connexions, which await me also. Life on earth is but a fleeting moment, but eternity endures, and throughout eternity we shall be with each other.

Blessed, yea, blessed are they who die in the Lord, for their works do follow them, and mine also will follow me!

O God of life, Judge of the dead! O merciful Saviour of sinners! my works also will follow me, the evil as the good! I look back with dismay at my past life. How often I may have erred, I do not even know. Lord, Lord, wilt Thou remember my offences? When Thou enterest into judgment with me, how shall I stand before Thee? The good that was in me was but feebly sustained by my will, and, alas! it was often set at naught by frivolity, thoughtlessness, or passion, while vanity frequently detracted from the merit of my best deeds. How often have I been failing in love, how often in perseverance, how often in meekness and humility!

Save me, O Lord, from the painful discouragement which takes possession of me when I think of my shortcomings and my errors, and of all in which, whether it be in secret or in public, I have offended against Thee and against my fellow-men; for through my own strength alone I shall never attain to that which I ought to be, in accordance with Thy will and with the teachings of Jesus. Could I not place my hope and my trust in Thy mercy, I should be disconsolate indeed at the thought of the future, and of the change that must come over me in death!

But thou, O Merciful God, art my comfort and my trust! Accept my will for half the deed, my endeavours for half success, my conflicts for half the victory. Forgive me my trespasses! Thou knowest how often I try to lift myself up, though I fall back each time in helpless impotence!

But perhaps life is but one long struggle against evil, and that he may find mercy before Thee who has had courage enough not to shrink from the combat, but to carry it on to the best of his power.

And I will never weary in this struggle after perfection. As Thy soldier I will die, full of faith, and full of hope in Thy Mercy, O Father, who ever granteth more than we deserve. Amen.

GLORIFICATION AFTER DEATH.

What, then, is mine ?   What life of bliss ?
  What quickening stream my dust flows through ?
O'er all my limbs what glow is this ?
  Is it my frame ?—I live anew ?
Can it be I ?   Are these my veins ?
  This Godlike glory, is it mine ?
I am not bound in death's cold chains ?
  Who calls ?   Whose throne doth yonder shine ?
Ah ! it is God—my trust—my own—
  Messiah, it is Thou alone !

O Lord, Thy truth it faileth never,
For Life renewed I thank Thee ever.
  In Revelation's light I soar.
All hail !   My foe subdued doth lie,
Death swallowed up in victory,
  And in the dust I rest no more—
Hail, Lord !   All honour, might, are Thine !
  Saviour ! from Thee my life doth spring.
The Angel choir I haste to join,
  And loudest Hallelujahs sing.

(1 *Cor.* xv. 36—50.)

IF I possess the right of citizenship in two worlds ; if I belong not only to the life here below, but shall hereafter, and perhaps soon, belong to a higher life also ; oh ! then it cannot be wrong for me to dwell at times on that which I have to look forward to, and which is ever drawing me toward itself by a feeling of indefinite longing.   It is as great a satisfaction to me to occupy my thoughts with the memory of the dear ones that have been separated from me by death, as it is to cultivate intercourse with those who still surround me in life, and are the joy of my existence. For the former also are still alive, though no longer abiding in earthly form. Though the body perish, the spirit lives. I still love you, ye distant ones, and can I doubt that ye still love me? Nay, spirits whom God hath united, no man can put asunder, neither can the grave.

It is true, that as to what will be my lot, and what I myself shall be on the other side the grave, I am left in ignorance; but it cannot be wrong that I should from time to time occupy my imagination with the subject; that I should endeavour, by comparison with what I experience here below, to divine what may take place hereafter. Here we live as yet by faith, not by sight. But even Jesus spoke in sublime images of the supersensuous state into which we shall enter after the death of the body. His disciples also loved to dwell upon the subject with their followers, or with those among them who entertained doubts as to the possibility of a resurrection of the dead.

The doctrine of the resurrection of the body had long been accepted among the Jews. The Pharisees taught it, but in a coarse and sensuous form, maintaining that the same flesh that is consigned to the grave was again necessarily to clothe, and to become the vehicle, of the spirit,—an opinion which was strongly opposed by the Sadducees, another Jewish sect. When called upon to pronounce as to which of the two conflicting opinions was correct, Christ showed that both the Jewish sects were in error on this point; and that immortality, or life in the world beyond the grave, or resurrection after death, would take place without the necessity for a corporeal resurrection, in the coarsely sensual sense in which they understood it; namely, that the soul required a body to be provided, as before, with all the earthly instincts necessary for its preservation and propagation. The Sadducees felt the truth of His words, and exclaimed, "Master, Thou hast well said!" (Luke xx. 27—39.)

That which Jesus but rarely touched upon in public, He seems to have developed more fully in His confidential communings with His disciples; for we find that they entertained the same views as He did as to the state of the spirit after death, and as to the Jewish doctrine of the resurrection. "Thou fool," says St. Paul, "that which thou sowest is not quickened, unless it die: and that which thou sowest, thou sowest not that body that shall be, but bare grain. It is sown a natural body; it is raised a *spiritual body*. Flesh and blood cannot inherit the kingdom of God; neither doth corruption inherit incorruption." (1 Cor. xv. 36—50.) The human body, composed of earthly substances, will return to earth. It is not capable of eternal life; being corruptible, it cannot inherit the incorruptible. It will rise from the dead a *spiritual body;* that is to say, when our earthly members separate from our higher self, this latter will rise with greater freedom above that which is dead, and as if transfigured or glorified, will be encompassed by a spiritual covering or body.

This doctrine, embodied in the Holy Scriptures as it was conceived in the spirit of Jesus and His disciples, is in wonderful harmony with what we discern here below as to the nature of man. It is unmistakeable that the spirit, while dwelling in the earthly body, is endued with a spiritual body, which is freed at the death of the former, and comes forth, as it were, as the blossom does from the seed.

Death is sometimes figuratively called the brother of sleep. And in reality it is so. Sleep is the retirement of the spirit and the soul within themselves,—a withdrawal, so to say, from the outward, coarser parts of the body. The same takes place in death. In sleep, however, the outward members of the flesh, though abandoned by our higher self, continue to be animated by the plant-life. Man lies there insensible, but the blood still flows through the veins; the lungs still breathe; all that is essential for the continuance of his plant-like life is in full activity, in the same manner as in the insensible flower or tree. This retirement of the spiritual part of man at regular intervals, seems to be necessary for the preservation of the earthly part, as this would otherwise by constant use be, as it were, worn out and rendered less efficient as an instrument of the spirit. If the plant-like life of the human body be left to go on unchecked by the activity of the spirit, it works more uninterruptedly, according to its own laws, and thus acquires new strength. Therefore it is that after every healthy sleep, we find that the body is refreshed and the mind cheered. In death, however, even the plant-life abandons the substances of which the body is composed, and which are held together by this force alone, and in consequence they decay.

Spirit and soul may, on the other hand, have abandoned the body, without the latter being apparently dead, though real death may be truly said to have taken place when the better part of man has left it. But the body breathes, its pulses beat; and it is said of the man: he is still alive. At other times it may happen that the vital power withdraws from certain parts of the body, and that these die, as it were, while the spirit and the soul still remain united with the other parts.

Sleep is one of the greatest mysteries connected with human life, and well worthy of our closest and most intelligent observation. But this observation is rendered doubly difficult by the fact, that the observing spirit is, in regard to the matters to be taken cognizance of, subject to the laws of corporeal nature, and must allow these to act without disturbance, in order that they may be restored and strengthened for its use. Sleep may be said to be the nourishment of the vital force. The spirit contributes nothing to this. The vital force is as independent of it as is the digestive process which converts the food of the body into blood, or as is the growth of the hair, or the various secretions that take place in the body. When we are awake, the vital force is consumed, it flows out and acts outwardly; when we are asleep, it is gathered in from without. Therefore, as you will observe, not only men and animals sleep, but also plants—they close their calyxes, or fold and hang their leaves when night sets in.

But what is the state of our higher self during its retirement from the outward senses? It can no longer receive impressions from without through eye or ear, through taste, or smell, or sensation. But shall we therefore say that the spirit is annihilated during those moments? Were this so, then our bodies would each morning belong to another spirit, another soul. But the spirit is perfectly conscious that it is ever the same, that it is no other to-day than it was yesterday. Though concentrated within itself, and withdrawn from the world of sense, and in consequence deprived for the time of the mediums through which it communicates with the outer world, the spirit lives and is active.

Dreams are a proof of the continued activity of the spirit during sleep. At whatever hour we may be awakened out of sleep, we are conscious of having dreamt, or when this is not the case, it is because the remembrance of the dream is obliterated by the strong impressions which are produced on the sudden re-awakening of the senses. And though on such occasions we may have no distinct recollection of our dreams, we have, nevertheless, a clear impression that on being awakened we have to turn our attention forcibly away from what was inwardly occupying it, to the outward objects which then lay claim to it.

In our dreams we are conscious of perceptions, desires, and feelings; but the outward senses being, as it were, closed, the spiritual activity goes on independently of outward objects. It rarely leaves a strong and lasting impression on the memory; nevertheless, it has taken place. Spirit and soul are consequently active even though we may not afterwards be able to remember the nature of their activity. Indeed, who can remember all the countless but fleeting ideas, that rise in the mind every moment of the day? But would we, therefore, maintain that our spirit, at the very time when it was perhaps most active and reflective, had no ideas?

In dreams, the self-consciousness of the spirit, that is to say, its knowledge of its own existence, is exactly the same as in waking life. In dreaming as when awake, it distinguishes itself from the objects of its perception. Without this self-consciousness, without this insulation, so to say, of the *ego* from the images of its own conceptions, it could not dream. Whenever we are able to recall to mind a past dream, we shall find that it was our *ego* which, with full consciousness of itself, lived and moved among the creations of its imagination. We may forget the various details of a dream, and even the entire dream, during which the impressions produced by the spirit on the sleeping body, through desires and feelings, were not very strong; consequently, we may also forget that the spirit was conscious of itself during the interval; but it does not follow from this that our self-consciousness, the spirit's knowledge of its own identity and existence, has for a moment ceased! There are persons who, even when merged in deep thought during their waking hours, become perfectly unconscious of what is going on around them. The mind, withdrawn from the outward parts of the body and the senses, is concentrated in itself, and occupied with itself alone; to all appearance these persons, at such moments, seem to be dreaming or sleeping with open eyes. But who will deny that, during these periods of deep thought, they are fully conscious of themselves, though they hear not with their ears and see not with their eyes? The very fact that we are able, when we are determined so to do, to awaken ourselves from sleep at a fixed hour, is another proof in favour of the continuance of our self-consciousness, and of the consciousness of our existence.

We cannot therefore say of a person, whether in light slumber or in deep sleep, that he has lost consciousness, for he retains the knowledge of his own existence, though he does not make it known to us. The spirit never loses the consciousness of its own being, and the soul never loses the consciousness of its identity, although when they return to the sphere of the outward senses, they may have lost the remembrance of having retained this in their sleeping state.

The same takes place during a swoon, when in consequence of the partial and temporary disturbance of the plant-life, the spiritual part of man withdraws into itself; for the spirit shuns what is dead, and is only bound to substances which are in themselves lifeless, by the bonds of the vital force. Although a person in a swoon gives no sign of self-consciousness, he is, nevertheless, as little without it as when asleep. Indeed, many persons on recovering from a swoon remember ideas which have occupied them during the period of apparent lifelessness, just as many, on awaking from sleep, remember their dreams, while others do not. Nay, there are physical conditions, such, for instance, as those of catalepsy, during which the body presents a pale, cold, breathless, motionless, rigid appearance, like that of a corpse; while the spirit, nevertheless, remains in connexion with some of the senses, and is perfectly cognizant of all that goes on around it, but is unable to give the slightest outward sign of life or consciousness.

There is another remarkable condition incident to human nature, which convinces us of the uninterrupted activity of the spirit, and of its never-ceasing consciousness, even during periods of which it subsequently loses the remembrance. I allude to the condition of the sleep-walker. He falls, to all appearances, into the ordinary state of sleep. His outward senses are closed. He hears not, sees not, feels not. Suddenly he seems to awake, not out of sleep, but in it. He hears, but not with his ears; he sees, but not with his eyes; he feels, but not through the skin. He walks, he speaks, he performs various acts, and to the utter astonishment of the spectators, often with greater skill and precision than he would be capable of when awake. In this state he has a vivid recollection of the events which have taken place during his waking life, and not unfrequently, indeed, of occurrences which entirely escape his memory when his senses are fully awake. After having remained in this state for some time, he again sinks into ordinary sleep, and when at length he rouses himself from this, he is perfectly unconscious of everything that has taken place. He has forgotten what he said and what he did, and often finds it impossible to believe, what those who have seen his sleep-walking tell him. But can we deny that his spirit has been self-conscious, and wonderfully active, during that sleep? When the somnambulist falls again into that state of outward sleeping and inward waking, he remembers while in this condition, which even to himself is incomprehensible, all that he did and thought, when previously in it, and of which when his outward senses are awake he knows nothing.

How is this to be explained? How is it that when asleep, when the outward senses are, so to say, closed, we nevertheless, in such cases as the one just alluded to, can hear and see not only as well, but better than when awake? It is because the body is nothing more than the outward shell or covering of the spirit; because in itself the body, independently of the soul, possesses neither the power of sensation nor perception, the eye of the soulless body being as sightless as that of a marble statue. It is consequently the soul, and the soul alone, that feels, sees, and hears what is going on outwardly. The eye, the ear, &c., are only special arrangements in the fleshly covering, skilfully adapted for conveying impressions from the outer world to the soul. There are, however, instances, as we have seen, in which the gross bodily covering being diseased, and having become injured in some way, the soul, as it were, comes forth from it, and continues its activity without the aid of the outward senses. In these cases it also acts upon an entirely different set of nerves than when the body is in its ordinary waking state; and through the increased vegetative force in these, it carries on its action against that which is in itself lifeless in man.

The soul is consequently the sensitive organ, not the body, and is therefore the true and real body of the spirit, and the body is only its outward framework, its shell and covering. Now, as we know from numerous instances and experiences that the activity and self-consciousness of the spirit never cease, not even during the moments in respect to which it may not be able to remember having been self-conscious; as we know, that when engaged in deep meditation the spirit may become unconscious of its own body and of all outward circumstances, or in certain diseases may be capable of acting on the members of the body, or, as in cases of somnambulism, is even capable of entirely dispensing with the aid of the bodily senses: there is no difficulty in conceiving how the immortal spirit, even after having entirely thrown off its gross and perishable body, can retain its self-consciousness and the feeling of its identity, though it can no longer manifest itself through the medium of the body to those who are still living in the flesh! We are thus able to conceive what is the *spiritual* body of which St. Paul speaks; what is the incorruption which is to rise out of corruption; what is the weakness that falls off, or is sown in the grave, and is raised in power, and soars towards heaven, being mature for the better life (1 Cor. xv. 43.) This, then, is the glorification after death; this is the spiritual resurrection. That which is born of the earth must return to the earth; but the spirit, invested with the glorified body, bears the image of the heavenly, as it has borne the image of the earthly (1 Cor. xv. 49.) The fleshly body, given over to corruption in the grave, feels no more; but in reality it has never felt through itself alone. It was the spiritual body, that is the soul, which in truth felt and perceived; and it will continue to do so even though dissevered from its earthly shell. Its power of feeling and perception will indeed be enhanced; and the spirit, continuing its self-conscious life in the spiritual body, will still see the glory of God in His creation, and will recognize and love the beings it loved before. But it will no longer have sensual or earthly wants and desires, and it will know no tears; it will bear the image of the heavenly from whence it descends.

What shall I feel, when Thou callest me, O my Creator, my God! When the time of my glorification shall arrive; when my living friends are weeping around me; when my glorified dear ones are drawing nigh and my heart blesses all with equal love! When I shall appear before Thee, sanctified through Jesus Christ, and having become a partaker of His kingdom, I will seek Him and will fall down before Thee, O Lord, and pray to Thee with increased thankfulness, with deeper reverence and awe, that my immortal spirit may ever ripen to greater perfection in every virtue! Amen.

www.ingramcontent.com/pod-product-compliance
Lightning Source LLC
Chambersburg PA
CBHW020232240426
43672CB00006B/504